The

English Spy's

Book of Wisdom

by

Harry Ferguson

By the same author:

Published by Bloomsbury

Kilo17
Lima 3
The Spy Handbook

Published by Random House

Operation Kronstadt

Book cover designed by:

Stefan P. from @pwaperpro on Fiverr

For Rebecca.

Preface

I am a former MI6 officer. As both an academic, lecturer and occasional television "expert" I have often pondered the question of how to convey to people the truth about spies and the way that we operate. This is an important goal because the work of spies changes our world almost every day and yet very few people know what spies actually do. The intelligence services of our own - and of foreign countries - involve us in conflict, manipulate our views and monitor our everyday life. Sometimes they even kill us. Citizens of every nation ought to have some understanding of spies, both their benefits and their threats.

But espionage is a complex field. It is difficult to explain. People have limited time and plenty of other problems to worry about.

And so we come to this little book.

Over the past forty years I have read hundreds of books, articles and news stories as part of my work and research. As a result, my notes are full of little sayings and anecdotes that seemed to me to say something useful about this so-called "wilderness of mirrors". It also seemed to me that a book of quotations, if supported by proper context and other information, would present the field of espionage in bite-sized chunks. By the time you have finished reading this book, I believe that you will be much better informed about the history, the tradecraft and, above all, the reality of modern espionage.

As for the structure of the book, this is not an exhaustive collection, I have omitted some very well known quotes. I could have simply run an internet search and dumped everything relevant into the word processor. But, this is a collection of quotations that seemed important to me as a former spy and some of the old quotations did not bear repetition. Similarly, there are certain authors and works – Malcolm Muggeridge's memoirs and Sun Tzu's *The Art of War* come to mind - which I could have raided for hundreds of quotes (and have done so rather more than I wished). But I have tried to follow the rule of only presenting to you those quotations that seemed most relevant to me and, if your curiosity is aroused by a particular topic, I recommend tracking down the relevant volumes.

Sometimes it is not the quote itself but the story behind it that interested me. So, if some quotes are not quite as quotable as others, it is because they are a doorway into a story or the subject behind it.

One final word of advice: You do not need to read this book from cover to cover. Dip into it whenever you feel like it and by the end of the book you will have learned one or two new facts and, maybe, will come out of the experience a little wiser. All of us need wisdom. Including spies.

Especially spies.

All the very best to you and yours,

Harry Ferguson,
London.
2024

Technical notes

The proper name of the United Kingdom's foreign intelligence service is the Secret Intelligence Service (SIS). However, during different stages of its history it has been referred to as MI6, MI1C or the Secret Service Bureau. As MI6 is the most commonly understood designation (and used on the Service's own website) I have used the term MI6 throughout.

As well as MI6, British Intelligence has had a number of different elements over the years. MI5 and MI6 were established in 1909. Before this (and after) the British Army and the Royal Navy had their own intelligence services: the Military Intelligence Department (MID) and the Naval Intelligence Division (NID) respectively. So, you may see occasional references to these bodies.

As for communications intelligence, Room 40 of the NID was the main centre for cryptanalysis (breaking the enemy's codes) during the First World War. This was succeeded by the Government Code and Cipher School (GC&CS) from 1919. GC&CS was run as part of MI6. During the Second World War the most important code breaking station of this organisation was Bletchley Park, home to Alan Turing and a legion of other code breakers. In 1946, communications interception and decoding was finally separated from MI6 and became the Government Communications Headquarters (GCHQ) that we know today.

Officers and agents: Use of the word "agent" often causes confusion. An "intelligence officer" is a member of an intelligence service such as MI6, the FSB, the Mossad or the CIA. Their job is to recruit sources who have access to intelligence. These sources are known as "agents". It is usually the agents who run the risks and, sometimes, pay the ultimate price. Both intelligence officers and agents are thought of by the public as "spies". This issue is confused by American agencies which sometimes refer to their intelligence officers as "agents." Meanwhile, the term "spooks" is often applied to MI5 officers as they are not really "spies" in the classic sense but "secret police". Welcome to the wilderness of mirrors.

Over the years, I may not have always noted down the correct attribution of a particular quote and some others may be missing. If you believe that your work has been quoted incorrectly or that there is some other error or if you have a suitable and sourced quote that you believe might be suitable for a future edition of this work, I would be glad to hear from you at the email address on the spyingtoday.com website or by direct message on TikTok @theenglishspy.

Contents: _____ Page No.

15

<u>A</u>

Accuracy

'On your own intelligence rely not.'

> *The Book of Proverbs*, Chapter 3 Verse 5. The problem is that intelligence from your allies can be even less reliable than your own and they may have their own intentions by feeding you certain reports such as the hope that you will take the action that they want. This is the eternal problem for a Reports Officer – a key and undervalued role in any intelligence service. The Reports Officer has to decide what to send to customers and what to hold back, what is reliable and what is distinctly dubious. Sometimes the best you can do, even in this advanced age, is go with your gut instinct.

'Since Vietnam, when it comes to predicting the nature and the location of our next military engagement, our record has been perfect. We have never once gotten it right.'

> US Secretary of Defence Robert Gates speaking to West Point cadets at their graduation in 2011 quoted in *Spies, Lies and Algorithms* by Amy B. Zegart (2022).

'Most intelligence reports in war are contradictory; even more are false and most are uncertain.'

> Carl Von Clausewitz *On War* (1832). Curiously, despite being one of history's leading military thinkers, Von Clausewitz has remarkably little to say about espionage. He seems to have considered it a discipline distinct from military conduct. Sun Tzu's approach in *The Art of War* is quite different.

'It is one of the more unfortunate characteristics of the sort of information supplied by secret agents that it becomes rarer and less detailed as the peril increases and the need for such information grows more urgent.'

> French political analyst Alexis de Tocqueville (1805-1859) in *The Old Regime and the Revolution* (1856). This is why intelligence agencies always need to be looking ahead and preparing for the next conflict. The War in Iraq is an example of this. Once the fight has started it is too late to be recruiting sources.

'The map is not the territory.'

> Attributed to the US Marines but in intelligence terms it means the following: satellites and hackers can provide you with any amount of intelligence detail, you can almost drown in it. But there is still no substitute for having a human source on the inside.

'There is no reliable majority among the American people at present in favour of Roosevelt's policy and of entry into the war.'

German Foreign Minister Joachim Von Ribbentrop to Adolf Hitler in August 1941. His intelligence was accurate but sometimes there is an element that cannot be foreseen – such as the Japanese attack on Pearl Harbour. Sometimes being accurate is not enough.

'You cannot photograph an intention.'

Attributed to Former Director of the CIA, James Schlesinger. And he is right – this is the second reason why accuracy in espionage may not be enough. Spy satellites and reconnaissance drones can send back intelligence that is 100% accurate - but it cannot tell you what will happen next. There is a chance that a human source can do this and that is why you will always need both - no matter how good the machines become.

Africa

'Africa is now the El Dorado of espionage.'

Unnamed "serving intelligence officer" quoted in *The Guardian* newspaper 25 February 2015. The officer was referring to the battle between China and the West for control of Africa's natural resources and contrary to what you might expect, this is the part of the world where many foreign intelligence agencies are most actively engaged.

Agent handling

'Concerning spies, you must always be suspicious of them.'

General George Monck (1608-1670) from his book *Observations on Military and Political Affairs, Chapter 12* (1670). Monck was a General and, as a military commander, was also Oliver Cromwell's spy chief in Scotland. He was in a key position to protect the new Commonwealth as Scotland was where a Royalist army was most likely to land and find support. To combat this threat Monck used spies at home and abroad. However, in his book, Monck seems to regard most spies as venal and untrustworthy. He believed that money was the best way to ensure that they did their job. As he said:

'The most effectual means to be well served by these kind of men, is to be very liberal to them, (i.e. to pay them well) *for they are faithful to those who give them the most.'*

So, of the four commonly accepted motivations for a spy: Money, Ideology, Compromise and Ego (of which more anon), Monck only appears to be aware of one - money. But then he was more of a soldier than he was a spymaster.

'In order to make them assent to us to the extent of their ability, we require to raise them a little bit in their own esteem and make them feel a little exalted...'.

Captain William Sleeman who smashed the Thugee cult in India in a little over four years. His system of "approvers" (informers) and profiling formed a model for future police work, decades ahead of its time. It was known as "Sleeman's machine". Quoted in *Thug* by Mike Dash (2005).

'Have a clear aim, a reason for meeting, know what it is you want to come away with; if you can't state your aim in a sentence, don't put the agent at risk of meeting. Think of everything, every reaction, however unlikely, everything that could go wrong, however unwelcome. Have a response to hand, no matter how trite or temporary, because it's bound to be better than blankness or panic.'

Alan Judd in his spy novel *'Legacy'* (2001). Judd is a frequent commentator on secret service matters. Although he is usually referred to in the media as a *"former Foreign Service officer"* which is deliberately vague, the intelligence service historian Stephen Dorril claims that Judd was a senior MI6 officer - See *MI6* by Dorril (2000). If Dorril is correct (and he usually is) then Judd is worth listening to.

'Remember, too, that the agent was also a human being, who had a life outside spying. As should you, if you were sensible. Let the agent see that you were human. Be professional at all times, but show that you have a soul, a heart, some humour. And finally, having thought of all of this well in advance, forget it.'

Alan Judd (see above) in *Legacy* (2001).

'Secret service activities must often come into provocative contact with the strongest emotions of the human soul. Love, hate, fear, revenge, greed: each, and all of these passions, play their part in such work.'

The journalist and *bon viveur* Hector Bywater was the most successful MI6 spy in the years preceding World War One. He was a fluent German speaker and his good-natured socialising with German naval staff led to many interesting snippets of intelligence. With his understanding of human nature he was a superb source handler. His codename at MI6 was "H2O" which, given his surname, is as poor a piece of tradecraft as you will come across. But it was alcoholism rather than enemy action that ended his life in 1940. Quoted in *Bywater* by William H. Honan (1990).

'...the feature which had superficially attracted him to it as an appropriate rendezvous for his organisation was the way in which the previous occupant had draped the walls of every single room with cretonne hangings of the Tree of Life pattern, and not merely the wall, but the doors and windows as well, so that nothing was to be seen round one but that pattern of teeming, barbaric life endlessly repeating in blood-red and powder blue ... there was no doubt that the effect on a person introduced for the first time to these draped, echoless, small rooms – there were half a dozen of them opening one into the other – was one of uneasy bewilderment. His stammering narratives seemed to get involved in the complications of the teeming design, and his anxiety over what might be hidden behind the draperies soon destroyed the confidence of the coolest liar.'

Author and MI6 officer Compton Mackenzie from his novel *'Extremes Meet'* (1928) Mackenzie was an MI6 officer in Greece during the First World War and although the book was written as fiction (because factual accounts of secret service were banned) the room really did exist and Mackenzie considered it one of his most useful weapons when questioning his agents.

'Above all, the mysterious manner should be avoided. It only engenders distrust. A frank and apparently open style generally gains confidence ... one can talk a great deal and say nothing.'

William Melville (1850-1918), police officer, private detective and, according to some historians, the godfather of the British Secret Service. Melville cut his teeth against Irish Republican dynamite gangs and European anarchists as a founding member of the Special Branch. After rising to the head of the Branch, he was then selected to be the private enquiry agent for the Military Intelligence Department. He was soon facing off against German spies and, in effect, became a one-man security service. Later, he trained some of the first officers to work for MI5 and MI6. Well known in his time, he is largely forgotten now. Quoted in *Spynest* by Edwin Ruis (2016).

'In general it is necessary to pay spies well and not be miserly in that respect. A man who risks being hanged in our service merits being well paid.'

Attributed to Frederick the Great.

'Money, however little, must be dropped in, like a touch of bitter in a mint julep, to validate the deal.'

Writer, broadcaster and MI6 officer Malcolm Muggeridge in *Chronicles of Wasted Time: The Infernal Grove* (1973). Muggeridge ran a one-man MI6 station during the Second World War at Laurenco Marques (now Maputo) in Mozambique. With MI6's genius for postings, they sent him to a Portuguese-speaking city and he didn't speak a word of Portuguese. The town was a key port on the supply routes that led to the Far East and Muggeridge fought a three-cornered battle against the German and Italian heads of intelligence (who did not always co-operate with each other.) He had an interesting war: he captured a U-Boat, recruited several key agents and, at one point, having survived an assassination attempt, he became so depressed that he tried to kill himself. To cap it all, his boss in London was the infamous traitor, Kim Philby. Like those other literary greats: Graham Greene, Compton Mackenzie and David Cornwell (John Le Carré) once he had seen the world of espionage he became thoroughly disillusioned by it.

'The only thing I ask is: treat me like a human being!'

This sounds like such a simple route to success for running spies and yet the history of espionage shows that so many agent handlers can't or won't do this. These were the words of GRU Major and American spy Piotr Semyonovich Popov to his American handlers in 1953. He volunteered to work for them by leaving a note on the windscreen of a CIA officer's car in Vienna. Popov worked as a double agent for the CIA between 1953 and 1958 but then was detected by the Russians and executed in 1960. Quoted in *The Literary Spy* by Charles E. Lathrop (2004).

Agent selection

'The first difficulty in espionage lies in finding reliable men.'

Colonel George Furse (1834-1906) in *Information in War: its Acquisition and Transmission* (1895). This book is regarded as one of the first intelligence handbooks written in the modern era and is widely quoted in intelligence service histories. Although, in this case, he perhaps should have mentioned women... He wrote a number of military histories including *"The Art of Marching"* - which certainly sounds like a book that could cure insomnia.

'Every man has his price and every woman is seducible.'

Not a very enlightened view but typical of the man: Colonel Sir Claude Dansey, Assistant Chief of MI6 and head of its ultra-secret "Z Organisation" in the 1930s. He was with the Service from its earliest days until after the Second World War. Some hated him, some loved him, but all admired his skill as an intelligence officer. (See more about him under "Dansey"). The Z Organisation was established because MI6 was no longer a truly secret organisation – many of its personnel and methods were known to the enemy. Dansey was even dismissed from the service in disgrace following a charge of theft so that the new organisation would be super-secret (it was all a ruse of course). But the Z Organisation barely lasted two years before it was blown to the Germans. Quoted by Professor Christopher Andrew in *Secret Service* (1985).

'Enlightened rulers and sagacious generals who are able to select intelligent spies will invariably attain great success.'

Sun Tzu, *The Art of War,* Chapter 13 Paragraph 27.

'Intelligence, as I have always insisted, is about people. You have to study people and weigh up your impressions with what you know of their national character, or even the character of their class. One of the secrets in spotting the potentially good German, I found, was to notice whether he had a sense of humour. If he had, then there was a good chance that he was potentially good ... of course the problem was to make sure it wasn't oneself the German might be laughing at.'

Sir Maurice Oldfield, Chief of MI6 1973-78. Oldfield joined MI6 just after the Second World War and rose to the highest position. There was widespread shock in intelligence circles when it was revealed that he had risen to the very highest post in MI6 while hiding his homosexuality. At that time homosexuality was a dismissal offence for MI6 officers. It is not known how many homosexual officers were dismissed while Oldfield stayed silent. When his sexuality was revealed in 1987, Margaret Thatcher, the Prime Minister, was forced to make a statement in Parliament because of the scandal. She said that his security clearance had been withdrawn shortly before his death in 1981. The ban on homosexuality in the UK intelligence services was not lifted until 1991 despite not being a criminal offence in the UK since 1967 - such was the level of homophobia in UK intelligence in those days. Incidentally, there is no truth in the story that Oldfield was the basis for John Le Carré's hero, George Smiley. However, the actor Alec Guinness (who played Smiley on television) did meet Oldfield during a lunch before portraying the character. Quoted in *'C': A biography of Sir Maurice Oldfield* by Richard Deacon (1985).

'Above all, the good spy has a thorough knowledge of human nature, especially its weaknesses, which he knows how to make full use of.'

Henry Landau (1892-1968), first head of MI6's Berlin station in his book *'All's Fair'* (1934). He was born in South Africa and spoke fluent German. In 1916, he joined MI6 and was posted to Rotterdam which was then the most active MI6 station in the world. He was No.2 to the station chief Richard Tinsley, a "maritime merchant". Neither of them had any training as spies. Yet Landau appears to have been a first rate agent runner and played an important part in processing the intelligence which poured through the station from networks of "train watchers" all across Europe. Knowledge of large scale troop movements was vital in predicting the location of German attacks and keeping a note of which regiments were being moved by train proved the best way of obtaining intelligence about them. However, thanks to recent work in the Dutch archives by an excellent young historian named Edwin Ruis (author of *Spynest*), it is now known that Landau was using his intelligence work as cover for paedophile activities (this appears to have been more than a smear story put about by the Germans). After the war and his posting to Berlin, Landau tired of peacetime intelligence work and resigned from MI6 in 1920. He tried various jobs around Europe, ran up massive debts and even became involved in jewellery smuggling. In 1925 he faked his own death by leaving his clothes on a river bank and making it seem that he had drowned while swimming (much as John Stonehouse was to do many years later). He later turned up in the United States. He earned money by writing several books about his intelligence work. MI6 wanted to prosecute him under the Official Secrets Act for this but they could never manage to have him extradited and he died in 1968 in Mexico.

'He who is not sage and wise, humane and just, cannot use spies. And he who is not delicate and subtle cannot get the truth out of them'.

Sun Tzu, *The Art of War*, Chapter 13, paragraphs 15 -17.

' – these people [secret agents] *are queer, and their motives more than doubtful. They are striving for recognition and must be handled very carefully'.*

Major Cyrus Regnart, the second officer to be appointed to MI6 just after its creation in 1909, assessing some of the very first people who offered to work as spies for the new service. Regnart, known to everyone as "Roy", was a Royal Marine who had worked undercover for the Naval Intelligence Division. He was loaned to Cumming as an assistant in 1910. Cumming had been appointed to lead MI6 but he knew nothing of intelligence work and was soon struggling. It was Regnart who guided Cumming through his very first experiences in espionage and helped him to create the worldwide service that we know today. Regnart left MI6 to return to the Royal Marines at the outbreak of the First World War in 1914. He survived the war but sadly, he committed suicide while posted to Ireland in 1921. Quoted in *The Quest for C* by Alan Judd (1999).

'It is useless to approach natives and expect them to betray their country. Some of the lowest class may consent, but they will of course betray us without scruple if it serves their purpose and they cannot be relied upon for the more important work.'

Mansfield Cumming, first ever Chief of MI6, writing in his diary in 1909, expressing doubt about whether foreigners could be recruited as spies. Quoted in *MI6: The Official History 1909-1949* by Keith Jeffery (2010). Keith was a kind man and a truly great historian. I still chuckle when I remember his frustration at all the cuts MI6 insisted on making to what he thought were perfectly innocuous accounts of our work. As if to prove a point, the journalist and historian Michael Smith wrote *SIX*, an unofficial history of MI6, published in the same year as the official history. He showed just how much detail it is possible to get from completely open sources. Sadly, Keith Jeffery died in 2016 and is a great loss to our profession.

'The trusted agent handling important matters and documents must needs be a person of intelligence, tact and address. He must be a linguist and, above all, a man of resource and a close student of his fellow men.'

"Doctor" Armgaard Karl Graves from his book *The Secrets of the German War Office* (1914). Graves was a con man who persuaded the German secret service to send him to Scotland as a spy in 1911. We are not even certain that Graves was his real name, it might well have been Max Meincke. He was certainly not a real doctor. He carried forged papers stating that he was an Australian medical student (he had travelled in Australia so he knew how to support the deception). Fortunately, when he applied for a post with a local GP in Glasgow, he was turned down on the grounds that he sounded "too German". His target was Rosyth naval base and he was actually pretty good at his job (although his landlady spotted him straight away – sadly no-one acted on her report. All spies need a bit of luck.) When he was arrested in 1912 he was already in possession of the plans of a new 14-inch naval gun. He was caught when one of his messages to Germany was intercepted and traced back to him. In April 1912, he was sentenced to 18 months imprisonment. The sentence was so light because, believe it or not, spying was not seen as terribly serious in the years before the First World War – even the most serious cases rarely got more than two years. But he did not even serve that. He was released after just six months – the government said it was for medical reasons,but Graves claimed it was because he had become a double agent and had been hired by MI5 to travel around Europe looking for German agents. Whatever the truth of the matter, he certainly appears to have spent a lot of MI5's money in Germany and Austria (this is on record) yet, surprise, surprise, no German agents were ever found. He was last heard of in America where he was perpetrating various crimes, including frauds and assaults on women, all while claiming that he had once been a great masterspy. However, the quote above is included not because he was an admirable man but because, like all great con men, he was a chameleon who could soak up knowledge from the real experts around him. This is one of the best definitions of a good spy that you will find.

'To be of any real value in an enemy country, a spy must be highly placed. The enemy must, in fact, buy someone who is in naval or military secrets, for even the ordinary citizen of the country is very rarely in a position to give useful information.'

Sir Basil Thomson, Director of Intelligence at the Home Office 1919-1921. Quoted from his book *Queer People* (1922). His post was established at the end of the First World War to deal with subversion in the UK and he might well have taken over at MI5 but instead made too many political enemies and was dismissed. He ended up is disgrace having been prosecuted for using the services of a prostitute in a public park in 1925. (He claimed that he was conducting research for a book.) Meanwhile, this quote shows how even someone who has worked closely with the intelligence services can get it wrong. In fact, the "ordinary citizen" is very often the person who has vital access. Perhaps the best example is Melita Norwood, "the grandma spy". Although she was only a secretary, she had access to key intelligence about Britain's nuclear weapons programme which she supplied to her KGB handlers. She was also a key contact for other agents. She remained undetected until 1992 just after the collapse of the Soviet Union when KGB archivist Vasili Mitrokhin smuggled hundreds of classified Soviet documents to the West. By then she was eighty years old and it was decided that she was too old and her betrayal was too long ago for her to be prosecuted. There was scandal when she was exposed as a traitor by the British press in 1999 but she remained unrepentant claiming that her work had averted a Third World War. She died in 2005 as one of the most damaging traitors the United Kingdom has ever had.

'Very clever – very doubtful – has been everywhere and done everything ... I must agree though, it is a great gamble.'

Diary of the first Chief of MI6, Mansfield Cumming, after his first meeting with Sidney Reilly, the so-called *"Ace of Spies"* (from the television adventure series about him starring Sam Neill). In fact, Reilly was a con-man, rapist and murderer who used MI6 as a way to carry out his own private schemes in Russia. His fame derives from the fact that a biography was written about him by Sir Robert Bruce Lockhart, a diplomat who fell for his outrageous stories. Like Doctor Graves above, Reilly's career shows how easily a con man can make it in the world of intelligence – and perhaps that is natural given that con-men and spies both spend much of their lives pretending to be something that they are not. The historian James Morton called Reilly *"the second most famous spy in history."* Presumably Mata Hari is the most famous – unless you count fictional characters like James Bond. That is probably right but it is interesting to note that neither Reilly nor Mata Hari actually did very much spying. Quoted in *Spies of the First World War* by James Morton (2010).

'The ideological volunteer if he is sincere, is a man whose loyalty you need rarely question, as you must always question the loyalties of people who work chiefly for money or out of a desire for adventure and intrigue.'

Former CIA Director Allen Dulles in *The Craft of Intelligence* (1963). While a good intelligence officer will bear in mind the advice of General Monck and other experts above (to <u>never</u> fully trust your spies), what Dulles says is largely correct. Of all the reasons for a spy to work for you, ideological motivation is usually the most reliable and the most highly prized.

'In a tight place he would have pushed his best friend in front of him, and if the friend had been killed, he would have picked his pockets while hiding under the corpse. Yet Waterlow would have sacked many of the people in his employment before Milton, and this afternoon he picked up his envelope with the confident expectation that if this gross, larded mountebank beside his desk said that he had secured something very hot, he was as likely as not to be right.'

Author and MI6 officer Compton Mackenzie in *Extremes Meet* (1928). Mackenzie was writing about one of his real Greek agents which goes to show that you cannot always work with angels in the espionage game – but that does not mean that "mountebanks" cannot also be bloody good agents.

Alcohol

'In any post I've ever been stationed, meeting and developing an individual is more often than not a very social business in which alcohol plays a major part.'

Former CIA operations officer Duane Clarridge in his book *A Spy for all Seasons* (1997) He's right and if you can't hold your drink, you are really going to struggle as a spy.

'Never get drunk; when you drink, you do not know what you say. If you are obliged to drink heavily on occasions, take two large spoonfuls of olive oil beforehand; you will not get drunk, but you can pretend to be so. If dealing with a suspect, make him drink as much as possible; he will probably tell you something interesting.'

> MI6 training manual from the First World War. Quoted in *SIX* by Michael Smith (2010). Actually, making your contacts drunk doesn't always work: during the Second World War, the James Bond author Ian Fleming, who was working for British naval intelligence at the time, took a number of high-ranking German POWs to a London hotel for a drunken party. He hoped that they would spill vital intelligence once the alcohol started flowing. In fact, the party became raucous and the management called the police because they were suspicious of all the loud German accents. Everyone was arrested. The experiment was not repeated.

'Can I tell you what's messed up about James Bond? "Shaken not stirred" will get you cold water with a dash of gin and dry vermouth. The reason you stir it with a special spoon is so as not to chip the ice. James is just ordering a weak martini and being snooty about it.'

> The actor Martin Sheen as President Jed Bartlett, *The West Wing,* Season Three, as written by Aaron Sorkin. There are so many inaccuracies in the James Bond novels (fun though they may be) that his image is probably the greatest single obstacle in trying to educate the general public about the benefits and the threats of real espionage.

'Many men are defeated by alcohol. This is a lamentable fact. Be attentive to how much you can imbibe without becoming drunk.'

> Yamamoto Tsunetomo in *Hagakure* (a guide for Samurai) 1716.

'I always carry a case of wine with me. This wine has often loosened the tongues of the most taciturn, and by its aid I was able to bring to justice some of the enemy's most stubborn spies.'

> Leutnant A. Bauermeister, German intelligence officer on the Russian Front, World War One in his book *Spies Break Through* (1934). Of course, if carrying a crate of wine around is a bit inconvenient, you could always just head to the hotel bar.

Allies

'Espionage today is really a branch of psychological warfare. The main objective is to sow mistrust between allies in the enemy's camp.'

> Graham Greene, novelist and MI6 officer. Quoted in *Literary Agents* by Anthony Masters (1987).

But sometimes you don't need to sow mistrust between allies because intelligence agencies are already creating it themselves:

'Spying among friends isn't on.'

> German Chancellor Angela Merkel after finding out that her mobile phone had been bugged not by Russian or Chinese but by the Americans. Quoted in *The Guardian* newspaper 12

November 2015.

But in fact, spying on their allies had become so commonplace that the Americans had stopped denying it at least fifteen years earlier:

'Yes, my Continental European friends, we have spied on you...'

> Former CIA Director R. James Woolsey in the article *"Why We Spy On Our Allies"* Wall *Street Journal* 17 March 2000.

and:

'There are no friendly services. There are only the services of friendly foreign powers.'

> Unnamed CIA officer. Quoted in *The Literary Spy* by Charles E. Lathrop (2004).

The French were at it as well:

'We are military allies, but economic competitors. Therefore, industrial espionage, even among friends, is a normal action of an intelligence agency.'

> Pierre Marion, former director of the DGSE (French foreign intelligence service), speaking in 1995 and confessing to spying on American companies during his time in charge. Quoted in *The Literary Spy* by Charles E. Lathrop (2004).

And, of course, Russia found her allies fair game:

'We are engaged in espionage against every country in the world – and this includes our friends...'

> GRU Colonel and double agent Oleg Penkovsky in *The Penkovsky Papers* (1966).

But of course, allies can be useful too. Well, sort of....

'Whenever we want to subvert any place, we usually find that the British own an island within easy reach.'

> CIA officer Frank Wisner quoted by the MI6 traitor Kim Philby in his book *My Silent War* (1968). Wisner was part of the OSS (American secret service) in World War Two and then joined the CIA where he served until 1958. He ran an operation to put agents into Albania that Philby betrayed. Many of the agents were captured and shot soon after they landed. Wisner became depressed about the loss of so many people in that operation and also in the Hungarian Uprising of 1956 (which he felt that the CIA-backed Radio Free Europe had encouraged prematurely). Sadly, this sense of guilt and other factors overwhelmed him and he eventually committed suicide in 1965. Another example of how mental health issues rather than enemy bullets can be the greatest danger for a real spy.

Americans

'It was rather easy to recruit Americans just by being friends with them.'

Former GRU Colonel Stanislav Lunev giving evidence to a Congressional Committee in 1998. Quoted in *The Literary Spy* by Charles E. Lathrop (2004).

Analysis

'Analysis ... is the Achilles' heel of intelligence.'

Stansfield Turner, former Director of the CIA in *Secrecy and Democracy* (1985). The reason is that intelligence rarely tells you the full story. Someone has to take the original report from the agent (known in the trade as *"raw intelligence"*) match it with other reports and open sources and then come up with a final report for customers (known as *"finished intelligence"*.) It is often at this stage that problems creep in. A good example would be the satellite intelligence used by US Secretary of State, General Colin Powell, in his presentation to the United Nations in February 2003. There was nothing wrong with the photographs – satellites can't lie – but Powell's analysts had told him that they showed evidence of weapons of mass destruction. They didn't. In fact, the analysis led him to make the following statement:

'Every statement I make today is backed up by sources, solid sources. These are not assertions. What we're giving you are facts and conclusions based on solid evidence.'

He was utterly wrong and a lot of good people died as a result.

Anti-Intellectualism

'I have less fear of Bolshies and Fascists than I have of some pedantic but vocal university professor.'

Colonel Claude Dansey, senior official at MI6 and head of MI6's ultra-secret "Z Organisation". Dansey's background was as a "gut-feeling" field agent who loathed the new university graduates who were being brought into the service. His main enemy was his fellow Vice-Chief of MI6, Colonel Valentine Vivian (known as "VV"), who thought that MI6 needed more graduates if it was to collect intelligence in the modern world. Dansey referred to VV's staff as *"a lot of old women in red flannel knickers"*. Quoted in *Secret Service* by Professor Christopher Andrew (1985).

'One Oleg Penkovsky is worth a hundred PhDs!'

CIA officer John Maury quoted in *Time* magazine 19 January 1981. Penkovsky was a GRU (Russian military intelligence) Colonel who volunteered to spy for the West. He was run jointly by MI6 and the CIA and was one of the most important spies the West ever recruited. He provided top level intelligence on Soviet nuclear weapons development at a crucial moment in world history. He was caught in 1961 and executed in 1962.

Apathy

'The Russian diplomat's file had been sent to me by a younger officer. Did I recognise him? Not really. It was a double agent case which had been running off and on for years. Did I have any ideas? Not really. When you join the Service every case looks different. When you leave they all seem the same.'

Peter Wright (who was an MI5 officer from 1955-1976) in his book *Spycatcher* (1987). Wright was an officer who became obsessed with his idea that the Russians had penetrated the British intelligence services and the Labour Party at the highest level. When he did not get the attention that he felt he deserved, he wrote a tell-all book expounding his theories and a lot more besides. When the government tried to have it banned, the resulting court case in Australia (where Wright was living) exposed all sorts of other problems and became a cause célèbre. One thing was true however: the intelligence services had become complacent and needed shaking up. Even though it was banned in the UK, young intelligence officers would import copies from America (which was perfectly legal) and display the books on their desk as a sign of rebellion.

'Yesterday there was a meeting of the Central "Stop the War" Committee. The only attendants were two lady police spies, who entered into conversation, neither knowing the other's occupation. At a subsequent election for vacancies on the committee both these ladies were elected – so I shall not be without information!'

Sir Basil Thomson, Director of Intelligence a the Home Office 1919-1921 in an extract from his war diary in *'The Scene Changes'* (1939). Today we would probably call them informants rather than "police spies" but it is interesting to note that in the early 1920s the police were using spies to infiltrate political groups. For more about Thomson see under "Agent Selection."

And, *plus ça change…*

'My section was tasked to investigate an extremist British nationalist group in the Midlands. Dressing myself to look like a young skinhead I paid for a party membership card and attended one of their meetings in the back room of a pub. It soon became clear that they were more interested in fighting each other than becoming a threat to the security of the state, so I never went back.

A year later, an envelope was forwarded to my cover address. It was from an international fascist group inviting me to their annual conference. It transpired that, in my absence, the party had elected me first as their regional representative, then as a member of their national council, and finally as their international "ambassador". All because no-one else had bothered to stand.

I forwarded the invitation to my head of section as a report attached to an internal e-mail. In the subject line I typed: "How to succeed in politics without really trying."'

Anonymous MI5 officer.

ARCOS Raid

'...an orgy of government indiscretion about the Secret Service for which there is no parallel in modern parliamentary history.'

ARCOS was the All-Russian Co-Operative Society, a body based in London which promoted trade between the UK and Russia. In May 1927, convinced by MI5 that it was a nest of Russian spies, the Government ordered its offices to be raided. But nothing incriminating was found. In fact, the Russians had been tipped off about the raid by their own spies in the British police. Questioned in the House of Commons, the Government tried to defend itself by quoting from illegally intercepted Russian telegrams and in the subsequent debate revealed that British intelligence services had broken the Russian secret codes. The Russians quickly changed all their codes and the secret service lost coverage for the next ten years. It was a (self-inflicted) intelligence disaster. Professor Christopher Andrew, the official historian of MI5, quoted in *Spies, Spin and the Fourth Estate* by Paul Lashmar (2020).

Assassination

'We don't wage war by those methods. We leave them to the Germans. Damn it all, we are gentlemen!'

The famous novelist W. Somerset Maugham in *Ashenden* (1927). Although fiction, the book is a barely concealed factual account of Maugham's life as a spy. He worked for British Military Intelligence in Switzerland in 1915. He then took a break from spying and spent much of 1916 in New York where one of his plays was being produced. In 1917 was approached by MI6 who wanted him to go on a mission to Russia. He travelled via Japan and the eastern Russian port of Vladivostok then across the breadth of Russia. He arrived in St Petersburg and managed to get a meeting with the Russian leader Kerensky. He then returned to England via Norway and a further visit to Russia was planned, but in the time he was away Kerensky's government collapsed and the Bolsheviks seized power. As far as anyone knows, that was the end of his espionage career but in that short time he left us one of the most vivid accounts of life as a spy at that time.

'No assassination instructions should ever be written or recorded.'

CIA operations manual from 1954 exposed during a Congressional inquiry into the overthrow of the Guatemalan government by the CIA that year.

'Certainly, we did very bad things. We did a lot of direct action. Assassinations. Although I was never involved.'

The novelist David Cornwell (John Le Carré) speaking of his time as an MI6 officer in Berlin in the 1950s. Quoted in *The Sunday Telegraph* 29 August 2010. This is a strange statement. The unwritten rule has always been that MI6 does not carry out assassinations. So Cornwell is either making a startling revelation or he is not being clear about which agency he is referring to.

'We have not yet reached that stage in our diplomacy when we have to use assassination as a substitute for diplomacy.'

Lord Halifax, British Foreign Secretary responding to a 1938 proposal to assassinate Hitler. Halifax was in favour of a policy of appeasement so it is not surprising that he did not want Hitler killed. However, even those determined to defeat Hitler also rejected the suggestion that he should be assassinated. The most famous proposal was codenamed *Operation Foxley*. It evaluated attacking his car with an anti-tank weapon, using a sniper to kill him on one of his walks at his holiday retreat in the mountains and even poisoning his drinking water. In the end, none of these methods were accepted on the grounds that Hitler would cause greater damage to the German war machine if he was left alive. There was also an *Operation Foxley II* study which proposed the assassination of Heinrich Himmler, head of the SS. Quoted in *The Secret Servant* by Anthony Cave Brown (1988).

'The French! Have you tried them? It's more their type of thing you know...'

MI5 officer Peter Wright in his book *Spycatcher* (1987). This was his response to the CIA who asked for assistance with an assassination attempt.

'There should be no fetters on reporters, nor must they tamper with the truth, but give light so the people will find their own way.'

Favoured motto of Gary Webb, the Pulitzer Prize winning journalist who, in 1996, exposed the CIA's involvement in supporting crack dealing gangs in Los Angeles. The CIA were using the money which this provided to fund insurgency in Central America. An internal investigation by the CIA found that most of Webb's allegations were true and his work led to the CIA being dubbed 'Crack in America' by black civil rights activists. This was not even the first involvement of the CIA in drugs running. Similar involvement had been uncovered during the Vietnam War in the 1970s and in support of the Nicaraguan Contras in the 1980s.

'Because of Gary Webb's work, the CIA launched an investigation that found dozens of connections to drug runners. That wouldn't have happened if he hadn't been willing to stand up and risk it all.'

Senator John Kerry, later a Presidential candidate, who chaired the Congressional Committee which investigated Webb's claims.

'I am scared. Look at what those people did to Gary Webb. Do something with your life – like enjoy it.'

Taped conversation between French journalist Paul Meoreira and an anonymous senior US media contact. Webb committed suicide in 2004 after he believed that his career and his marriage had been destroyed by the CIA. Those officers who may have hounded Webb to his death have since been rewarded with high ranking academic and media posts ... which shows that in espionage there is more than one way to skin a cat.

'Assassination? In general, it is an effective tool.'

Dani Yatom, Director General of Mossad (the Israeli foreign intelligence service) 1996-98. Quoted in *Inside the Mossad*, TV documentary, 2019). The Israelis assassinate more of their enemies than any other country. Mossad even has a specialist assassination section named *Kidon* which is Hebrew for "Bayonet".

'Who will rid me of this turbulent priest?!'

Attributed to King Henry II of England. Thomas a Becket, the Archbishop of Canterbury, was assassinated by a team of four knights as a result of this outburst. There have been several recent and reliable reports that decisions by the US President to assassinate targets on the US "Kill List" use similarly oblique language. Perhaps the most famous version of this desire to avoid the word "assassination" in the West is the phrase *"Terminate With Extreme Prejudice"* attributed to the CIA but not officially recorded.

'To the little gentleman in the black velvet waistcoat!'

This was the toast of secret supporters of the Stuart monarchy in England in the early eighteenth century. They had mounted several unsuccessful assassination attempts against King William III. He was finally killed in 1702 when his horse stumbled in a molehill and threw him to the ground. He died of later complications including pneumonia. Stuart supporters frequently drank a toast to the tiny, unknowing assassin. William had left only a childless daughter and they thought their time had come. But the English monarchy survived.

Australia

'The Soviets always seemed to be a step ahead of us. If we put on an operation, it failed.'

ASIO (Australian Security Service) officer Molly Sasson who had earlier worked for MI5 in Britain. She was convinced that the reason that so many early ASIO operations failed was because there was a mole. She claims that the CIA station chief in Canberra confirmed it to her. Quoted by ABC TV Australia, 17 August 2015.

'Don't open this can of worms.'

ASIO deputy director Colin Brown's reaction when Molly went to him with her fears. Quoted as above. And indeed, an ASIO investigation was never held. However, by 1974 the suspicions were so strong that a Royal Commission held an investigation into ASIO. But it was too late. The Commission could reach no firm conclusions and the mole was never caught. In fact, from the earliest days of the organisation it had been suspected that it was penetrated by the KGB. One of the first people who helped to set up ASIO was senior MI6 officer Charles 'Dick' Ellis. It was subsequently shown that Ellis had worked as a double agent not only for the KGB (which he didn't admit) but also for the Nazis (which he did admit). But when all this was discovered (in 1965) he was not prosecuted because, in the wake of Philby, Burgess, Maclean, Blake, etc there was a fear that British intelligence could not stand the revelation of yet another double agent. Ellis died in obscurity in 1975 and is probably the greatest British traitor you have never heard of.

B

Bay of Pigs

'Perhaps that will stop them lecturing us quite so frequently about our traitors.'

Dick White, Chief of MI6. He had been trying to rebuild MI6's reputation after a series of disasters including Burgess, Maclean and Blake. The incident that White was referring to was the CIA's calamitous attempted invasion of Cuba known as "the Bay of Pigs." That evened the score somewhat. On the other hand, Kim Philby, the so-called "Third Man" (of the Cambridge Five) was yet to be exposed. Quoted in *A Spy Called Cynthia* by Anonymous (2021).

Belgians

Their espionage work in the First World War *'... is the best answer to the often heard opinion that the Belgians as a race are devoid of courage. My experience is that there are no risks which they are not ready to undertake, and that the remuneration for which they are prepared to undertake the is, in most cases, absurdly small.'*

Colonel Reginald Drake of British Military Intelligence cited in *Armour Against Fate* by Michael Occleshaw (1989). Following their surrender in WWI the Belgians had a reputation for cowardice rather as the French did following their surrender in WWII. But it was their intelligence activity behind the lines that helped to defeat Germany, especially trainwatching networks such as *La Dame Blanche* which tracked German troop movements. Thousands of Belgians were involved and many were recognised with bravery awards after the war. Belgian's female spies were particularly noteworthy including Gabrielle Petit and Marthe McKenna. They are largely forgotten today but they rank amongst some of the world's greatest spies.

Betrayal

'This is why we should never trust the British'.

Bill Harvey, senior CIA officer speaking after the VENONA project reveals that that the US atomic programme was riddled with British spies working for Russia. Quoted in a PBS Documentary by Oxford Digital Media (2016). VENONA was one of the most valuable intelligence operations ever mounted. US signals intelligence had captured a great deal of enciphered Soviet traffic. Because it was enciphered it initially appeared to be of little use. However, someone decided that while it may not yield much current intelligence, deciphering the messages one day might yield a great deal of valuable historical information such as the identity of agents. So, a long-term decryption operation was set up and did indeed yield all kinds of valuable material including confirmation of the penetration of the Manhattan project by the Russians. Coming on top of the Burgess and Maclean revelations this was a bit too much for some US spies including Harvey. Many felt that they could never fully trust the British intelligence services again. In fact, the Russians learned of the VENONA operation from one of their American agents almost as soon as the operation commenced in 1945 (so it wasn't always the British at fault). There wasn't anything the

Russians could do since the material was already in US possession but it did make them more careful with their transmissions. But, despite its considerable intelligence value, most people in the West have never heard of VENONA because it was kept secret well into the 1990s. The operation ceased in the 1980s.

'One traitor in a main cryptographic centre can probably do his country more harm than in any other situation.'

John Bruce Lockhart quoted in *Intelligence: A British View* (1984). He was an MI6 officer during and after World War Two. He rose to be Deputy Director of MI6 so he knew his stuff. He should not be confused with his uncle Robert Bruce Lockhart who wrote about Sidney Reilly (see under "Agent Selection") and who was a diplomat, not a spy. What John Bruce Lockhart said is even more true now than it was in the 1960s. Computers have revolutionised the amount of information that is easily available. In 2010, Chelsea Manning, a lowly US army intelligence analyst, was able to steal more than half a million classified documents, while in 2013 Edward Snowden, an IT contractor, was able to steal 1.7 million classified documents from the NSA (US signals intelligence). Spies used to be happy if they could steal just one classified document. Those days are long gone.

Bettaney (Michael)

'As the commission says, his stress went unrecognised and untreated by his superiors, and eventually he became a traitor.'

Miranda Ingram, former MI5 officer quoted in *The Observer* newspaper 12 May 1985. Michael Bettaney was an MI5 officer who suffered a mental breakdown and offered to work for the Russians in 1983 by the simple method of posting his offer through the letterbox of the KGB Resident (head of station) in London. Unfortunately for him, the Deputy KGB Resident in London, Oleg Gordievsky, was a double agent working for MI6. He promptly informed them and Bettaney was arrested. Bettaney was convicted and sentenced to 23 years in prison of which he served 15. He lived quietly after his release but never quite overcame his alcoholism which eventually killed him in 2018. While one must not forget that Bettaney was a traitor, Ingram is right in pointing out the role that mental health had in his story. This mental rather than physical risk so beloved of spy thriller writers, is one of the largely unexplored aspects of espionage. It is also something largely ignored by the services themselves where a request for mental health treatment can all too easily be seen as a career-ending move.

Bias

'It is easier for a man to burn down his own house than to get rid of his own prejudices.'

English philosopher Roger Bacon from his *Opus Majus* (1267). See under "Codes and Ciphers" for more about Roger Bacon.

'An intelligence officer needs a well balanced mind. As much of the news which he will get will be contradictory, questionable and often entirely false, he must abstain from according too much faith to any reports which reach him.'

> Colonel George Furse in *Information in War* (1895). See under "Agent Selection" for more about Furse.

'A desk is a dangerous place from which to watch the world.'

> MI6 officer David Cornwell (John Le Carré) in his novel *The Honourable Schoolboy* (1983)

'A man who isn't a socialist at 20 has no heart and a man who is still a socialist at 40 has no head.'

> Attributed to William Casey, former Director CIA. There are many variations of this saying around the world so while he may have said this, he was almost certainly not the first.

Blackmail

'Sometimes even private indiscretions may serve the spy, and blackmailing is resorted to. This is a method never used by the British, but it is one in which the Germans are past masters.'

> Henry Landau, MI6 officer in *'All's Fair'* (1934).

And yet…..

'Once information has been handed over, the informer is forced as a rule into giving further information by fear or threat of betrayal, until eventually he becomes a regular spy in the pay of the country in question. Such a man, if he is in some state department, becomes a very valuable agent.'

> Henry Landau again in *'All's Fair'* (1934). See under "Agent Selection" for more about Landau.

And there is evidence that this second view was the right one:

Our... *'best source is a Belgian who has a hold on a German officer in Brussels. The latter goes to Holland about once a week for unnatural purposes, and our Belgian got to know of this, and threatens to denounce him.'*

> Major Walter Kirke talking of a source in a British military intelligence network in October 1916. Quoted in *Armour Against Fate* by Michael Occleshaw (1989).

But, a modern intelligence source would disagree:

'This service does not use blackmail, partly because most of us would find it repugnant and partly because, unless you control the environment within which your target operates, as in a totalitarian state, it is rarely effective for long and is never a guarantee of loyalty. The analogy often used is that we would not push a man off a ski-slope in order to break his leg, but we like to keep close behind him so that if he does fall we can offer help, and then make it easy for him to repay us, if he wishes.'

Alan Judd, "former Foreign Service" officer in '*Legacy*' (2001). See under "Agent Handling" for an explanatory note about Judd.

So, which is true? In fact, for all intelligence services (including the German service in the period that Landau was writing about) persuasion will always provide a better agent than coercion. The idea of intelligence officers as black-hearted puppet masters is (well, usually is) very far from the truth. Not because spies are more moral than normal people but because kindness often works better than force. However, there is another rule in espionage: never say "never" where national security is concerned. There may always be a case for an exception.

And finally, a poet has probably said it best:

'He that complies against his will is of his own opinion still'.

Samuel Butler (1612-1680) from his poem *Hudibras,* lines 547-549.

Bletchley Park

'I told you to leave no stone unturned, but I didn't expect you to take me so literally.'

Sir Winston Churchill to Arthur Denniston, the head of Bletchley Park, upon finding that the new staff who had been hired included academics, chess grandmasters and an expert on porcelain from the British Museum. Churchill shouldn't have been surprised: in World War Two, Bletchley Park was the successor to the First World War codebreaking centre named "Room 40". This name referred to one of the rooms in the Admiralty, a department led by Sir Winston. The principle of hiring "oddballs" for codebreaking was established by Room 40 which employed people such as ancient history experts, actors, poets, novelists, businessmen and Alfred "Dilly" Knox who used to do his codebreaking while sitting in a warm bath. (And just in case you think I am making that up, the bath is now on display at the Bletchley Park museum.) Quoted in *The Code Book* by Simon Singh (1999).

'...the geese that laid the golden eggs and never cackled.'

Sir Winston Churchill speaking about Bletchley Park staff after the war and reflecting not only their achievements but also the fact that they remain so tight lipped even though it meant that many of them never received the recognition they so truly deserved. Today only Alan Turing is widely remembered but there were many others who were equally, if not more, deserving of fame. Incidentally, the same rule did not apply to Room 40 staff after the First World War as many of them listed their Room 40 service and their home telephone numbers in *Who's Who?*

But it wasn't all good news:

'It was something of a disappointment to a young woman ...'

Pamela Rose, in charge of Naval Hut 4's indexing section. Quoted in her obituary in *The Guardian* newspaper 6 November 2021. Too few parties apparently.

Blunders

'Once in a while, just often enough to give intelligence officers a false sense of confidence, a secret operation almost goes according to plan.'

Former CIA officer William Hood in his book *Mole* (1993)

'Fucking unbelievable!'

Comment by an unnamed CIA officer to *Guardian* journalist Luke Harding after President Trump revealed Top Secret Israeli intelligence about Russia to Russian Foreign Minister Sergei Lavrov. Trump even revealed the city where the Israeli source was based. It is an absolute rule of intelligence that you do not disseminate intelligence from an ally without their express permission. Quoted in *Collusion* by Luke Harding (2017).

'Pollard had once collected so much data that he needed a handcart to move the papers to his car, in an nearby parking lot and the Pentagon security guards held the doors for him.'

Seymour Hersh in *"The Traitor – The Case Against Jonathan Pollard"* in *The New Yorker* 18th January 1999. Seymour Hersh has probably broken more important intelligence stories than any other journalist currently working. Pollard was a civilian intelligence analyst for the Navy working at the Pentagon. He passed thousands of items of classified US intelligence to Israel. He was caught and sentenced to life imprisonment in 1985. But after years of pressure from Israel, he was released in 2015 and flown to Israel where he was greeted as a hero. Yet the greatest damage that Pollard caused was not to America but to hundreds of other Jewish intelligence officers around the world. Pollard was Jewish and his defence had been that he had become a traitor because he believed that Israel deserved to have the intelligence. Security chiefs began to wonder if their Jewish staff were a similar security risk – which is of course a terrible slur. But you can see why they asked the question.

BND (Bundesnachrichtendienst – German foreign intelligence service)

'You don't see people making fun of them anymore.'

Tyler Drumheller, former head of the CIA in Europe. The service was mocked as clumsy and ineffectual during the Cold War but has re-invented itself since the creation of a united Germany and is now one of the best in the world. Quoted in *The Guardian* newspaper 18 March 2011.

Bond (James)

'James Bond is a highly romanticised version of a true spy.'

Ian Fleming. (No he isn't.)

'James Bond, in the real world of espionage, wouldn't survive four minutes.'

H. Keith Melton quoted in *Smithsonian* magazine (July 2001). Melton is one of the world's leading experts on espionage and real spies would endorse his view. Including the following officers:

'...a fantasy figure embodying all a sick generation's obsessive interest in secrecy, violence and sex at its most debased.'

Malcolm Muggeridge, author, broadcaster and former MI6 officer from the introduction to *British Agent* by John Whitwell (1966). Whitwell was the pseudonym of Leslie Nicholson, an MI6 officer who had been head of station in Prague and Riga in the 1930s before working in other roles for MI6 during the war. Muggeridge described Nicholson as *"gentle and rather like Bertie Wooster"* but he was an excellent agent runner. See under "Agent Handling" for more about Muggeridge.

'... the ultimate prostitute...'

Former MI6 officer and novelist David Cornwell (John Le Carré.) Quoted in *Literary Agents* by Anthony Masters (1987).

'An Etonian version of Mickey Spillane.'

Malcolm Muggeridge again. Quoted in *Literary Agents* by Anthony Masters (1987).

'Bond's adventures were, of course, preposterous. There was nothing in them really that was measurable in the experience of most Western intelligence agencies or agents...'

Howard Hunt, veteran CIA officer and author. He was commissioned by the CIA to write a series of Bond-like thrillers which the Agency hoped would boost its reputation just as Ian Fleming's Bond had done for MI6. His *Peter Ward* thrillers were not a similar success.

'... the hyaena who stalks the capitalist deserts ...'

David Cornwell (John Le Carré) again. Quoted in *The Observer* newspaper 9 October 2022.

But he does serve one function for real spies:

'...the best recruiting sergeant the Service ever had...'

Former MI6 Chief Colin McColl quoted in the article *Fiction, Faction and Intelligence* by Nigel West in *Understanding Intelligence in the 21ˢᵗ Century* edited by L V Scott and P D Jackson (2004). And it is true that the exciting James Bond image does get new recruits "through the door". The trouble is that you then have to start dismantling that image and showing them what real espionage is about: a lot of it is routine or boring or requires months of painstaking research. At which point many of the recruits go back out through the door again – hopefully, before they have learned too many secrets.

Occasionally Fleming gets it right:

'The Bond situations are so ridiculous. I mean, this man is supposed to be a spy and yet everybody knows he's a spy.'

Roger Moore, one of the actors who portrayed Bond on screen. Quoted in *The Independent* newspaper 17 October 2005. Oddly enough, although much of the Bond persona is rubbish, this is one aspect in which Fleming is correct. It is almost impossible for a spy to remain secret all his or her life, but that does not mean their career is over. Most heads of stations of all services are "avowed" to the government of the country where they are based and the identity of others are known through counter intelligence work or the media. Such officers serve two purposes 1) it is useful to have someone for defectors and other people who might offer valuable intelligence to contact and 2) they distract attention from other, still secret, spies.

Perhaps Fleming himself suspected the truth about the character of Bond:

'What are you? You are a common thug, a blunt instrument wielded by dolts in high places.'

The villain Blofeld to James Bond in *You Only Live Twice* (1964).

And finally:

'Throughout all of Bond's adventures nobody English does anything evil.'

Kingsley Amis. He was talking of the Bond books and also different era of world history. English villains are now rather common in spy thrillers. Perhaps the world's perception of the English has changed...

Boredom

'It would be terribly disappointing for the livelier fantasies of people who have written about me in that capacity, if they knew how boring my life had been. And how humdrum is the world of intelligence in many ways.'

David Cornwell (John Le Carré) novelist and former MI6 officer. Quoted in *Literary Agents* by Anthony Masters (1987).

'There is nothing especially dramatic (contrary to popular opinion) about the operations of a spy. If they are caught red-handed, their work may have dramatic enough results, but many of the routine duties of espionage add up to a merely dull and rather undramatic business...'

Lt. Col. A. P. Scotland in his book *The London Cage* (1957). During the Second World War, Scotland, who spoke German fluently from his childhood in South Africa, was one of the UK's finest interrogators. During the First World War he had been an undercover spy so natural with the Germans that they assumed that he was one of their own. A film inspired by his First World War adventures was made in 1958 (*The Two-Headed Spy* starring Jack Hawkins). His appearance at the Nuremburg trial led to him being hailed by one fevered newspaper as *"Britain's Masterspy!"*. He wasn't, but he was damned good. Interestingly, he worked for British Military Intelligence and not for MI6.

'For sheer excitement and danger in the performance, routine spying often compares unfavourably with even a good fast football game.'

Lt. Col. A. P .Scotland (see above).

'It must seem odd to consider the possibility of facing boredom in this sort of work, but boredom is as much a part of the experience as the exciting bits. You should always be prepared for the tedium of waiting for a weary to knock at your door, sitting outside a police station for twelve hours until your last comrade is released or taking part in a week of mind-numbing discussions on political theory.'

From the tradecraft handbook of the Special Demonstration Squad, an undercover police unit discredited and subject of the Pitchford Inquiry after it was revealed that officers had used their undercover roles to seduce and sometimes rape female targets. A "weary" was SDS slang for a political activist. Their abuse of power is a good example of what happens in the world of espionage when there is no oversight.

'Spy novels ... paint a romanticised or highly dramatised picture of espionage. A novel depicting the true life of a secret agent would probably bore the reader to death.'

Espionage historian David Stafford in *The Silent Game* (2013).

Bribery

'Nothing is beyond the reach of the power of gold.'

Unnamed French historian writing of the great successes of Marlborough and how much of the success was down to the fact that agents reporting to Marlborough were able to bribe French officials to give up the secret plans of the French War Ministry. Quoted by the historian Richard Holmes in *Marlborough* (2008).

British Security Co-ordination (BSC)

'BSC may have been the largest single covert operation in British intelligence history.'

BSC was the MI6 front organisation in the United States, formed in 1940, when the US was still neutral and British intelligence activities were still regarded with suspicion by isolationists (including the FBI under J. Edgar Hoover who hated the British). To be effective and to make the best of secret support from friendly elements in the US government, a new way of working was needed. William Stephenson provided it. He was a highly successful businessman and self-trained spy appointed to the job personally by Winston Churchill. BSC is probably one of the greatest intelligence operations the public has never heard of. Quoted in *Spies, Spin and the Fourth Estate* by Paul Lashmar (2020).

'To have established a US-wide intelligence operation on the scale and with the influence that Stephenson succeeded in doing was as great an achievement as there has ever been in the world of intelligence.'

The anonymous author of *A Spy Called Cynthia* (2021). He is believed to have been a senior diplomat who was part of the operation.

'Throughout the neutral Americas, and especially in the US, BSC ran espionage agents, tampered with the mails, tapped telephones, smuggled propaganda, disrupted public gatherings, covertly subsidised newspapers, radios and organisations, perpetrated forgeries – even palming one off on the President of the United States –violated the Aliens Registration Act, shanghaied sailors

numerous times, and possibly murdered one or more persons in this country.'

Ernest Cuneo, liaison between British intelligence and the US government during the Second World War. He may not sound like a fan but the BSC provided inspiration for the formation of the CIA. Quoted in *Spies, Spin and the Fourth Estate* by Paul Lashmar (2020).

Bugs

'Nothing beats an agent in the right place. Bugs can't tell you who is sleeping with whom, who is jealous of his superiors and fed up with his job – and who is drinking.'

John Bingham, MI5's head of counter-subversion, a staunch traditionalist who disliked electronic devices and was a great believer in well-place agents. Yet he was surely wrong. A well placed bug or intercept can reveal all of the points above. Quoted in *Literary Agents* by Anthony Masters (1987).

Bureaucracy

'We have no use for the "usual channels", except in the early morning.'

Favourite saying of Mansfield Cumming, the first chief of MI6, quoted by Alan Judd in *The Quest for C* (1999). He was of course referring to the channels at the bottom of public urinals. Charming. On the other hand, it does rather sum up the Service's attitude to outsiders.

'I disagreed with Maurice on one thing. He was all for moving people about from one area to another every three years or so. I argued that a particularly good man in his own area needed to be kept on...'

Anonymous MI6 officer quoted in *'C': A biography of Sir Maurice Oldfield* by Richard Deacon (1985). This moving of MI6 intelligence officers may seem strange but Maurice (Oldfield – Chief of MI6 1973-78) supported it for a very good reason. In the early days of MI6 some officers remained in post for very long periods. This led to inefficiency, complacency and, on more occasions than it is comfortable to note, outright corruption. Intelligence work requires imagination and ideas – you never want to repeat the same trick twice if you can help it. Freshening up the pack every so often helps in that endeavour.

Burgess (Guy, one of the Cambridge Five who secretly worked for Russia)

'Morally afflicted, the personification of evil'

MI6 officer Malcolm Muggeridge only met Burgess once - but he clearly made an impression. Quoted in *Literary Agents* by Anthony Masters (1987).

'We gossiped about life in London; he gave me messages for former lovers. The theme that he constantly reverted to was the possibility that he might some day be able without danger to come home to England.'

Tom Driberg, notorious homosexual, Labour MP, and agent for the KGB and MI5 as well as, possibly the Czechs. Burgess (who was homosexual and this was the basis of his friendship with Driberg) never meant to defect. Burgess, like Blunt, Philby, Maclean and Cairncross, the other members of the Cambridge Five, he wanted to stay in the UK and brazen it out. You see – and it may seem strange to say this given what he did - he had no particular love for Russia. He really only wanted to oppose Hitler and saw Communism as the best way to do it. However, someone had to go with Maclean when he defected because the Russians thought that he was not mentally tough enough to make the journey. Burgess, who was also under suspicion, reluctantly went along. By the end of his life, Burgess hated Russia, missed the UK desperately (he often wept when he talked about it) and eventually drank himself to death. Meanwhile, Driberg was also very good friends with Maurice Oldfield, the Chief of MI6 who was also homosexual. At the time, homosexuality was illegal in the United Kingdom so there was already a bond of secrecy between many people. Oldfield was at absolutely the other end of the spectrum of loyalty from Burgess. Sometimes the lines between friends and enemies in espionage are very blurred.

C

Cambridge Spies (Philby, Burgess, Maclean, Blunt, Cairncross)

'Everyone knew that the Cambridge Apostles, an elite intellectual society to which Burgess belonged, was a hotbed of Communist sympathies, everyone that is except MI5. Their stuffed-shirt officers, bedecked with old school ties, never bothered to investigate persons who were so obviously "one of us"'.

Professor Donald Cameron-Watt. Quoted in *Defending The Realm* by Mark Hollingsworth and Nick Fielding (1999). In case anyone doesn't know, the Cambridge spies were students from that university who joined various sections of British intelligence and the Foreign Office (where there was also access to secrets) and betrayed secret to the Russian intelligence service during the 1940s. Almost all were members of "The Apostles", an elite debating society. The most notorious of the five was Kim Philby who became a senior officer at MI6. The others were Donald Maclean (Foreign Office), Guy Burgess (MI6), John Cairncross (MI6) and Anthony Blunt (MI5). They are sometimes referred to as the Cambridge Five although there were in fact more than five spies in the circle, it is just that these five achieved the greatest success.

'Sometimes the price of liberty is eternal inefficiency.'

Robert Cecil, 1ˢᵗ Viscount Chelwood (1864-1958). Cecil was speaking in the House of Lords and answering those who pointed out how useless British counter-espionage had been in failing to catch Maclean and Burgess who had just fled to Russia. He was implying that those who wanted to live in a system which would have caught such men should perhaps go and live in Russia. It's a fair point but doesn't quite excuse the fact that British intelligence security at this time was so useless that members of the Communist Party could simply walk into sensitive posts just because "they were the right sort of people". There is a better balance between security and liberty than inefficiency. Cecil was not an MI6 officer but he was the Foreign Office's advisor to 'C' (the Chief of MI6, Stewart Menzies) and so was very close to the Service. He remained so for the rest of his life.

'If I had a choice between betraying a friend and betraying my country, I hope I would have the guts to betray my country.'

The novelist E. M. Forster, but supposedly a favourite saying of Guy Burgess.

'To betray, one must first belong. I never belonged.'

Kim Philby in answer to the question of whether he was a spy or a traitor. He always insisted that he was a Russian penetration agent and not a traitor as he had offered his services to Russia and then deliberately got himself hired by MI6. It is a fine point and probably not one that the agents he betrayed and who paid with their lives might have appreciated.

'All through my career, I have been a straight penetration agent working in the Soviet interest. My connection with MI6 must be seen against my total prior commitment to the Soviet Union...'

Kim Philby in *My Secret War* (1968). No person ever thinks he does wrong. There is always a way of justifying your actions to yourself. Philby had an intellectual justification for his treachery.

'My God, how I despise you now. I hope you have enough decency left to understand why.'

Nicholas Elliott of MI6 to his old friend Kim Philby after the Soviet defector Anatoly Golitsyn had revealed that Philby was a Russian agent. Elliott had been sent to Beirut where Philby was living in semi-retirement. His mission was to bring Philby back. But either from incompetence or collusion (no-one is quite sure which) Elliott gave Philby one night to think about things and, of course, Philby ran for it. He made it all the way back to Russia where he lived out the rest of his rather sad life. Quoted in *The Fourth Man* by Andrew Boyle (1979).

'It's like being a lavatory attendant: it stinks but someone has to do it.'

Donald Maclean trying to justify his treachery. Quoted in *KGB* (1990) by Christopher Andrew and Oleg Gordievsky. Interestingly, Gordievsky himself was a KGB double agent who eventually defected to the British. He betrayed his country's secret for years (and thank goodness that he did.) But does a perception of treachery depend on viewpoint or is it a human reaction to the personal cost?

'The Cambridge Spies were not only traitors; they were also, in different but closely similar ways, monsters of egotism.'

The historian John Keegan in *Intelligence in War* (2003). This is true but then I have met dozens of agents over the years and I have yet to meet an agent who did not have a very high opinion of him or herself. One of the main reasons for becoming a spy is to feel that your life matters. It is not an aspect of character peculiar to the Cambridge Spies.

'Got you, you swine.'

Goronwy Rees who lay dying in a hospital bed when he heard that Anthony Blunt, the "Fourth Man" had finally been exposed. The first three were Philby, Burgess and Maclean but many people were sure that there must be others. The public exposure of Blunt and Cairncross came much later. Rees was a journalist, academic and a friend of Guy Burgess. Just after the war, he worked briefly for MI6. He had been trying to convince people of Blunt's guilt for years. Quoted in *Blunt* by Miranda Carter (2001).

Case Officers

'To be a good case officer, you have to be a bit of a shit.'

Unnamed MI6 officer to the journalist and historian Michael Smith in his book *Foley* (1999). What does this mean? I have often asked this question – and I worked there. A case officer is usually a good friend of an agent. You cannot be a good agent runner unless you respect (at least in some regard) your agents and the risks that they are running. But I think what this officer was driving at is that a case officer must always remain objective and sceptical. That is because, on very rare occasions, it may be necessary to take a harsh decision for the good of the operation. Either that or this officer was a real bastard.

Children

'It was during the third stage of the contract that I started to make use of children to obtain information'

Bill Graham, MI6 agent who, once having obtained access to a Soviet compound under the guise of a double glazing contract, found that the children of KGB spies can inadvertently give up a lot of useful intelligence about what their parents are up to. Quoted in *Break In* by Bill Graham (1987).

China

'Power, money and politics are going east, that's the political reality we need to adjust to.'

Alex Younger, Chief of MI6 2014-2020, speaking to students at St. Andrews University in November 2018.

'From a perspective of threat against the United States national security and our interests, China is number one by far.'

William Evanina, Director of the US National Counterintelligence and Security Centre. Quoted by BBC News in December 2018.

'Adapting to a world affected by the rise of China is the single greatest priority for MI6.'

Speech by Richard Moore, Chief of MI6 from 2020 to the International Institute of Strategic Studies on 30th November 2021.

Churchill

'Churchill stood head and shoulders above his political contemporaries in grasping the importance of intelligence. Secret service with all its romance and melodrama, trickery, deception, plot and counter-plot, certainly appealed to the schoolboy within him.'

The historian David Stafford quoted in *Spymaster* by David Ramsay (2008).

'How much ?!'

One of the great "What Ifs?" of history. In January 1915, Admiral Hall of Naval Intelligence (NID), instigated a campaign to persuade Turkey to drop out of the war using three NID agents based in Constantinople: Edwin Whittal, Gerald Fitzmaurice and George Eady. Hall authorised his agents to pay the Turks up to £4 million. Churchill found out on 13th March 1915 and stopped further negotiations, reportedly using these words. If he had not intervened, it is possible that the disasters of Gallipoli and Kut might never have happened and tens of thousands of British lives would have been saved. It might not even have cost the British Treasury a penny since the Turks had two warships interned in Britain valued at

£4 million each. These could have been returned. Churchill was not always right. Quoted in *Spymaster* by David Ramsay (2008).

'In the years I have been in office since [British codebreaking] began in the autumn of 1914 I have read every one of those flimsies [reports] and I attach more importance to them as a means of forming a true judgement of public policy in these spheres than to any other source of knowledge at the disposal of the State.'

From *Churchill and Secret Service* by David Stafford (1987). By chance, Churchill was First Lord of the Admiralty when Britain first began reading the world's communications through its very first codebreaking centre (known as Room 40). It can be said that codebreaking changed the course of the war because it brought America in on the Allied side (via the revelation of the Zimmerman Telegram). Churchill quickly understood the power of this new facility and never let it go. Even when he was no longer First Lord and had moved on to other posts such as Chancellor, he demanded the right to see intercept intelligence. Together with the fact that he was also seeing most MI6 intelligence which was brought to him (quite irregularly) by a senior officer, this wealth of knowledge must have given him a tremendous advantage in public life. Historians are still evaluating just how much.

CIA

'We do espionage.'

Former CIA Director George Tenet from an interview on 23 June 1998 quoted in *Studies in Intelligence,* Volume 42/1.

That seems a straightforward statement. But consider this:

'What the hell do those clowns do out there at Langley?!'

Langley being, of course, the headquarters of the CIA. This was Richard Nixon speaking in 1970 shortly after hearing of the overthrow of Prince Sihanouk in Cambodia, a major US ally. Quoted in *The Memoirs of Richard Nixon* (1978). Those with a well-developed sense of intelligence *schadenfreude* should look out a good history of the CIA where they will find dozens more examples of where the CIA intelligence assessments predicted almost the opposite of what actually happened such as: the chances of Taiwan surviving more than a year against China, the strength of Viet Cong forces, the extent of Soviet nuclear arsenals, etc. etc.

'Selecting one of the principal leaders of the torture programme is actually a hostile act against the CIA, designed to make the agency worse, not better.'

Alberto Mora, general counsel of the Department of the Navy, 2001-2006 speaking of the appointment of Gina Haspel as Director of the CIA. Haspel had run a CIA torture site in Thailand and drafted the orders for all evidence of such torture at CIA sites around the world to be destroyed so that the torturers could never be prosecuted. Mora was suggesting that President Trump had appointed her as an act designed to weaken the CIA rather than picking the best person for the job. Trump's lack of respect and trust for America's intelligence services is well documented. Quoted in *The Guardian* newspaper 17 March 2018.

'Gina [Haspel] has her defenders. Some on the left. Some who are very reputable people. They depict her as being very competent, thorough and professional. But no one ever accused the Nazis of being sloppy, inept and amateurish. They were accused of war crimes.'

Larry Beinhart speaking in April 2019. Beinhart is an expert on the intelligence services and the author of the famous political novel *American Hero.*

'After World War Two, the CIA, with ramifications all over the world, came to outclass our once legendary Secret Service as a sleek Cadillac does an ancient hansom cab.'

Malcolm Muggeridge, author, broadcaster and former MI6 officer. Quoted in *MI6* by Stephen Dorril (2000).

'Uncertain allies.'

George Young, former MI6 officer. Quoted in *MI6* by Stephen Dorril (2000).

'We had some awful things in mind ... some of which we carried off.'

In 1967 the US magazine *Ramparts* exposed the CIA's subversion of the National Students Association. The CIA was not supposed to carry out operations against US citizens inside the USA. For more than a year the CIA used all kinds of terrible revenge against the journalists responsible for the article including smears, bugging, surveillance and blackmail. Quoted in *Spies, Spin and the Fourth Estate* by Paul Lashmar (2020).

'And ye shall know the truth and the truth shall make you free.'

Motto of the CIA. It is inscribed on the wall of the entrance lobby at Langley.

'When I joined the CIA I believed in the need for its existence. After twelve years with the agency I finally understood how much suffering it was causing...'

Philip Agee, former CIA officer from his book *Inside The Company* (1975)

'I was never worried about the CIA catching me. I knew how inept the organisation was.'

Aldrich Ames quoted in *Confessions of a Spy* by Pete Earley (1998). Ames was the CIA's most notorious traitor. He worked for Russian intelligence 1985 -1994 and betrayed as many as fifty top agents. At least ten of these were shot. It is hard to be sure as Robert Hanssen, an FBI officer, was also spying for the Russians during this period. Hanssen echoed Ames words saying that he had not feared detection and described FBI security measures as "pathetic."

'There has not been a foreign policy event that the President could not have understood better by reading the daily press than by relying on the CIA.'

Robert E. White, former US ambassador writing in the *Los Angeles Times* 12 March 1997. Interestingly, the same accusation was levelled at MI6 by the Franks Inquiry into the intelligence failures of the Falklands War.

Ciphers and Codes

'A man is crazy who writes a secret in any other way than one which will conceal it from the vulgar.'

Roger Bacon (c1220 - c1292) from his *Epistle on the Secret Works of Art and the Nullity of Magic*. Bacon was a medieval philosopher and an expert in physics, mathematics and other sciences. He was working at a time when there was always a danger that others might steal one's knowledge and he knew how to protect it. One such secret was the formula for gunpowder which was a dangerous secret indeed if it fell into the wrong hands (although he did not invent it – it came from China).

'I am very lovely when wet.'

Key phrase in a letter to Commander James Stockdale from his wife who was being held in North Vietnam's infamous torture centre, the "Hanoi Hilton". The letter (which had passed the Vietnamese censors) included a photograph of a woman who was supposed to be his mother but clearly wasn't. Stockdale puzzled over this for days. Finally he got it. The phrase was supposed to tell him to soak the photograph. He did so and it came apart revealing a secret message and a carbon paper for secret writing which would enable him to get messages out without detection in his normal letters home. Captured in 1965, Stockdale survived an incredible 2621 days of confinement and torture before being released in 1973. The messaging system started by this simple phrase eventually expanded to the point where the POWs imprisoned with Stockdale even had their own short wave radio with which to communicate. The Vietnamese guards, who read every letter, never suspected a thing.

'Cypher ... is a kind of Magick.'

Abraham de Wiquefort, a Dutch diplomat of the 17th century quoted in *Espionage in the Reign of Charles II* by Alan Marshall (1994). This was in a period when the term "diplomat" was little more than code for "legitimate spy". Everyone expected ambassadors to do a little bit of spying. It was only in the Victorian era that this changed and espionage became the realm of specialist spies.

'Detective stories or crossword puzzles cater for the majority; the solution of secret codes may be the pursuit of a few.'

John Chadwick in his book *The Decipherment of Linear B (1958)*. The techniques required for understanding ancient and forgotten languages is one reason why most early cipher centres such as Room 40 at the Admiralty in World War One and Bletchley Park in World War Two, employed ancient historians as well as mathematicians.

'Deciphering is, in my opinion, one of the most fascinating of arts.'

Charles Babbage, creator of the first mechanical computer, from his book *Passages From the Life of a Philosopher,* Chapter 18 (1864). There is a considerable correlation between inventors and an interest in codes – Leonardo Da Vinci is another example.

'Real mathematics has no effect on war. No one has yet discovered any warlike purpose to be served by the theory of numbers.'

British mathematician G H Hardy in *The Mathematicians Apology* (1940). He was writing just before it came to be universally accepted that coding was a matter of mathematics rather than of linguistics which had been the skill used for deciphering ancient texts. This is largely because of changes that were being made to codes and ciphers to make them harder to break.

'Whichever country gets there first [the development of a quantum computer] *will have the ability to monitor the communications of its citizens, read the minds of its commercial rivals and eavesdrop on the plans of its enemies. Although it is still in its infancy, quantum computing presents a potential threat to the individual, to international business and to global security.'*

The Code Book by Simon Singh (1999). The development of such computers will enable all previous codes to be broken. That is one reason why all intelligence services across the world are storing up unbroken coded messages because even if they are old, they will still reveal useful secrets.

However it seems that the advantage would not last for long ...

'Quantum cryptography would mark the end of the battle between codemakers and codebreakers, and the codemakers emerge victorious. Quantum cryptography is an unbreakable system of encryption.'

The Code Book by Simon Singh (1999). If you want to know why, read Singh's excellent book. He explains it far better than I ever could.

'The war of cryptographer against cryptanalyst has been won by the cryptographers.'

David Kahn in his book *The Codebreakers* (1996) Kahn's work is seminal and always worth a read. He is the godfather of cryptography historians.

But as an intelligence officer, part of me cannot accept that this is true. There must be a way in! The following statement gives me hope:

'There may be perfect systems, but there are no perfect users.'

Attributed to the American NSA and quoted in *The Literary Spy* by Charles Lathrop (2004). In information security terms this is known as *social engineering* – manipulating the users rather than attacking the system. A good example of this approach would be the uber-hacker Kevin Mitnick. In the early 1990s he was America's most wanted hacker. He seemed to have almost legendary abilities to hack into even the most protected of systems. Investigators assumed that he must be a programming genius. But as he tells in his book *The Art of Deception* (2002), much of the time it was not his programming skills but his ability to fool users that really enabled him to break into key systems. He was considered so dangerous that four and half years of his five year sentence were served in solitary confinement in case he taught other criminals some of his skills. Today he is a "white-hat" hacker, using his skills for good.

Class

'If there's any one thing about England that Cayce finds fundamentally disturbing, it is how "class" works – a word with a very different mirror world meaning, somehow. She's long since given up trying to explain this to English friends.

The closest she can come is that it's somewhat akin, if only for its enormity, to how the British seem to feel about certain American attitudes to firearms ownership – which they generally find unthinkable, and bafflingly, self-evidently wrong, and so often leading to a terrible and profligate waste of human life. And she knows what they mean, but also knows how deeply it runs, the gun thing, and how unlikely it is to change.'

William Gibson, *Pattern Recognition* (2003). Class is an issue that bedevils British Intelligence. If you want to rise to the very top in any of the British services then there are certain private London dining clubs of which you should be a member. But they only invite people from the right class. In its way, it is almost as poisonous to the country as the influence of the gun laws in America – and equally mystifying.

Cold War

'My strategy for the Cold War is: we win, they lose.'

US President Ronald Reagan. Simple and fun, but rhetoric like this very nearly destroyed the world. From his public utterances, the Russians thought that Reagan was so fanatically anti-communist that he would launch a nuclear first strike. They were so afraid that they thought they might have to strike first. Fortunately, intelligence provided by MI6 agent Oleg Gordievsky (Codename: OVATION) demonstrated to Reagan just how worried the Russians were. He was shocked. He had never thought that they were so weak. This led, at least in part, to a revision of his position and to his much more pragmatic relationship with Russian leader Mikhail Gorbachev. That eventually led to the collapse of the Soviet Union and the end of the Cold War. It is one of the few times in history when intelligence really has made a difference.

Communications Intelligence

'War is ninety per cent information.'

Attributed to Napoleon.

'By the frequent inspection of letters a king soon knows the temper of all his principal and active subjects.'

Sir Samuel Morland, 17th Century spy and inventor. Quoted in *Espionage in the reign of Charles II* by Alan Marshall (1994).

'It is not possible to be a great statesman without opening packets (i.e. letters)*.'*

Phillippe de Comminges – French diplomat. Quoted in *Espionage in the reign of Charles II* by Alan Marshall (1994).

'Gentlemen do not read each other's mail.'

Attributed to US Secretary of State Henry Stimson shortly before shutting down the US Cypher Bureau in 1929.

However:

'Gentlemen do read each other's mail – if they can get their hands on it.'

Former CIA Director Allen Dulles writing in *The Craft of Intelligence* (1963).

'To read an opponent's messages is to read his mind.'

Angelo Codevilla in *Informing Statecraft* (1992). As so often, Codevilla says it more succinctly than anyone else. And this statement has become even more true since our "messages" now include all of our internet activity. Truly, if you can see all of that, there is very little that a person can keep secret. That is why intelligence agencies collect so much of it, store it permanently and analyse it. This is known in the trade as *"data mining"*. They tell citizens that they do not use this information. And they won't. Not until you become a problem....

'Metadata absolutely tells you everything about somebody's life'.

Metadata is the mass result of everyone's internet activity. Intelligence agencies always claim that it is impossible to single out individuals from this and therefore citizen's have nothing to fear if they collect it. However, this is Stewart Baker, former general counsel at the NSA (US signals intelligence), commenting on the whistleblower Edward Snowden's observation that supposedly anonymous metadata can in fact be used to get information about almost anyone. Quoted in *The Guardian* newspaper 17 May 2016.

One of the very first mentions of espionage in English state papers, possibly the first, concerns mail interception. It occurs in a royal writ dated 18 December 1324. It is addressed to officials in ports around the English coast and berates them for not observing previous orders:

'...to make diligent scrutiny of all persons passing from parts beyond the seas to England ... to stop all letters concerning which sinister suspicions might arise' and to send these to the king *'with the utmost speed.'*

Quoted in *Plots and Paranoia* by Professor Bernard Porter (1988).

It may have been a technique which Shakespeare was aware of:

'The king hath note of all that they intend,
By interception which they dream not of.'

William Shakespeare, Henry V, Act II Scene II.

'...a gift more precious than a dozen Fabergé eggs.'

Sir Winston Churchill in 1914 reacting to the gift of a copy of the German Imperial Navy's code book and cipher key. Quoted in *Churchill and Secret Service* by David Stafford (1987). Admiralty interception units could soon read all German naval signals which were invaluable in allowing the Royal Navy to maintain the economic stranglehold that eventually brought Germany to its knees. The gift was from Russia. How times have changed.

'Our intelligence service has won and deserved world-wide fame. More than perhaps any other Power, we were successful in the [First World] War in penetrating the intentions of the enemy.'

Sir Winston Churchill in *The World Crisis* (1923). The activities of Alan Turing and Bletchley Park tend to get all the attention these days (e.g. the movie *The Imitation Game*) but the United Kingdom had been a world leader in cryptography long before that. Churchill was referring specifically to the interception and decryption of German radio communications by 'Room 40' of the Admiralty. This forerunner of GCHQ had been set up at a meeting on 5th August 1914 between Sir Alfred Ewing, Director of Naval Education, Rear Admiral Sir Henry Oliver, Director of Naval Intelligence and Churchill, who was then First Lord of the Admiralty. Oliver was wondering what he could do with the flood of enciphered German radio signals that he was receiving. Ewing, who was an amateur enthusiast for both radio telegraphy and decryption (he had even designed his own cipher machine) believed that it was possible to decrypt those signals and then to intercept and decrypt even more. Churchill was fascinated by the prospect of being able to read his enemies secret thoughts and gave them the green light. Room 40 became one of the most crucial weapons in the First World War.

'Today this business requires a huge investment and Britain just doesn't have that.'

Lt. Gen. William Odom, head of the American NSA (US signals intelligence 1985-1989) explaining why the UK is no longer a leader in the field of communications intelligence Quoted in *UK Eyes Alpha* by Mark Urban (1987).

'No matter how benign the original intent, large collections of personal data, especially combined with the economic pressures of a deep recession or a government interested in data mining for security purposes, are fraught with the potential for evil.'

Seth Finkelstein, Technology Correspondent for *The Guardian* newspaper in an article dated 26 March 2009.

'A programme in which the end justifies all means, in which everything that is technically feasible is then acted out, violates trust and spreads mistrust. In the end, it produces not more but less security.'

Angela Merkel, Chancellor of Germany speaking of US interception in the light of the Edward Snowden revelations. Quoted in *The Guardian* newspaper 30 January 2014.

'The human spy, in terms of the American espionage effort, has never been terribly pertinent.'

Aldrich Ames, the CIA traitor. What Ames was getting at was this: The CIA was founded in 1947. By that time signals intelligence was already having a major impact (one only has to think of how ULTRA material shortened the war by two whole years according to some claims.) The influence of signals intelligence has only continued to grow since and that growth has accelerated with the dawn of the internet. Therefore, in American intelligence terms, human sources of intelligence have always played second fiddle to the massive scope of American signals intelligence. But it is still true that the right agent in the right place can have a devastating effect. You just have to find and recruit them. That's the real problem.

'The deciphered telegrams of foreign governments are without doubt the most valuable source of our secret information respecting their policy and actions.'

Lord Curzon talking of the value of the work of Room 40 of the Admiralty and MI1b of the War Office during the First World War. It shows that the value of signals intelligence (known in the espionage world as "Sigint") is not something that was discovered in the internet age but has been true right the way through the twentieth century. Quoted in *Inside Room 40* by Paul Gannon (2010).

'Hello Scottish bastards.'

Early in World War One, it was discovered that messages sent over field telephone cables could be intercepted remotely because the wires did not have proper earthing. This meant that the signal could be carried over some distance by rivers or barbed wire or even the ground itself depending on conditions. Messages could be intercepted up to a range of one thousand yards. The Germans were first to exploit this with their Moritz listening sets. One Highland regiment, newly moved up to the front lines, was surprised to be greeted by a banner in the German trenches reading: *"Hello Scottish bastards."* The Germans had learned of their arrival from Moritz sets. Moritz II soon followed and had an even greater range. Moritz sets are believed to have given away the key date of the Somme offensive and allowed the Germans to be ready. Until 1916 when better communications discipline was introduced this method was thought to have yielded more intelligence than all other German methods put together. The Fullerphone was then introduced by the Allies. This scrambled messages and meant that they had to be decoded even if they were intercepted. The British first used French sets and then developed their own. Quoted in *Armour Against Fate* by Michael Occleshaw (1989).

Commitment

'No. Communists don't take holidays.'

The reply of Anne Neill, also known as *"the ASIO spying housewife"* (ASIO is the Australian security service.) She was already in her fifties when her espionage career began. At the time of this quote (in the 1950s) she was elderly and sick and had been spying on the Australian Communist Party for almost ten years. But when her ASIO handler suggested that she should step down, she refused. He later wrote: *"It was incredible commitment. I haven't come across any other agent with quite that drive."* At one point, the Communists became suspicious and interrogated her for several hours but they could not crack her story. She gathered her intelligence by simply staying in the background and waiting for opportunities: she did all the thankless tasks for the organisation from cleaning the offices to making marmalade for fund raising. It was the perfect cover. One communist said that they didn't suspect her because she was so motherly to all the younger party members. But it could not last for ever: eventually her position became too dangerous and ASIO pulled her out. The cover for this was that she was giving up politics to spend more time on her religious interests. When her story came out in the Australian press in 1962, the Communists claimed that they had known about her all along. Pity that they gave away so many secrets then. She died in October 1986. The interesting point about Anne Neill is that she was a marvellous spy but she never had any training. So does espionage training really matter? I have trained spies all over the world including Asia and Africa and the truth is that, while training can improve natural abilities, every trainer I have ever met agrees that there are some people who are simply natural spies. We had one on the BBC TV series *Spy*. Her name was Nicola and all of the trainers working on the show including Mike Baker from the CIA and even the retired SAS troopers who ran the surveillance exercises spotted her ability. No-one can really explain why this should be so. It requires a very special balance of qualities. The real trick for intelligence services is to spot and recruit such people. Quoted by ABC (Australia) 22 February 2022.

Computers

To allow someone to snoop on your internet traffic is to allow them to put a television camera in your room, except that it will tell them a whole lot more about you than the television camera.

Tim Berners-Lee (creator of the world wide web). And he would know. Quoted in *The Guardian* newspaper 26 March 2009.

Conspiracies

'When once a government encourages spies and informers, it becomes part of their business to commit such forgeries and create such terror.'

The playwright Richard Sheridan (1751-1816) speaking in the House of Commons. There are many modern observers who might agree with him. Quoted in *Plots and Paranoia* by Professor Bernard Porter (1988).

During the 1980s, in the wake of the exposure of Anthony Blunt as a Russian spy, there was an accusation by some right-wing intelligence officers that Roger Hollis, former Director General of MI5, had been a Russian spy and part of a deep-rooted Russian conspiracy that was yet to be uncovered. It was one of the central allegations of Peter Wright's sensational *Spycatcher* book which the British government tried, and failed, to ban. The Russians had a different view:

'... when the KGB saw the chaos caused by the allegations against Hollis, their laughter made Red Square shake.'

Oleg Gordievsky, KGB officer and Soviet defector quoted in *Defending The Realm* by Mark Hollingsworth and Nick Fielding (1999).

'A very close German friend has confided to my informant that an effort will be made to blow up the Lusitania at Liverpool after arrival there across the ocean.'

The *Lusitania* was a passenger liner travelling between the United States and Britain during the First World War. Neville Chamberlain, a Conservative party politician, received warning of an intended attack on the *Lusitania* from an old acquaintance in Germany. On 30 March 1915 he wrote to Vernon Kell, head of MI5, and warned him of the attack. But Chamberlain got two things wrong: first, he said that the contact told him that there would be a bomb hidden in a passengers' luggage and second, that there absolutely would not be an attack at sea by a U-boat. Six weeks later, just off the Irish coast, the *Lusitania* was torpedoed and sunk by a U-boat. 1,193 passengers and crew were killed. 123 of these people were Americans which was a neutral country at that time. The deaths of these people helped to shift America's attitude to the war and eventually America entered the war on the Allied side in 1917. There has long been a conspiracy theory that the British government, including Winston Churchill, ignored the intelligence that the *Lusitania* would be attacked because they wanted American citizens to perish thus making it more likely that America would join the Allies. It seems unlikely and most historians believe that the warnings were not acted on because of the usual inefficiencies of government. The 9-11 attack in America in 2001 happened for much the same reason: there was plenty of intelligence about the impending attack but none of it was acted upon. As for Chamberlain's "close German friend" was he (or she) trying to help Britain by warning of the attack or lulling suspicion by saying that there absolutely would not be an attack by a U-boat? That remains a mystery. Quoted in *Spies of the Great War* by James Morton (2010).

Counterespionage

'On the whole I am heartily sorry for spies; they have a rotten time and a nasty end – unless they are exceptionally lucky.'

Quoted in *Traitors Within* by Herbert Fitch (1933). Fitch was a Police Special Branch officer and a leading spy hunter during the First World War. It is true that German spies did have a pretty rough time in the UK – 12 of them were executed (there is a memorial to ten of them in the cemetery at Plaistow in London). At least another nine died in UK internment camps. Perhaps the worst fate was reserved for female spies. Rather than being executed they were condemned to asylums on the grounds that they must be mad to work for Germany. And they died there too. But despite Fitch's impression of the work, the general picture for spies is not quite so bad. For intelligence officers the risks are surprisingly low: for instance MI6 has never lost an officer on a intelligence operation (very far from the James Bond image). The CIA figure is higher but that is because they are a quasi-military service and more often involved in combat situations. The loss rate for agents is much greater. This is because it is the agents, not the officers, who run all the risks. But even so, I would estimate an agent's chances of survival to be 90%. (See the Preface for an explanation of the difference between officers and agents.)

'Fortunately for us (the British), we are as a nation considered by the others to be abnormally stupid, therefore easily spied upon. But it is not always safe to judge entirely by appearances'.

Lord Baden-Powell in *My Adventures as a Spy* (1915).

'It is essential to seek out enemy agents who have come to conduct espionage against you and to bribe them to serve you. Give them instructions and care for them. Thus doubled agents are recruited and available for your service.'

Sun Tzu, *Art of War*, Chapter 13 Paragraph 21. This is the ultimate goal of counterespionage: not just to catch the opposition's spies and prevent them from spying on you, but to turn them around and use them as a weapon against your enemy. The best example of this is the "Double Cross" operation by the United Kingdom against Germany during the Second World War. So many German spies were turned into double agents (not always willingly) that the Nazi espionage operation was crippled for the duration of the conflict.

'Jesus Christ only had twelve – and one of them was a double agent!'

Attributed to the FBI Director J. Edgar Hoover. This is supposed to be what he said on being told that one of the top MI6 men in Washington (Kim Philby) had been a Russian spy. If he did indeed says this, he may have been referring to the fact that many of the Cambridge spies were members of a university politics and debating society known as "The Apostles".

Counter Surveillance

'The trick in evading surveillance, they were told, was not only to get away but to give the impression you weren't looking for surveillance because you were innocent of anything that would merit it.'

Alan Judd, former "Foreign Service officer" in *Legacy* (2001). See under "Agent Handling" for more about Judd.

'SV teams [Surveillance teams] reckon they can always tell the difference between – say – a KGB officer approaching a meeting, brush contact, emptying or filling a DLB – dead letter box – or whatever – and one who's just done it, because afterwards he's relieved and his pace quickens.'

More from Alan Judd in his spy thriller *Legacy* (2001). Having worked as a surveillance officer, I can confirm that this is true. If you watch a target for many weeks, you get to know them so well that you can often tell from a slight change in their actions that something important is about to happen.

Courage

[The courage of a spy] *'...is something greater than the ordinary bravery of a soldier in action, who is carried on by the enthusiasm of those around him under the leadership of an officer, and with the competition and admiration of others. The pluck of the man who goes out alone, unobserved and un-applauded, and at the risk of his life, is surely equally great.'*

Lord Baden-Powell in *My Adventures as a Spy* (1915). When outlining the key qualities of a successful spy during lectures I always use the word "nerve" rather than courage. Courage suggests something immediate such as attacking an enemy position, but a spy may be under continual strain for many months, even years. That takes something more than courage. A good example would be the German spy Robert Rosenthal (see under "Last Words"). He was, no doubt, a courageous man, but in the end his nerve failed him, otherwise he might have got away.

'Spying brings with it a constant wearing strain of nerves and mind, seeing that it involves certain death for a false step in war or imprisonment in peace. The Government promises to give no help whatsoever to its servant if caught. He is warned to keep no notes, to confide in no one, to use disguises where necessary, and to fend for himself entirely'.

Lord Baden-Powell in *My Adventures as a Spy* (1915). This is true but only to an extent. Modern spying is much more of a team game than it used to be. Modern technology means that it is much easier to be in touch with headquarters or to call on support. Intelligence operations may only have one officer "up front" but there can be dozens of others behind the scenes planning, analysing and supporting in other ways. Of course, sooner or later, the operation rests with the man (or the woman) in enemy territory and that is when Baden-Powell's words ring true. But the "Great Game" is not quite the same as it was in his day.

'The person who has nothing for which he is willing to fight, nothing which is more important than his own personal safety, is a miserable creature and has no chance of being free unless made and kept so by the exertions of better men than himself'.

John Stuart Mill, the English philosopher, from his book *Principles of Political Economy* (1848).

'Nothing is lost as long as courage remains.'

Attributed to Napoleon.

'I will be arrested alone; I will be shot alone; if I fall, I will be replaced.'

Gabrielle Petit, Belgian secret agent of the First World War, talking to her associate Helene Segard and explaining that she would never give up her fellow agents no matter how she was tortured. She was true to her word. Petit's colleague, Marie Collet, who was arrested at the same time as Petit, was released because Petit would not implicate her. Petit was executed by firing squad on the 1st April 1916. She was just 22. Quoted in *Gabrielle Petit* by Sophie De Schaepdrijver (2015).

'There are no hopeless situations, there are only men who become hopeless about them.'

Admiral Reginald "Blinker" Hall, quite possibly Britain's greatest spymaster. Quoted in *Spymaster* by David Ramsay (2008).

And finally:

'And how can man die better
Than facing fearful odds,
For the ashes of his fathers,
And the temples of his gods.'

From Stanza 27 of the oft-quoted poem *Horatius* by Thomas Babington Macaulay. These were some of the favourite lines of an agent I knew who worked for a foreign service. By some strange quirk of fate, some years later I heard that he had been killed on an operation – alone and outgunned but with his mission a success. For reasons of security, no-one will ever know about him. Such is the lot of the spy.

Cover stories

'Be as you wish to seem.'

Socrates, 469-399 BC. These six words contain a wealth of wisdom. The key to a good cover story – and you only find this with the very best spies - is to actually _believe_ that you are who you are pretending to be. This is something that is very hard to teach but some people naturally have this ability and trainers in intelligence services are always on the lookout for them. In the TV series _Spy_ we found a young Scottish secretary who was a natural at assuming cover stories. Experienced officers contributing to the programme were astonished at her natural ability in this area. Certain con men have this ability as well which is why they are so successful – their victims "buy into" what the con men believe about themselves. It is also one of the key ways of beating a polygraph machine. If you have this ability, you are streets ahead of other spies.

'I remember an old scout in Rhodesia, who had done many queer things in his day, once telling me that the secret of playing a part was to think yourself into it. You could never keep it up, he said, unless you could manage to convince yourself that you were it.'

The novelist John Buchan in his classic thriller _The Thirty-Nine Steps_ (1915). Buchan was not a spy but he did know a great many spies from his work at the Ministry of Information during the First World War. He was partly responsible for inspiring the greatest ever MI6 spy, Sir Paul Dukes, the only MI6 officer to be knighted for his work in the field.

The greatest risk to the new officer working under-cover is that he has: '... _no sooner settled himself in his first class corner with his bundle of currency safe in his pocket, than he experiences a burning desire to tell some one of his fellow passengers all about his secret mission.'_

Mansfield Cumming writing in the preface to the very first MI6 agents' training guide written in 1918. This is so true and every officer I have ever discussed this with has admitted to it. It is even worse when you are on your way back from a successful mission and desperately want to tell the world about it. This is known as _Post Mission Elation_ - the time when you relax because you think the operation is over and the work is done. A good example of this is from the movie _The Great Escape_ where an escapee is just about to board a bus, having passed through all the German security checks, when he falls for the old trick of reacting to a casual comment in his native language. This is where experience in the field counts. Quoted in _The Quest For C_ by Alan Judd (1999).

'N'avouer jamais.'

'Never confess'. The watchwords of Baschwitz Meau, one of the leading British spies of the First World War. Quoted in _Secrets of the Rue St Roch_ by Janet Morgan (2004). It cannot be emphasised how important this is. The history of spying is littered with those who have been caught when they gave up and confessed because they thought the evidence against them was stronger than it actually was. As a spy you must always remember: they have not actually "got you" until you finally admit it.

'Let's all pretend to be someone else and then perhaps we'll find out who we are.'

The MI6 officer and novelist David Cornwell (John Le Carré) in _A Perfect Spy_ (1986).

'Have a good cover and always give a certain amount of time to your supposed occupation.'

MI6 training manual of the First World War. Quoted in *SIX* by Michael Smith (2010). This point has become even more relevant in the internet age when it is so easy to check up on a suspect's employment history. These days there is a greater chance than ever that you might be recruited as a spy because your work gives you perfect cover – so you never know!

Covert Action

'First let each wiser art be tried; bribe them or win them or divide. Such was the counsel of the spy.'

> *The Ramayan Of Valmiki*, Book 6, Canto 20: The Spies. Quoted in *The Enemy Within* by Terry Crowdy (2006). In most espionage situations, anything is better than resorting to the bomb or the bullet despite what the movies (and certain world leaders) would have you believe.

'Acts of sabotage, too, are directed by the Secret Service. These are often planned in peace time to permit immediate action being taken on the declaration of war before necessary protective measures can be adopted by the enemy.'

> MI6 officer Henry Landau in *All's Fair* (1934). For more about Landau see under "Agent Selection." Notice that he says "directed". Despite the images from the books and movies, it has always been the procedure, at least in the British services, that offensive action is undertaken by the military and not by intelligence officers. (However, remember the first rule of intelligence which is to "never say never".) This approach is slightly different in the CIA where their training is quasi-military and they will sometimes undertake covert action missions - which is also one reason that their casualty rate is so much higher than other Western services.

Although not all CIA officers are convinced it is a good idea:

'The Six Phases of US Government Sponsored Covert Action: Enthusiasm – Disillusionment – Panic – Search for the Guilty – Punishment of the Innocent – Praise and Honor for the Nonparticipants.'

> Sign on the wall of the CIA's Central American Task Force office in 1982 cited by former CIA Officer Duane Clarridge in *A Spy For All Seasons* (1997).

But some American politicians do:

'I cannot accept the proposition that the United States is debarred from acting in the gray area between diplomacy and military intervention.'

> Henry Kissinger (US National Security Adviser 1969-75) in *The White House Years* (1979). And sure enough the CIA has been used to launch military operations to overthrow regimes in Iran, Guatemala, Chile, etc. etc. Usually followed by an inquiry into what went wrong.

'Go out and kill me 10,000 Soviets until they give up.'

CIA Chief William Casey to Operations Officer Milt Bearden in 1986 when sending him to oversee a programme providing weapons to the Afghan mujahideen. Quoted in the *Washington Post* newspaper 12 December 1998. Sounds awful but it <u>did</u> work. The Soviet casualty rate rose so high that they were forced to withdraw in 1989. That would be fine except that the America did not learn the lesson and invaded Afghanistan themselves in 2001 before being forced to withdraw in chaos in 2021. "Those who do not learn the lessons of history etc. etc. ..."

'Covert policy is usually policy to which insufficient thought has been given.'

Angelo Codevilla in *Informing Statecraft* (1992). Once again Codevilla says it better than anyone else.

'The real tragedy is when special operations as they are called become a way of life, and then they escalate and are often staged when it is quite unnecessary. Surely Watergate taught us that?'

Sir Maurice Oldfield, Chief of MI6 (1973-78) quoted in *C: A Biography of Maurice Oldfield* by Richard Deacon (1985). Oldfield, a tubby, bespectacled type, was often accused of being shy of covert action. It was not that but rather that he believed that it should only be used when it was absolutely necessary. When questioned, two examples he gave were to rescue a colleague or to rescue a defector. For more about Oldfield see under "Agent Selection."

'Truly shocking...'

The reaction of British Labour MP Ben Bradshaw to allegations in 2023 that MI5 had failed to investigate claims by Sergei Cristo, a Conservative Party activist, that an FSB agent, Sergei Nalobin (political first secretary at the Russian embassy in London) had offered to supply money to the British Conservative Party via Russian companies. The Intelligence and Security Committee which oversees the British secret services had found "credible evidence" in its "Russia report" in 2020 that MI5 had failed to investigate Russian interference in UK democracy including the Brexit vote – the result of which favoured Russian aims. Now this second allegation of failure had emerged. Cristo had first tried to raise the alarm as long ago as 2011. Ten years later there was still no action. Nalobin had quite a track record. His father and brother were both spies and he was subsequently expelled from Estonia where he was working as a diplomat and was trying exactly the same trick. Such undermining of the political process of a country is classic covert action. Quoted in *The Observer* newspaper 22 January 2023. Russia's tactic, the use of its spies for covert action, takes us back to Sun Tzu:

'Supreme excellence lies in breaking the enemy's resistance without fighting.'

Sun Tzu, *The Art Of War*, Chapter Three, Paragraph Two.

Cryptanalysis

[The cryptanalysts of Bletchley Park] *'...lived in a world of their own. They were an eccentric, pernickety lot. My work in SIS often brought me into contact with them. One day, one of them showed me a German message he had been working on. It was about a meeting to take place at the Brenner Pass between Mussolini and someone else. The cryptanalyst said the original message had*

*the second person's name but he hadn't been able to get all the letters. All he had was "H-TL-R".
He asked me if I had any ideas. Straight away I said: "Hitler. It's got to be Hitler!" He looked at
the message again and after a while he said sadly: "Well, yes. But there's not a shred of
cryptological evidence for such a conclusion. Not a shred."'*

Kim Philby quoted in '*Philby – KGB Masterspy*' by Philip Knightley (1988).

*'39 shall expect more assistance in 87 from 197 and 202 than any numbers ... he would take care of
securing an election for 202, for 39 does not think it absolutely necessary to have him in 108 this
winter...'*

A simple number substitution code used by the Duke of Marlborough to his wife Sarah
Churchill advising her of the importance of the Woodstock parliamentary election in August
1710. 39 = Duke of Marlborough, 87 = Parliament, 197 = Cadogan, 202 = Sir Thomas
Wheate, 108 = England. The post at this time in England was notoriously insecure. Quoted
in *Marlborough* by Richard Holmes (2008).

Although many complex codes can be invented... *'The industry of men whose wits are sharpened by
necessity and by self-interest, will not fail to discover the key to them.'*

Francois de Callieres, *The Practice of Diplomacy* translated by A F Whyte (1919).

*'Really expert cryptographers can never be found ready-made: only experience can make "expert"
the individual who possesses the necessary mental and qualifications and aptitude for the work.'*

Secret government assessment of the work of Room 40, the UK's cryptanalysis section in
the First World War. Quoted in *Inside Room 40* by Paul Gannon (2010).

*'Successful codebreakers combine the pedantry of the grammarian with the logic of the linguistic
philosopher and the flair of a chess grandmaster.'*

John Ferris in *The British Army and Signals Intelligence During the First World War*
(1992).

*'No code ought to be insoluble given a sufficient quantity of material, a proper method of work, the
necessary qualities in the would be solvers and sufficient time between changes of the codebook...'*

US Army Intelligence Report 1918. Quoted in *Inside Room 40* by Paul Gannon (2010).

'His wit was worth a guinea a minute.'

British Labour MP Tam Dayell recalling Frank Adcock, who had been one of his tutors in
the 1950s. He was Professor of Ancient History at Cambridge for more than 25 years.
Adcock was not a member of Room 40 or Bletchley Park, but was a talent spotter for those
organisations in two world wars – for instance, he brought in Alan Turing in during WWII.
Quoted in *Spymaster* by David Ramsay (2008).

Cumming (Mansfield – first chief of MI6)

Many of those who worked for him in the early days did not know who he was:

'The initial of C was used to justify everything, but who C was, where C was, what C was and why C was, we were never told.'

This is from one of Compton Mackenzie's memoirs (but I am afraid I can't remember which volume.) Mackenzie, who was MI6 head of station in Greece during the First World War, was probably being a little disingenuous. He probably did know Cumming's name but was not allowed to publish it – although it does seem to be true that he was sent out to Greece without actually meeting Cumming, so he might have only known him by his initial for quite some time. However, the quote still encapsulates an essential truth which is that in those days, the physical distance and difficulties of communication meant that intelligence officers had an almost completely free hand and almost no interference from London. They also tended to be sent out without any training (as no proper training course had been set up at this time). This situation continued at least as long as 1919 when Sir Paul Dukes was sent on a highly dangerous mission in Russia with no training whatsoever. Then Augustus Agar was sent to rescue Dukes but wasn't even allowed to know his name!

'... a sidelined naval officer, with no relevant experience in intelligence gathering...'

Edwin Ruis, one of the Netherlands' leading intelligence historians in his book *Spynest* (2016).

'A clever officer with a great taste for electricity ... knowledge of photography ... speaks French .... draws well.'

Captain, later Admiral, Walter Hunt-Grubbe. Quoted in *The Quest for C* by Alan Judd (1999).

'If a Staff College man were in Cumming's place, we should never have the slightest trouble, as he, like ourselves, would be working for the common good, and not for self-aggrandisement.'

Major Walter Kirke of British Military Intelligence, from his War Diaries, quoted in *Armour Against Fate* by Michael Occleshaw (1989).

'He is most economical, travelling second class even though he is entitled to first.'

Admiral Bethell, Director of Naval Intelligence, summing up Cumming's performance in 1911. Quoted in *The Official History of MI6* by Professor Keith Jeffery (2010).

'*The mysterious Mr Smith*'

Smith was his birth name. He sometimes used it when undercover. He changed his name to Smith-Cumming when he married so that the name of his wife's family should not die out and then again to simply Cumming towards the end of the First World War.

'*Thick set, short, gingery*'

Not exactly James Bond. This is a description by a Mrs Vetcher who knew him well. Quoted in *The Quest for C* by Alan Judd (1999).

'The man with the Punch-like chin...'

Author and MI6 officer Compton Mackenzie who knew Cumming well. Mackenzie was comparing him to the Victorian "Mr Punch" puppet which had an enormous pointed chin. Cumming greatly admired Mackenzie and his piratical ways. Mackenzie tended to ignore the rules and do whatever seemed right to him at the time – a classic field intelligence officer in the James Bond mould. At one point Cumming suggested that Mackenzie should be his successor but Mackenzie had made too many enemies for that idea to succeed. From Mackenzie's memoir *Greek Memories* (1939).

'Obstinate as a mule, with a chin like the cutwater of a battleship'

Compton Mackenzie from *Greek Memories* again. His sheer strength of will is demonstrated by the fact that on 2nd October 1914, having been involved in a car crash which killed his only son, he cut off the remains of his own leg with a pen knife so that he could reach his son's body in a vain attempt to render first aid. His son died in his arms. He was back at work again by 11th November. Cumming had a wooden leg for the rest of his life. And if Cumming had not been such an obstinate personality, MI6 would never have survived. It was only ever supposed to be a two-man section for processing informants who were offering to sell information, not the world-wide organisation it has become.

'...the cheeriest fellow I've ever met, full of the most amusing yarns'.

Major Walter Kirke of British Military Intelligence again. Quoted in *Secrets of the Rue St Roch* by Janet Morgan (2004).

'We get ... still shots taken from a major feature film which we will never see'.

Alan Judd from *The Quest for C* (1999). The point that Judd is making is that Cumming's personal papers and much of the official record has been destroyed. Therefore much remains unknown about Cumming's life. Judd was given privileged access to Cumming's remaining diaries which are held at MI6, before which almost nothing was known about him. Today, thanks to the efforts of numerous historians, we know a great deal. His story was certainly an amazing one. It even appears that he may have been Ian Fleming's inspiration, not for James Bond, but for Commander Caractacus Potts, the inventor of *Chitty Chitty Bang Bang*. Perhaps one day that feature film will be made after all.

'... like Toad in The Wind in the Willows, he adored inventions and acceleration. Room could always be found in 'C''s diary for a meeting to set up a new society for the enjoyment of a faster means of locomotion or for an appointment to examine a new technology: electrical gas detection apparatus; metal said to be invisible in sunlight.'

Quoted in *Secrets of the Rue St Roch* by Janet Morgan (2004). This is a wonderful description of Cumming and absolutely nails a key aspect of his character. His father and elder brother were both famous engineers and Cumming had an enormous workshop both at his house and at his office where he could tinker with new inventions. He once confessed that he found this far more interesting than intelligence work.

'I have heard that he spoke no foreign language; but he made up for any shortcomings in this respect by other qualities of mind and an unfailing flair for picking men who did.'

Quoted in *The World Of Action* by Valentine Williams (1938). This is not quite right: Cumming spoke some schoolboy French and a few words of German but he was certainly not a linguist. This makes him unusual in intelligence circles as one of the key skills for an intelligence officer is knowledge of at least one foreign language. However, it is typical of Cumming, always inventive, that he found a way around the problem.

' ...you have come to bury C sir, not to praise him.'

Sometime in 1923 a farewell dinner was thrown for Cumming at which Admiral "Blinker" Hall, the other great British secret service leader of World War One, gave a speech that summed up Cumming's monumental achievements. Cumming is supposed to have replied with these words. He had been ill with heart trouble for some time and his successor had already been selected, but he did not survive to retirement. On 23rd June that year his secretary found him dead on the sofa of his Melbury Road office. He had just briefed his last agent. Quoted in *The Quest for C* by Alan Judd (1999).

D

Dansey (Claude) – Deputy Chief of MI6 in the 1940s

'Claude Dansey? He was the best of them.'

Victor Cavendish-Bentinck, Chairman of the Joint Intelligence Committee (JIC). The JIC is responsible for assessing all the intelligence that the British services produce and deciding which intelligence is worth sending to ministers. The intelligence for JIC-selected intelligence reports is used to produce a document known as "the Red Book" for each area or subject. So, Cavendish-Bentinck may have been assessing Dansey's reports but then again he didn't have to work with him. Quoted in *Colonel Z* by Anthony Read and David Fisher (1985).

'England had in him one of the ablest and most single minded servants she has ever known. Our debt to him is beyond computation.'

Brendan Bracken, Minister of Information under Winston Churchill. Quoted in *Colonel Z* by Anthony Read and David Fisher (1985).

'...an utter shit; corrupt, incompetent, but with a certain low cunning.'

Hugh Trevor-Roper, former MI6 officer who later became Lord Dacre.

'The sort of man who gives spying a bad name.'

Edward Crankshaw, expert on Russia who knew Dansey well. Quoted in *The Secret Servant* by Anthony Cave Brown (1988).

And the truth? Probably the best person to ask is one of his most capable enemies:

'It came to me, when I heard he was dead, that I had really rather liked him. Nefarious as his influence on the Service was, it gave me a pang to think that that crusty old spirit was still for ever.'

The Cambridge Spy, Kim Philby. Quoted in *Colonel Z* by Anthony Read and David Fisher (1985).

Deception

'I'll fill these dogged spies with false reports.'

Shakespeare, *King John*, Act IV, Scene I.

'His power went out in such distractions as beguiled all spies.'

Shakespeare, *Antony and Cleopatra*, Act III, Scene 7.

'In warfare, practice deception, and you will succeed.''

Sun Tzu, *The Art of War*, Chapter 7, Paragraph 15.

'Conceal your dispositions and you will be safe from the prying of the subtlest of spies, from the machinations of the wisest brains.'

Sun Tzu, *The Art of War*, Chapter 6, Paragraph 25.

'It may be accepted as a truism that the man who spends his life in deceiving those with whom he comes into contact will have little compunction in deceiving his employers – the Government - if it be in his interests to do so.'

Sir Henry Blake from his work *The Irish Police* quoted in *The Origins of the Vigilant State* by Professor Bernard Porter (1987).

Defectors

'There is no way that anyone would consider defecting to the UK from Russia. The British authorities have proved that they are not able to protect anyone who needs and deserves to be protected'.

Boris Karpichkov was an officer of the Latvian KGB who defected to the UK in 1996. His address was passed to the Latvians by the UK's National Crime Agency in response to an official request to extradite, but it was a trick by the Russian intelligence services. Fortunately, a court refused to agree to the extradition request. Karpichkov was moved to a new address but he was being monitored because in January 2022 the following note was later sent to his new house: *"No matter how much you change your residence, you cannot avoid your punishment. Traitors like you have no place on earth. Wait, death is on the way for you."* The UK refused to move him again on the grounds that he had already been moved once and it was too expensive. There was also some indication that they did not believe his story. But, in the wake of the assassinations of Alexander Litvinenko in 2006, the attempted assassination of Sergei Skripal in 2018 and the suspicious deaths of numerous other Russians living in the UK, Karpichkov believes that his days are numbered. The Russians' aim is to curb the number of defectors by demonstrating that no-one is beyond reach of their assassins.

However, note that a basic rule of espionage is being followed here: *"Spies do not kill spies"*. Although they use assassins, the Russians are killing defectors not UK intelligence officers. That is not the way the Great Game is played. This is different from the images that the movies would have you believe. Russia sees traitors as different from "regular" spies and therefore fair game. Incidentally, many defectors to the UK have complained about their treatment once they arrive in the country. One even chained himself to railings in Whitehall as part of his protest. Not quite the glamorous life that they expected. The Americans have less trouble – largely because they have more money - which is why most defectors head for the States. Quoted in *The Observer* newspaper 27 February 2022.

'Whereas former secret agents in Britain tend to defect to the Russians, in America former secret agents tend to defect to their publishers.'

> Television personality David Frost during an interview with former Director of the CIA Richard Helms speaking in 1978. Helms was there to promote his new book – twenty-three years before Stella Rimington broke the mould and wrote her memoirs. Her defiance of this rule - which had applied to all other British intelligence officers - led to a great deal of criticism. Quoted in *The Literary Spy* by Charles Lathrop (2004).

Denial

'As a general rule always deny everything when in the hands of the police. They cannot do anything if you persist. If you are formally denounced by someone, deny what they say. If confronted, continue to deny. You must continue to deny everything. If two people are confronted with you, continue to deny all the same. It is all in your advantage if you continue to deny, nothing can be done if you do. If you are confronted with other agents, who have been arrested and have confessed, and it is known that you were often in their company, do not deny that you know them, admit it, but state that you made their acquaintance in such and such a manner, but that you were ignorant of what they did and, under no circumstance, admit that you work with them. Never admit anything. Never make a confession.'

> From an MI6 training manual of the First World War. Quoted in *SIX* by Michael Smith (2010).

Deniability

'...contrary to what is usually thought, there have been very few, if any, examples of friendly relations being seriously damaged by espionage. Politicians are too routinely cynical and relations between states, more a matter of interest than emotion, usually too complex to be disrupted by a spy case.'

> Alan Judd in *The Quest for C* (1999). For more about Judd see under "Agent Handling."

'Denial is the black art all intelligence services long ago perfected.'

> Gordon Thomas, espionage writer and expert on the Mossad in *Gideon's Spies* (1999). And he is right. For instance, one of the reasons stated by the Curzon Committee in 1909 (when MI5 and MI6 were created) was that they should "act as a screen" for the government. One of the most basic considerations for any espionage operation, by any service, is deniability. That is the key reason why governments have secret services.

'Menzies, what would happen if I were to ask you the name of our man in Berlin?'
'I should have to say, Sir, that my lips were sealed.'
'Well, supposing I were to say "Off with your head"?'
'In that case, Sir, my head would roll with the lips still sealed!'

> Supposed conversation between King George VI and Menzies. Quoted in *Secret Intelligence Agent by* Montgomery Hyde (1982). Hyde was an SOE and MI6 officer and later a historian. At one point, his wife ran off with "Biffy" Dunderdale, the MI6 head of station in Paris. Apparently the two men remained on good terms.

Detail

'Even minutia should have a place in our [intelligence] collection, for things of a seemingly trifling nature when enjoined with others of a more serious cast may lead to valuable conclusions.'

> George Washington. Quoted widely. This protection for even the smallest details of an espionage or military operation is known as OPSEC (Operational Security.)

Diplomats

'A diplomat has as much right to consider himself insulted if he is called a spy as a soldier has if he is called a murderer.'

> Alfred Duff Cooper, British ambassador to Paris explaining why he did not want an MI6 officer under-cover at his embassy. Quoted in *The Official History of MI6* by Professor Keith Jeffery (2010). This might be true today (it depends which country you are from) but for a long time it was "understood" that an ambassador was always going to do a little spying as part of his work (see the quote below). Spying in this sense i.e. for diplomatic and economic intelligence, as opposed to military spying, was known as *espionage civile* and was considered almost respectable, a thing that Princes did. The ambassador's role evolved out of the use of merchant's agents who were sent on particular missions of inquiry or negotiation. Soon it seemed to make sense to have someone based in a country permanently to handle these and other questions. One of the very first ambassadors to the UK arrived in 1330 when Genoa sent an "Envoy Plenipotentiary", Count Niccolino del Fiesco, to the court of Edward III to complain about a Genoan ship which had been seized off Bristol. The king and Niccolino must have got along very well because a few years later he acted as Edward's secret agent in Avignon at the Papal Court. So, one of the very first diplomats sent to this country was not just a spy but a double agent.

One military attaché wrote: *'I would never do any secret service work. My view is that the Military Attaché is the guest of the country to which he is accredited and must only see and learn that which is permissible for a guest to investigate. Certainly he must keep his ears open and miss nothing, but secret service is not his business and he should always refuse to have a hand in it.'*

> Quoted in *William Le Queux, Master of Mystery* by Chris Patrick and Stephen Baister (2007). William Le Queux was a thriller writer in the early years of the twentieth century whose widely-syndicated potboilers led, in part, to the nationwide spy scare in England that led to the creation of MI5 and MI6. It is ironic that Britain's secret services were created (at least to an extent) by a spy thriller writer.

'Above all, do not get into any trouble; for I suppose you that, if anything happened to you, it would be of no use to talk about your mission. We should be obliged to know nothing about you, for ambassadors are the only avowed spies.'

> A last briefing for Casanova from *The Memoirs of Jacques Casanova* (1797).

Disability

'The woman who limps is one of the most dangerous Allied agents in France. We must find and destroy her.'

Gestapo memorandum quoted in *Sisterhood of Spies* by Elizabeth P. McIntosh (1998). Known as "the Limping Lady", Virginia Hall is one of the outstanding spies of history. She wore an artificial leg after losing the limb below the left knee following a shooting accident in the 1930s. After the outbreak of the Second World War, she joined the British SOE in 1940 as she spoke fluent French. By August 1941 she was living in France organising resistance networks under cover of being a reporter for the *New York Post* (the US was, of course, neutral at this time). In 1943 she was forced to flee to Spain when her work became known. She returned to London and in April 1944 she joined the fledgling OSS (the American version of SOE). She then went back to France, trained more than three hundred agents and at the end of the war was awarded the Distinguished Service Cross (the second highest military award for valour) as well as many other honours. She is truly proof that anyone can be a spy no matter what they think might hold them back.

Disguises

'My voice was flat and colourless, and I had a face that seemed easily forgotten. Indeed I was, and still am, an unusually ordinary-looking individual. Not that those, attributes, have ever displeased me, for in the world of espionage and security they are a man's finest asset: a defensive camouflage of immeasurable value.'

> Lt. Col. A P Scotland, *The London Cage* (1957). For more about Scotland see under "Boredom."

'It is the silent and secretive man who attracts suspicion.'

> H. C. Bywater, MI6's most successful spy in World War One. Quoted in Fifty Amazing Secret Service Dramas (1937). For more about Bywater see under "Agent Handling."

'But suddenly I remembered a thing I once heard in Rhodesia from old Peter Pienaar. ... He was the best scout I ever knew, and before he turned respectable he had been pretty often on the windy side of the law, when he had been wanted badly by the authorities. Peter once discussed with me the question of disguises, and he had a theory which struck me at the time. He said, barring absolute certainties like fingerprints, mere physical traits were very little use for identification if a fugitive really knew his business. He laughed at things like dyed hair and false beards and such childish follies. The only thing that mattered was what Peter called 'ammosphere'.

If a man could get into perfectly different surroundings from those in which he had first been observed, and – this is the most important part – really play up to those surroundings and behave as if he had never been out of them, he would puzzle the cleverest detectives on earth. And he used to tell a story of how he had once borrowed a black coat and went to church and shared the same hymn-book with the man that was looking for him. If that man had seen him in decent company before he would have recognised him; but he had only seen him snuffing the lights in a public-house with a revolver.'

> John Buchan in *The Thirty-Nine Steps* (1915).

'The matter of disguise is not so much one of theatrical make-up – although this is undoubtedly a useful art – as being able to assume a totally different character, change of voice and mannerisms, especially of gait in walking and appearance from behind. This point is so often forgotten by beginners, and yet it is one of the most important'.

Lord Baden-Powell in *My Adventures as a Spy* (1915). Early spies were almost obsessed with the idea of disguise. Mansfield Cumming, the first chief of MI6, who knew nothing about spying except what he had read in books, used the services of a theatrical costumier in Soho named Willie Clarkson. Clarkson was flamboyant and notorious but he didn't know much about spying either. Cumming ended up in a series of outrageous disguises usually involving some kind of false hairpiece. One of these slipped off when he removed his hat during a visit to the German embassy and very nearly led to his capture. Fortunately, he was able to replace it before anyone seemed to notice. Also, for many years there was a myth that the way to throw off surveillance was by changing your clothes in a department store or alleyway. But if a suspect changes their appearance that is almost proof positive that they are a spy which is exactly what you don't want. The skill in losing surveillance is to lose them without them realising that it was a deliberate move. Today disguise has come back into play as a serious espionage tool in order to evade facial recognition devices.

'For a quick change, it is wonderful what difference is made by merely altering your hat and your necktie. It is usual for a person addressing another to take note of his necktie, and probably of his hat, if of nothing else, and thus it is often useful to carry a necktie and a cap of a totally different hue from that which you are wearing, ready to change immediately in order to escape recognition a few minutes later'.

Lord Baden-Powell in *My Adventures as a Spy* (1915).

'The one article which I frequently changed was headgear. It is astonishing how headdress can impart character (or the lack of it) to one's appearance.'

Sir Paul Dukes in The Story of *ST-25* (1938). Dukes was MI6's most successful spy ever, known as *the Man of a Hundred Faces* – but then, in the chaos of post-revolutionary Russia, you could get away with that sort of thing.

'It was all very boy scout – false beards were quite the thing.'

Author, broadcaster and MI6 officer Malcolm Muggeridge remembering his time in MI6 in the 1940s. Quoted in *Literary Agents* by Anthony Masters (1987).

'I believe they (the KGB) failed to spot me because of a very simple error: they allowed themselves to be taken in by superficial appearances. From the moment I walked into the Trade Delegation until the moment I walked out of it, I was, to them, an ordinary Irish working man, with a duffle coat and scruffy shoes, who liked a joke and a chat and was a bit too fond of his drink.'

Bill Graham who bugged and burgled the Soviet Trade Delegation in London for about a year in the 1980s. Quoted in *Break In* by Bill Graham (1987).

Dissemination

'Next to the acquisition of information, its distribution to those who may be able to use it is the most important duty of the Intelligence Branch.'

Lt Col David Henderson, in his *Field Intelligence, Its Principles and Practice* (1904).

Diversity

'We have to approach, cultivate and recruit people to be agents, to work for us. That does not work so well if everybody looks like me.'

> Andrew Parker, Director General of MI5 2013-2020. Quoted in *The Guardian* newspaper 1 November 2016. And yet, four years later, his successor looked just like him.

Donovan (William 'Wild Bill' – the founder of OSS, the wartime US intelligence service)

'The sort of guy who thought nothing of parachuting into France, blowing up a bridge, pissing in Luftwaffe gas tanks, then dancing on the roof of the St. Regis hotel with a German spy.'

> The film director John Ford quoted in David Stafford's *Churchill and Secret Service* (1987). And so a legend is born. In fact, there is growing evidence that many of his staff found him tiresome and even a liability. He liked to be called "Wild Bill" but his staff tended to call him "Seabiscuit" (after the famous American racehorse) because of his tendency to run around from Front to Front. He was even accused by some of "war tourism". But this is the image he wanted to project and it's still a great quote. To misquote the movie *The Man Who Shot Liberty Valance*: *"when fact conflicts with the legend, print the legend."*

Double agents

'Clandestine intelligence organisations are, generally speaking, as easy to penetrate as a co-operative store. They consist largely of personnel who either are, or become neurotics, and, therefore, are easily turned round or turn themselves round ... Even in the case of the USSR there have been many more defections among senior intelligence officers than in any other branch of the armed forces.'

> Author, broadcaster and former MI6 officer, Malcolm Muggeridge, in *Tread Softly For You Tread On My Jokes* (1968).

'I begin to wish I had never started this affair. To spy and cheat on one's friends, it's not nice, it's dirty.'

> Eddie Chapman, MI5 double agent codenamed "Zigzag". Quoted in *Agent Zigzag* by Ben MacIntyre (2007).

'Running a team of double agents is very much like running a club cricket side. Older players lose their form and are gradually replaced by newcomers. It is not always easy to pick the best players to put into the field. Some of the players required a good deal of net practice before they were really fit to play in a match.

> Masterman, head of the MI5 "Double Cross" network during the Second World War, arguably the most successful double agent operation in the history of espionage. Quoted in *The Double Cross System* by J C Masterman (1972).

'I have heard of the work you do and I want to serve you. I have no scruples and no fear of danger. Whatever you order me to do, I will accomplish.'

Gilbert Gifford, an English priest in Rome, from a letter offering his services to spymaster Francis Walsingham in 1585. Taking on a priest was a calculated risk – he might well have been working for the Papacy (which would have made him a triple agent). But Walsingham took the chance and Gifford proved true to his word. Walsingham used Gifford to break the Babington Plot in 1586. Quoted in *The Code Book* by Simon Singh (1999).

'I should have preferred the role of a double agent to that of a spy, but I was advised that my services would not, after all, be needed.'

Graham Greene, novelist and MI6 officer in WWII. But even before he joined MI6, in 1924, when post-war tension between Germany and France was at its height, he had very nearly been recruited by the Germans. And then was almost recruited by the French! Quoted in *Literary Agents* by Anthony Masters (1987).

'Varus! Give me back my legions!'

Supposedly the words screamed by Roman emperor Augustus upon hearing of the Battle of Teutoberg Forest. Native scouts working for the Roman army of occupation in Germania conducted Roman General, Quintilius Varus through the Teutoburg Forest. The scouts were thought to be loyal but in fact were working for the Germanic chieftain, Arminius. Over the course of several days the legions were led into a carefully planned trap and the Romans were slaughtered to a man. Legions XVII, XVIII and XIX were wiped out. Such was the disaster that their legion numbers were never used again. The Romans were forced to retreat back across the Rhine. This was quite possibly the greatest double agent operation of all time.

Double Cross

'Owing to a sequence of wrong information coming from you which has much misled us, we are herewith dispensing with your services.'

If you cannot persuade an agent to become a double, there is still one course open to you. This is a message from the German secret service to their agent Karl Muller in late 1915. They had recently paid him £400 and awarded him the Iron Cross for his valuable work spying in the UK. There was only one problem. Karl Muller was dead. He had refused to become a double agent, had been tried in secret and executed in the rifle range at the Tower of London on 23 June 1915. The German operation was kept running by MI5 in the hope of trapping more spies. No spies were trapped by this route but the £400 came in handy (it was used to buy a car for further surveillance operations). Quoted in *Spies of the First World War* by James Morton (2010).

Drones

Drones have revolutionised several aspects of the intelligence world by providing a direct observation, eavesdropping and electronic intelligence gathering capability.

'We are the ultimate Peeping Toms. No one's gonna catch us. No one's going to hear or see a

Predator drone flying at the distance and height that we flew at.'

Brandon Bryant, USAF Predator pilot. Quoted in *Sudden Justice* by Chris Woods (2015).

But they do have other uses:

'Ah, what's the best way to put this? We think it's the first electronic capture in history.'

AAI's Director of Corporate Communication, Adam R. Fein, confirming that Iraqi troops had on two occasions surrendered to circling unmanned Pioneer reconnaissance drones during the First Gulf War in 1991. These were surprising surrenders because the drones were unarmed but of course the poorly trained Iraqi troops did not know this. Predator drones armed with Hellfire missiles first appeared in 1995 and they are now regularly used to assassinate enemy targets. Surrender is no longer an option.

'We can turn it into a flying nose!'

Stephan Sessan of the European Aerospace Defence and Space Company unveiling a new and practically silent microdrone in Munich in November 2003. He was suggesting that the drone could be combined with sensing equipment to sniff for traces of explosives and bioweapons. Quoted in *New Scientist* magazine 6 December 2003.

With drones often operated by staff sitting in safety thousand of miles away there is not the sort of physical risk that spies are often exposed to. However, there is another cost – and it is one that intelligence officers are familiar with:

'If you wanted to talk to a therapist about it, they would say "well if you do, your security clearance is going to be taken away." And that scared a lot of people because security clearance is sacred.'

Brandon Bryant, Predator pilot. He suffered PTSD after leaving the USAF. Quoted in *Sudden Justice* by Chris Woods (2015).

'When you are exposed to it over and over again it becomes like a small video, embedded in your head, forever on repeat, causing psychological pain and suffering that many people will hopefully never experience.'

Drone footage analyst Heather Linebaugh. Quoted in *Sudden Justice* by Chris Woods (2015). (If you have any interest in how drones are used then I highly recommend this book.)

Many more spies have been damaged by the psychological effects of intelligence work than have ever been killed on operations and yet, as with drone pilots, it is an aspect of the work that is hardly ever talked about. For instance, very few intelligence officers are killed in the field but the sense of responsibility for running an agent who is killed creates a sense of guilt that never goes away and ends many careers.

Drugs

'In those days the Germans were just as keen to get hold of morphia or cocaine as addicts are nowadays with heroin. I had a great deal of difficulty in getting permission to do this drug-pushing,

in fact, I had to go to the Prime Minister, to Lloyd George, to get his authority to buy large quantities of morphia tablets and cocaine. With this I was able to suborn quite a number of people in the German army.'

Sigismund Payne-Best OBE, MI6 officer during World War One. While nothing in the field of intelligence should be ruled out, Payne-Best was working in the early days of modern agent running and this tactic is unlikely to be used today. Not because spies are more moral than they used to be, but if your agent is a regular drug user or even just dealing in drugs, his intelligence is likely to be dubious at best. Quoted in *Armour Against Fate* by Michael Occleshaw (1989).

Dr Zhivago

'... more important than any other literature that has yet come out of the Soviet Bloc.'

CIA Memo describing the famous novel by Pasternak. You may not think that this was a matter for spies but this was banned in the Soviet Union and in 1957 MI6 managed to obtain a copy of the unpublished manuscript from one of Pasternak's western contacts. The CIA then published it widely in the West and made sure that copies went back to the Soviet Union. This was considered important propaganda move in undermining the Soviet system because Pasternak was a national hero but the central character in the book rejects Bolshevism. It may not have caused a revolution in Russia but it was another small step towards winning the Cold War. Quoted in *The Guardian* newspaper 11 June 2014.

E

ECHELON

'ECHELON was at the heart of a massive, billion-dollar expansion of global electronic surveillance for the 21st Century. ... The NSA and its partners had arranged for everything we communicated to be grabbed and potentially analysed.'

> The journalist, Duncan Campbell. The existence of the ECHELON programme had been known since 1988 thanks to Campbell but no-one realised the true extent of its reach until the whistleblower Edward Snowden released his documents in 2013. Quoted in *Spies, Spin and the Fourth Estate* by Paul Lashmar (2020).

England

'Without her spies England is helpless.'

> Michael Collins, leader of the IRA in the 1920s quoted in *Churchill and Secret Service* by David Stafford (1987). Collins backed his words with action. On 21 November 1920, teams of IRA assassins that he had organised, struck at the home addresses of almost all of the officers comprising Dublin District Special Branch. The Branch was seen as a threat because of the success it was having but it was also heavily infiltrated by IRA agents who allowed the movements and home addresses of the officers to be monitored. Fifteen men were killed (not all were members of Special Branch) and five people were wounded, effectively wiping out Special Branch in Dublin. Several of the corpses were mutilated by the assassins. But in the end it didn't matter: the Branch was re-constituted under new leadership and this time the IRA failed to penetrate it. By August 1922, Collins was dead, killed by the very same men he had once led so ruthlessly.

Escape and Evasion

'If you are hemmed in on all sides in a patch of land there is only one chance of escape. You must stay in the patch, and let your enemies search it and not find you.'

> John Buchan in *The Thirty-Nine Steps* (1915). The principle is easy, it's the practice that is hard. Especially if the patch where you are trying to hide in is full of thistles...

'On a recent occasion in my knowledge a man was hunted down into a back street which was a cul-de-sac, with no exit from it. He turned into the door of a warehouse and went up a flight of stairs, hoping to find a refuge, but, finding none, he turned back and came down again and faced the crowd which was waiting outside, uncertain which house he had entered. By assuming extreme lameness in one leg, hunching up one shoulder and jamming his hat down over a distorted looking face, he was able to limp boldly down among them without one of them suspecting his individuality'.

> Lord Baden-Powell in *My Adventures as a Spy* (1915). This must have been the most stupid mob in history – but I have heard of similar escapes where agents could not believe they could not get away with it yet did: in one case by simply running back past his pursuers

shouting: "I'll phone for help!"

'Another secret that one picked up at the game of Hide-and-Seek was, if possible, to get above the level of the hunter's eye and to "freeze" – that is, to sit tight without movement, and, although not in actual concealment, you are very apt to escape notice by so doing. I found it out long ago by lying flat along the top of an ivy-clad wall when my pursuers passed within a few feet of me without looking up at me'.

Lord Baden-Powell in *My Adventures as a Spy* (1915). Again, this sounds dumb, but it does work. One of the basic rules in rural surveillance (a specialist role in which officers are trained to keep an area under surveillance from an area in which there is no cover) is to remain perfectly still as even a slight movement at a distance can catch the target's eye. One of the hardest parts of that role is staying absolutely still for long periods of time. Another is learning how to use cling film to assist in certain bodily functions - but I haven't found any quotes about that yet.

Expense

'Knowledge is never bought too dear in defence of the realm'.

Attributed to Sir Francis Walsingham, Elizabeth I's spymaster.

'No war can be conducted successfully without very early and good intelligence. Such advices cannot be had but at very great expense.'

John Churchill, Duke of Marlborough. Quoted in *Marlborough* by Richard Holmes (2008).

'To remain in ignorance of the enemy's condition simply because one grudges the outlay of a hundred ounces of silver in honours and bribes is the height of inhumanity.'

Sun Tzu, *The Art of War,* Chapter 13, Paragraph 2.

'Every spy caught is worth a new cruiser!'

Alfred von Tirpitz, head of the Imperial German Navy before World War One. Quoted in *Bywater* by William H. Honan (1991). If he had paid as much attention to the importance of communications security he might have been better off. The German Navy lost key battles because British naval communications interception and decryption was so advanced.

'A hundred ounces of silver spent for information may save 10,000 spent on war.'

Ancient Chinese proverb.

Exploitation

'The tussle between making effective use of intelligence and protecting its source for future use is an age-old one and there is no easy resolution.'

Quoted in *Inside Room 40* by Paul Gannon (2010).

Eyebrows

'In regard to disguises, hair on the face such as a moustache or beard are very usually resorted to for altering a man's appearance but these are perfectly useless in the eye of a trained detective unless the eyebrows also are changed in some way'.

Lord Baden-Powell in *My Adventures as a Spy* (1915). Again, I am not sure that eyebrows are very often a spy's greatest concern but it is true that with a cover story, an officer can get all the big details right and yet it is something apparently trivial that just doesn't seem quite right and makes someone else suspicious. It can be a manner of talking, the use of certain words, an expensive watch, an unfashionable item of clothing, even the way that someone stands, the list is almost endless. But the skill in both disguise and cover (the two are almost always entwined) is to be aware of those small details that might give you away. To get those right you have to *inhabit* the role you are to play. Hard to define but that's where the skill lies.

<u>F</u>

Fame

'We're the CIA. If we wanted applause we would have joined the circus.'

From the film *Argo* (2012) about CIA rescue of American embassy staff trapped in Iran. Tony Mendez who was awarded the agency's highest honour, the Intelligence Star, for his part in the rescue of American hostages from Iran, but then was promptly told that no-one must know on the grounds that the public must not know about the event. This quote reflects reality up to a point but it also doesn't. For instance, Mendez wrote four books about his time in the CIA and in 2012 a high-profile movie was made about the operation. (The CIA now actively seeks participation in certain movies and other projects in order to enhance the image of the Agency. MI6 does not do the same not for reasons of morality but because it does not have the CIA's budget.) Meanwhile, many of those field officers who have done the greatest work may never be known. But those in senior management, who consider themselves a different breed, are often happy to tell their stories.

'The man who fights and kills and plunders is honoured; but he who serves his country as a spy, no matter how faithfully, no matter how honestly, lives to be reviled or dies like the vilest criminal.'

James Fenimore Cooper (1789-1851) in *The Spy* (1821), one of the first ever spy novels. It is the story of a double agent and supposedly based on a real case. He also wrote *The Last of the Mohicans.*

Fear

'I seldom slept more than three hours in twenty-four. Oh, the agony of wakefulness! It is then that the mind marshals its fears and cares into battalions ... from where was one to get the courage to stumble through yet another day? ... I was groping my way through life, dazed and bewildered. No casual onlooker would have credited it; one had returned from the war with life and limb whole; all was well.'

George A. Hill, former MI6 officer talking about his difficulty in adjusting to civilian life after working as a spy in Bolshevik Russia in *The Dreaded Hour* (1936).

'There is one evil that I dread and that is their spies.'

George Washington talking during the American Revolutionary War against the British (1775-1783).

Fleming (Ian)

'Find immediately the twelve top German naval commanders and make each one one write ten thousand words on why Germany lost the war at sea.'

The James Bond creator's final (and deliberately humorous) message to the member of 30 Assault Unit, the specialist commando group that he formed in World War Two. The Unit was one of the inspirations behind such later special operations units such as the UK's SBS, US Navy Seals, etc.

Franks Report

'... witness after witness described how crucial intelligence reports were ignored, forgotten about, mislaid, withheld from ministers, or misinterpreted. It was difficult to know whether or not civil servants responsible for distributing intelligence reports to decision-makers in Whitehall were incompetent buffoons or devious manipulators. Whitehall, it seemed, learned nothing from the last inquiry into intelligence failings – the Franks Report.'

Richard Norton Taylor, journalist for *The Guardian* newspaper and one of the best connected defence correspondents in Fleet Street. Quoted in *MI6* by Stephen Dorril (2000).

'...the changes in the Argentinian position, were, we believe, more evident on the diplomatic front and in the associated press campaign than in the intelligence reports.'

Or as one intelligence officer commented:

'You would have been better informed if you just read the bloody papers than the MI6's so-called "intelligence.'

The Franks Report into the Falklands Conflict, paragraph 316 (1983).

G

Gadgets

'Intelligence is the battle of minds and brains, and the role of the gadgets and improvements is to assist the human being in his conceptual challenge.'

> Meir Amit, head of the Mossad 1963-8. Quoted in *Every Spy A Prince* by Dan Raviv and Yossi Melman (1990).

'You can tell a good spy from a bad spy by the amount of equipment he carts around with him.'

> Unnamed MI6 officer.

Garbology (the art of producing intelligence from trash)

'He did not like wastepaper baskets. For five months now he had been receiving from the agent known as Keats two or three times a week, the fragments of the wastepaper baskets in the German Legation.'

> Author and MI6 officer Compton Mackenzie in *Extremes Meet* (1928). Several major cases have begun through the product of garbology including the infamous Dreyfuss Case. So, be careful of what you throw away – or what you think you have deleted on your computer – you usually haven't. But while garbology can be useful in certain circumstances, you do have to think carefully about your cover story if you are using it: two French intelligence officers who were caught rifling through the bins of an American official in the 1970s claimed to be *"looking for grass cuttings to repair a hole in the embassy lawn."* That is one cover story that didn't work.

Gathering Intelligence

'... gadgets cannot divine a man's intentions.'

> Former Director of the CIA Richard Helms at an awards dinner in May 1983. The point Helms was addressing was the astonishing rise in the amount of intelligence gathered by technical means such as satellites and other signals interception. Some people were asking what is the value of human spies these days? For Helms the answer was simple. Quoted in *The Literary Spy* by Charles Lathrop (2004).

'... the most difficult task in intelligence is not to obtain the information, but to determine exactly what information one wants to get.'

> Ivone Kirkpatrick, War Office Intelligence Officer attached to the MI6 station at Rotterdam during the First World War. He studied under Lt. Col. Laurence Oppenheim who revolutionised the collection and exploitation of intelligence and made Rotterdam the most productive MI6 station of the war. Quoted in *The Inner Circle* by Ivone Kirkpatrick (1959).

'The good spy, when he is obliged to seduce those who hold information he needs, will never offer to purchase it. After he definitely knows his victim is in possession of important information he leads him on to make the offer himself by methods of casuistry or enticement in which he is well versed. For example, he tells his man on one occasion that he has a great personal friend, A, in the B government; and then, a few days later, he makes a casual remark that country B would give anything for the type of information the victim can give.

If now the bait is taken and he is asked to act as an intermediary, he is horrified. "I can't possibly have anything to do with it. Do be careful, old man. Of course, if you want to take a trip across the border, you can drop in and see A. I will give you the address. Tell him you are a friend of mine. He will be delighted to see you." And so, uncompromised himself, he sends the victim on his way.'

> MI6 officer Henry Landau in *'All's Fair'* (1934). For more about Landau see under "Agent Handling."

'The means by which enlightened rulers and skilful generals have controlled and conquered others, even when they were vastly outnumbered, was advance knowledge. Advance knowledge cannot be gained from ghosts or spirits, it cannot be inferred from omens, it cannot be read in the stars or the weather. It must be gained from men for it is the true knowledge of the enemy's situation.'

> Sun Tzu, *The Art of War*, Chapter 13, Paragraphs 4-6.

'Now, there are five sorts of spies: there are native spies, internal spies, double spies, doomed spies and surviving spies. When all these five types of spies are at work and their operations are successfully clandestine, it is called "the divine manipulation of threads." It is a sovereign's most precious faculty.'

> Sun Tzu, *The Art of War*, Chapter 13, Paragraphs 7 and 8

'All intelligence is gathered by treachery and ... we must have what we can get, not get what we would have.'

> An English Member of Parliament commenting in 1667 during Parliament's examination of the Dutch assault on the Medway. The Dutch raid had been a disaster for the English who had thought that they had good intelligence about Dutch intentions. But this is a quote which has to be interpreted carefully: in the first part he is saying that we need sources in the enemy's camp, not that "treachery" is the only motivation. The second part is not saying that they should only have that intelligence that their spies can easily pick up – it is the job of an intelligence service to go out and get the difficult stuff – rather he is saying that a nation must not just listen to the intelligence that it expects to hear. This was one of the problems with the Medway attack: the English did not think the Dutch Navy was capable of it and discounted any intelligence that suggested that they were. In case you think that this is an old fault in espionage, note that the War in Iraq was initiated (in part) due to a very similar error. Quoted in *Espionage in the reign of Charles II* by Alan Marshall (1994).

GCHQ (UK communications intelligence agency)

'[The current laws are] ... *a blank check to carry out whatever activities they deem necessary.'*

> Conclusion in March 2015 of an 18 month inquiry by the ISC – the Intelligence and

Security Committee (the Parliamentary body that oversees the British intelligence services). The 149 page report found that the legal framework governing the UK intelligence services was so complicated that they were able to do almost anything they wished. This meant that they could spy on almost any section of society in the UK, not just on the nation's enemies. In particular, it found that GCHQ that was gathering *"bulk personal datasets"* on individuals - much of which was gathered without any statutory authority. Some of the data came from abroad (particularly America which was, of course, not covered by UK law), from other government organisations or from private companies. In the report in March 2015, the ISC concluded that laws governing intelligence agencies needed a complete overhaul. That overhaul is yet to occur. In GCHQ's defence, the Director said that the agency does not spy on ordinary citizens and this is true – as long as the citizens do not cause any trouble. But as soon as the agencies decide that political protest or some other form of dissent has reached an unacceptable point (in their eyes) then they have stores of intelligence, built up by communications intelligence, ready to use. It was that aspect that the ISC considered was dangerous as there is no meaningful oversight. Quoted in *The Guardian* newspaper 13 March 2015.

The agency's contribution ... *'must be of sufficient scale and of the right kind to make a continuation of the Sigint alliance worthwhile to our partners ... This may entail on occasion the applying of UK resources to the meeting of US requirements.'*

From GCHQ staff handbook in 1994 explaining why GCHQ staff spend so much of their time working for the NSA (US signals intelligence).

'We don't suddenly lose our souls the moment we swipe into the Doughnut."

Sir Iain Lobban, Director of GCHQ (2008-2014), speaking at his leaving event and trying to explain that GCHQ staff aren't sinister but "normal human beings". The "Doughnut" is the nickname of the main GCHQ building in Cheltenham, a circular, state-of-the-art building completed in 2003 at great expense (see below).

'The original estimate of £40 million for the cost of moving their computer systems all in one go may be the most inaccurate estimate I have ever seen.'

Edward Leigh MP, referring to the building of the GCHQ "Doughnut" (see above) at the Commons Public Accounts Committee, July 2003. The final bill of £337million was seven times the original estimate. While all government projects tend to have cost overruns, this was so extreme that the Committee concluded that they might well not have approved the new facility if Parliament had known the true cost. But then, intelligence services, in part because of the very secrecy they maintain, often get away with bloated expenditure. This is because it is almost impossible for anyone outside the secret service to know what an agency actually needs and then the costs are often hidden within several different budgets.

Glory

'"Legendary" is precisely what all Intelligence Brass, in my experience, wanted to be. They were all in their own estimation, the central character in a Kiplingesque thriller, in which, when their agents were caught, tortured and finally executed, they always died with the words: "Tell the colonel I have kept the faith", on their lips.'

Author and former MI6 officer Malcolm Muggeridge in his memoir - *Tread Softly for You Tread On My Jokes (1968)*. Notice that he says "Intelligence Brass", in other words, he was talking about the managers who stay nice and safe at headquarters in London. This aspect tends to ring true. You almost never find this desire for fame from field officers, many of whom simply want to forget their operational lives and move on to a more peaceful, less-ethically challenged existence.

GRU (Russian military intelligence)

Standing outside GRU headquarters:

'Suvorov: "What kind of fish are swimming there?"
Boss: "There are only one kind of fish in there – piranhas."'

Viktor Suvorov, (real name Vladimir Rezun) - a former GRU officer who defected to the UK in 1978, from his book: *Aquarium – The Career and Defection of a Soviet Military Spy* (1985). "The Aquarium" is the nickname given to the GRU headquarters in Moscow.

Guantanamo (American torture camp in Cuba).

'What psychopathic nightmare land of ogres and shadows do the security services inhabit?'

Kenneth J Moss to the Independent letters page on 17 March 2006 after the news broke that two agents working for MI5 (UK Security Service) had been handed over to the Americans to be tortured at Guantanamo Bay and then had been asked to work for MI5 again. Not all agent handling is sensitive and skilful.

'A vision of hell, beyond Orwell, beyond Kafka.'

Former MI6 officer and novelist David Cornwell (John Le Carrè) in his foreword to *Guantanamo Diary* (2015) written by Mohamedou Ould Slahi, an inmate who was held there – without being charged with any offence – for over 14 years.

'What you have to understand is that these are bad men.'

Chris Mullin, British Foreign Office Minister, defending the treatment of inmates at Guantanamo. Quoted in *The Independent* newspaper 17 March 2006.

Guns

'I never saw a spy who carried a gun, apart from James Bond.'

Former KGB officer Mikhail Lyubimov quoted in *The Philadelphia Inquirer* 22 February 2001. What he says is largely true. The reason is that, although almost all intelligence officers are trained in firearms, carrying a gun, in many situations, automatically marks you out as suspicious. Usually, if there is any shooting to be done, an intelligence service will call on military backup. But that occasion is rare: contrary to what the movies would have you believe, being an intelligence officer is not usually a dangerous occupation – at least not physically.

'A true secret agent only shoots once in his life – when he has no other way out.'

i.e. to commit suicide. Kim Philby talking journalist Vadim Kassis in January 1988. Of course, the situation that Philby was talking about (and is depicted in so many movies) rarely happens. He was actually making a broader point: that the best agents don't quit, they keep going no matter how bleak the situation seems. The history of espionage, especially in wartime, is packed with instances of such determination. Interestingly, when he died in May 1988, the official story was that he died of heart failure. However, there was a rumour that he had committed suicide in despair at the mess that the Soviet Union had become. The Soviet Empire that he had fought for collapsed just two years later.

'The OSS gave me a gun, but I never carried a gun. I thought: "What the heck was I gonna do with a dumb gun?"'

Stephanie Czech, OSS agent and inaugural recipient of the Virginia Hall award for her outstanding courage and work as an American spy during World War Two. Quoted on the official CIA website.

'"I have told your father time and time again," she said moving the gun about as she talked in a way that would have made a grown man faint, "he is not to leave revolvers in the side drawers of guest rooms."'

Charlotte Bingham's mother having found one of her husband's many revolvers. He was a senior MI5 officer (and never shot anyone in his life). Her mother also complained that the knuckleduster in her husband's jacket-pocket pulled his suits out of shape. (I am willing to bet that he never hit anyone with it.) But some officers just like to pose – either with weapons or in their use of the sense of secrecy. Perhaps it makes them feel more important. Quoted in *MI5 and Me* by Charlotte Bingham (2018).

<u>H</u>

Hacking

'They wanted Donald Trump to win, they wanted Hilary to lose, but most of all they just wanted to fuck with us.'

Former CIA Deputy Director David Cohen speaking after a bipartisan Senate Intelligence Committee concluded that Russia had attempted to interfere in the 2016 Presidential election. It estimated that Kremlin-designed content had been seen by more than 126 million people in the US. This shows how the world of intelligence has changed in the past twenty years and how foreign agencies can have a scope and influence they could have never dreamed of in the days of traditional espionage. Quoted in *Spies, Lies and Algorithms* by Amy B. Zegart (2020).

Reginald "Blinker" Hall (Director of the British Naval Intelligence Division during the First World War – arguably Britain's greatest ever spymaster.)

'He did not conform to my rather stereotyped ideas of a retired British admiral. Small, like Nelson, it is true, the top of his imposing head was bald – but it was his face and eyes that caught one's attention. A majestic nose over a rather tight-lipped mouth and a firm, cleft chin made one feel instinctively that this was not a man with whom one could take liberties.'

Patrick Beesley, naval historian upon meeting Hall at a dinner later in life. Quoted in *Spymaster* by David Ramsay (2008).

'...no man could fill his place, a perfectly marvellous person, but the coldest-blooded proposition that ever was – he'd cut a man's heart out and hand it back to him.'

American attaché Edward Bell describing Reginald"Blinker" Hall during World War One. Bell liaised with Hall regularly and was one of the main links in bringing America to the Allies' aid in 1917 which turned the course of the war. Quoted in *Spymaster* by David Ramsay (2008).

'Hall is one genius that the war has developed. Neither in fiction nor in fact can you find any such man to match him. The man is a genius – a clear case of genius. All other secret service men are amateurs by comparison.''

US Ambassador Walter Page writing to President Wilson. Quoted in *Spymaster* by David Ramsay (2008).

'If I had any, I certainly wouldn't tell you!'

Hall addressing Lord Northcliffe who had just asked him how many agents he had in Zeebrugge. Northcliffe, the odious proprietor of the *Daily Mail,* had wormed his way into government with a responsibility for propaganda. He had arrived in Hall's office at the Admiralty and, without even the good manners to take off his hat, had started telling Hall how inadequate he thought Britain's secret services were. He demanded to know what

Hall's agents were up to? Having regarded Northcliffe with astonishment, Hall had called for his uniform cap. Having seated that firmly on his head, Hall told Northcliffe where he could stuff his concerns. Quoted in *Spymaster* by David Ramsay (2008).

'If I had a big proposition to handle and could have my pick of helpers, I'd plump for the Intelligence Division of the British Admiralty.'

The novelist John Buchan, who was a big fan of Hall. Quoted in *Literary Agents* by Anthony Masters (1987). It is a common error, if one thinks of it at all, to assume that all British spies were run by MI6. In fact, both the Army and the Navy had very capable intelligence organisations of their own.

'If you are the undertaker, my man, you are too early.'

Hall on his death bed to a plumber who had wandered into the wrong room. This being Claridges, the exclusive London hotel, he was dressed in black suit and tie. Quoted in *Spymaster* by David Ramsay (2008).

Hippies

'The "Practical English" of the past are being replaced by long-haired "planners" injecting themselves into everything.'

Claude Dansey, senior officer in MI6 and head of its ultra-secret "Z Organisation". He was writing, in 1945, to his good friend Sigismund Payne-Best, a monocle-wearing MI6 spy who he had known for years. He was deploring the new sort of officer that MI6 was hiring – young and educated. The "long hair" probably only reached the men's collars but that was too still much for Dansey. He strongly believed that spying was a game for men of experience who had been out in the world, not sheltering behind books. Quoted in *Secret Service* by Professor Christopher Andrew (1985).

History of Spying

'Diplomats and intelligence agents, in my experience, are even bigger liars than journalists, and the historians who try to reconstruct the past out of their records are, for the most part, dealing in fantasy.'

Author and former MI6 officer Malcolm Muggeridge in his memoir *Chronicles of Wasted Time: The Infernal Grove* (1973).

'The Lord of Hosts is with us.'

Watchword of Sir Francis Walsingham (1532-1590), one of England's most successful spymasters. Quoted in *Espionage* by Margaret Richings (1934).

'There is perhaps in every thing of any consequence, a secret history which it would be amusing to know, could we have it authentically communicated.'

James Boswell in his *Life of Samuel Johnson* (1791). The first part of this is not in doubt. It is the second part that is tricky.

Homosexuals

'I thought men like that went out and shot themselves.'

> King George V reacting to the revelation that the Liberal cabinet Minister, Lord Beauchamp, was homosexual. It was also the revelation by the Naval Intelligence Division to the King that German spy Roger Casement was a homosexual that removed George V's support for clemency in his case. Casement was a British diplomat and Irish nationalist condemned to hang because he took part in a German-supported plot to encourage rebellion in Ireland. His record as a champion of human rights very nearly saved him, but the revelation by the intelligence services that he was a homosexual condemned him. Quoted in *Spymaster* by David Ramsay (2008).

'Oh, don't worry, we have quite a few bachelors,' my father told me shortly. 'And quite a few friends of Dorothy too.'

> John Bingham, senior MI5 officer in the 1950s talking to his daughter Charlotte Bingham who had just been hired as an MI5 secretary. Although homosexuality was officially banned in the British intelligence services and supposedly a reason why positive vetting status (access to secret documents) would be refused, many gay men worked in both services and those around often knew of them. Quoted in *MI5 and Me* by Charlotte Bingham (2018).

'There were three communities – those who embraced change, those who opposed it openly or in the background by their actions and those in the middle who drifted in the wind according to events.''

> MI6 officer quoted on the BBC News website on 28th February 2021.

The MI6 ban on homosexuals ended astonishingly late, on 23 July 1991. However, despite denials by the Service, this did not end the discrimination there:

'There was no amnesty for those who joined before the ban was lifted, so many of us lived in fear even afterwards.'

> Anonymous MI6 officer.

'Throughout the 90s there were direct discriminatory impacts on families and partners, allowances, pensions, promotion, career management and postings.'

> As so often in life, what the rules say and what actually happens in practice are two different things. Both quotes above are from the BBC News website story dated 28 February 2021.

Honey Traps

'On becoming a spy, you will have to learn to deal with feminine wiles. Always remember: the temptation of a beautiful woman can be your downfall - if you're lucky.'

> Groucho Marx in *'How To Be a Spy'* from *This Week*, 16 February 1946. Quoted in *The Essential Groucho'* edited by Stephen Kanfer (2000).

'I let my defences down.'

The words of former British Ambassador to the Soviet Union, Sir Geoffrey Harrison. In 1968 had an affair with an attractive chambermaid working at the embassy, Galya Ivanova. She was of course a honey trap. The KGB tried to blackmail him and sent him photos of the encounter. Sir Geoffrey did the smart thing, confessed and was immediately recalled. Such women, usually sent by the Second Chief Directorate, were known in the KGB as "swallows". Quoted in *Collusion* by Luke Harding (2017).

'I must admit that the behaviour of the accused was more foolish than evil. She permitted herself to be so carried away by her involvement that she laid open to him secret telegrams.'

The prosecution counsel at the trial of British diplomat Rhona Ritchie in November 1982. She had been posted to the British embassy at Tel Aviv in July 1981. It was her first posting. She met an attractive young man at a drinks party at the Egyptian embassy and fell for him. But he was a Romeo spy named Rifaat al-Ansari. He was an Egyptian intelligence officer, married and with children – although of course he never told her that. Soon she was passing secret documents to him. Shin Bet, the Israeli security service had Ritchie under routine surveillance. They quickly discovered the relationship, monitored it and then informed the British when it seemed to them to be taking a dangerous turn. In some ways she was lucky. Although humiliated, the relationship was ended before she did really serious damage. The court clearly took pity on her as often happens when the victims of these rather cruel espionage tricks are discovered. She was only given a suspended sentence. Of course, the British press had a field day, this was spying straight out of the pages of Ian Fleming. *"Virgin Diplomat cheated by Romeo of Cairo"* read one headline. Quoted in *Every Spy a Prince* by Dan Ravi and Yossi Melman (1990).

'Women in love were more dangerous than men because everything was used to reinforce the physical attraction. They were liable to reveal diplomatic secrets in the same spirit as they revealed that little amount of more leg.'

Author and MI6 officer Compton Mackenzie in *Extremes Meet* (1928) on why Romeo Spies are so dangerous. This was a common sexist view at the time but Mackenzie was underestimating just how much damage male spies could do because in the male dominated intelligence services they were the ones with all the access – and to some extent still are.

Honour

'That name? No, I cannot give that. I have pledged my word of honour.'

German spy of World War One Carl Lody when asked in court to say who had sent him. The information might have saved his life. He was sentenced to death but stuck to his principles to the end which earned much admiration from his captors as the quote below illustrates. Quoted in *Spies of the First World War* by James Morton (2010).

'I suppose you would not wish to shake hands with a German spy?'
'No. But I will shake hands with a brave man.'

Lord Athlumney, the Provost Marshall, who had come to fetch German spy Carl Lody from the execution cell in the Tower of London at dawn on 6 November 1914. Lody was a

German naval officer. He had worked for the Hamburg America Shipping Line before the war and spoke good English with an American accent so he was sent to England in the first months of the war under cover as an American - but with almost no training or other preparation. He was picked up when his messages home were intercepted by the postal censor. He was shot in the Tower of London rifle range, the first person to be executed at the Tower in more than 150 years. Several other German spies were to follow him as the war progressed but many others were never caught. Quoted in *Sixty Years in Uniform* by John Frazer (1939).

'The word "spy" conveys something as repulsive as "slave."'

Sir Garnett Wolseley, *The Soldier's Pocket-Book* (1869).

'There are few archbishops in espionage. He's on our side and that's all that matters.'

Former CIA Director Allen Dulles talking about the CIA's work with former Nazi Richard Gehlen. The CIA recruited many former Nazis including those found guilty of war crimes because of their technical knowledge (e.g. responsible for much of NASA's success), their knowledge of Soviet agents, or sometimes just because of their contacts. Quoted in *Spying for America* by Nathan Miller (1989).

'Would <u>you</u> betray a friend? I would rather die a thousand deaths.'

Confederate spy Sam Davis when offered his freedom in return for the names of his agents. He had been operating behind Union lines making drawings of Union defensive positions and collecting other sources of intelligence. He was hanged on 27 November 1863.

I

Imagery (aerial intelligence)

'In the hunt for Osama Bin Laden, we have made extensive use of our multi-billion dollar satellite surveillance capability. So far, all we can confirm is that he is not hiding on a roof anywhere'.

> Frustrated CIA officer talking to the author in 2005. Despite OBL being America's number one terrorist target and despite the unrivalled technical coverage which US intelligence agencies have across the entire globe, it would be another six years before he was finally discovered.

'I could take a random image of any land mass in the world and say there is a 'unicorn training camp' and I promise you it would wind up in some form or another of publication.'

> Allison Puccioni, former US imagery analyst pointing out that despite the fact that satellite imagery is available to the public (and amateur espionage sleuths) as never before, very few people actually know how to use it. Quoted in *Spies, Lies and Algorithms* by Amy B. Zegart (2020).

In four words

(A) ' nasty, dangerous, thankless task.'

> Special Branch officer and leading spycatcher Herbert Fitch in *Traitors Within* (1933). For more about Fitch see under "Counterespionage."

'...the instruments of darkness...'

> Banquo from Shakespeare's *Macbeth*. Quoted by long-time scientific intelligence officer (and one of the great characters in British intelligence history) Professor R.V. Jones in his memoir *Most Secret War* (1978).

'A battle of wits.'

> Gustav Steinhauer. He was a former naval officer and an ex-Pinkerton detective who became head of the British section of German naval intelligence in the years before World War One. He later wrote a rather less than truthful memoir: *"I was the Kaiser's Master Spy"*. Quoted in *Spynest* by Edwin Ruis (2016).

'The Game of Foxes.'

> Ladislas Farago, US author, historian and intelligence expert from his book of the same name. Incidentally, he referred to those who were not spies as 'rabbits'.

'A Game of Moles'.

> Desmond Bristow, MI6 officer (1940-1953). He believed that many leading British

intelligence figures were working for Russia and wrote the book of the same name.

'A War of Brains.'

> Charles Lucieto, French secret service officer during World War One and spy novelist. From his memoir *On Special Missions* (1927).

'A wilderness of mirrors.'

> A well-known quote attributed to James Jesus Angleton but originally from T.S. Eliot's poem *Gerontion*.

'The Looking Glass War.'

> The title of a thriller written in 1965 by John Le Carré (MI6 officer David Cornwell).

'A (sort of) legalised illicit affair.'

> Alan Judd, former "Foreign Service officer", in his spy novel *Legacy* (2001). For more about Judd see under "Agent Handling."

'(A) distasteful but vital necessity.'

> Dwight D Eisenhower speaking in 1960. Quoted in *The Literary Spy* by Charles E. Lathrop (2004).

'Not for the fainthearted.'

> Former Director of the CIA Richard Helms in his book *A Look Over My Shoulder.* (2004).

'The game without rules.'

> Quoted in *The World Of Action* by Valentine Williams (1938).

'We of the Game'

> From *Kim* by Rudyard Kipling (1900). Still one of the best books about espionage ever written. Variations of Kim's Game are still used as a test of memory in secret service training courses all over the world. Those who have played the real "Great Game" are forever branded by it.

In more than four words

'One of the toughest games played.'

> David Nelligan from his memoir *The Spy in the Castle* (1968). Nelligan was a notorious double agent working during the war for Irish independence for the Irish police and MI5 but in fact for the IRA. Espionage should be full of sporting comparisons but this is one of the few I could find.

'One of the more potent aphrodisiacs of power.'

Historian David Stafford in his book *Churchill and Secret Service* (1987).

In three words

'A silly thing.'

Malcolm Muggeridge, author, broadcaster and MI6 officer in the Second World War. Quoted in *Literary Agents* by Anthony Masters (1987).

'...an unpleasant necessity...'

King William III of England (as a soldier he felt that secret service was somehow dishonourable but he knew the value that intelligence might bring.) Quoted in *Espionage* by Margaret Richings (1934).

'England's guiltiest pleasure...'

Film critic Terence Rafferty in *The New York Times* newspaper on 12 October 2003.

In two words

And it is probably right that the last word should go to the man who, in many ways, started it all in the modern age:

'Capital sport!'

Captain Sir Mansfield Cumming, first chief of MI6.

Inspiration

'If you are thrown out the door, then re-enter through the window.'

Old Mossad maxim. Quoted in *Every Spy a Prince* by Dan Raviv and Yossi Melman (1990).

'This judgement I have of you – that you will not be corrupted with any manner of gift, and that you will be faithful to the State, and that, without respect of my private will, you will give me that counsel which you think best.'

Attributed to Elizabeth I and also a notice which the Vice Chief of MI6, Claude Dansey, kept behind his desk as a credo.

'Mistakes may be forgiven, but God himself cannot forgive the hanger-back.'

Favourite saying of "Blinker Hall" arguably Britain's greatest ever spymaster. Quoted in *Spymaster* by David Ramsay (2008).

Intelligence

'The shock of meeting somebody connected with Intelligence work who could understand immediately what was wanted and why it was wanted, proved too much for my nerves.'

Author and MI6 officer Compton Mackenzie talking about his first meeting with Sir Eric Holt Wilson. Contrary to what you might expect, studies show that the intelligence services (of all countries) are not known for attracting the brightest brains: the pay is low and the work often goes unnoticed. Holt-Wilson's intelligence was a rarity. He rose to become deputy-head of MI5. Quoted in *Armour Against Fate* by Michael Occleshaw (1989).

'The most important limitation on intelligence is its incompleteness. Much ingenuity and effort is spent on making secret information difficult to acquire and hard to analyse ... it is often, when first acquired, sporadic and patchy, and even after analysis may still be at best inferential.'

From the Butler Review into intelligence failures during the hunt for Iraqi weapons of mass destruction which led to the Iraq War (2004).

'Intelligence is information on which action can be taken.'

The definitive view by the first chief of MI6, Mansfield Cumming, in the preface to the very first MI6 officers' training guide written in 1918. In the scramble to keep up their quota of reports, intelligence officers often produce material which is not particularly useful and, as numerous inquiries have shown, sometimes it isn't even secret. Quoted in *The Quest for C* by Alan Judd (1999).

'Secret Service is not a matter which can be organised or controlled entirely by correspondence. In this work above all other the personal touch and inspiration are what is most required.'

Colonel Reginald Drake, Head of the British War Office's Military Intelligence Branch I(b) in World War One. Quoted in *History of Intelligence (B), British Expeditionary Force, France* (1918).

'Good intelligence is often the mother of prevention.'

Private correspondence of I. Basire 17 May 1665. Quoted in *Intelligence in the reign of Charles II* by Alan Marshall (1994).

'Nothing should be valued as highly as intelligence, nothing should be as generously rewarded as intelligence and nothing should be as closely guarded as the work of intelligence.'

Sun Tzu, *The Art of War*, Chapter 13, Paragraph 14. This is fine as far as it goes but it also illustrates the problem with aphorisms. Valued highly? Yes, but intelligence must also be rigorously tested. Generously rewarded? Well maybe, but too much money leads to inefficiency in secret services and unreliability in agents. Closely guarded? Yes, but overuse of secrecy can mean that intelligence is not properly exploited. (A Senate Committee concluded that this was one of the reasons for the successful terrorist attack on the Twin Towers on 9/11.) In the intelligence services, use of secrecy other than to protect operations can lead to inefficiency, corruption and nepotism.

Intelligence and Security Committee (the Parliamentary Committee which oversees the British intelligence services).

'I asked the Home Secretary, Ken Clarke, if we could interview the then head of MI5, Stella Rimington. Clarke refused. However, Rimington, in an effort to improve the image of the service, had been privately briefing newspaper editors. How come, I asked Clarke, the head of MI5 was permitted to meet with the unelected but not with the elected? At which point he came out with his hands up. Half a dozen of us were invited to lunch with her.'

Chris Mullin, MP who was then on the Home Affairs Select Committee which had the oversight responsibility before the ISC was formed. Quoted in *Spies, Spin and the Fourth Estate* by Paul Lashmar (2020).

'If the American oversight committee had produced such an anodyne document they would have been ridiculed. Instead the silence has been deafening.'

The reaction to the ISC's first ever report in 1996 by James Adams of the *Sunday Times* newspaper.

'How can we have proper oversight if the people you are overseeing are the very people who are determining the information that you get?'

Yvette Cooper, MP and former member of the ISC. Quoted by Stephen Dorril (2000).

'...the result is that we cannot then put our hands on our hearts and tell the public ... that all is well ... because we are not in a position to know'.

Tom King, MP and former head of the ISC. Quoted in *MI6* by Stephen Dorril (2000).

'Oversight of intelligence, whoever carries it out, is inescapably political.'

Quoted from *Intelligence in an Insecure World* by P. Gill and M. Pythian (2012).

Internet

'Many of the sort of things for which officials once would have turned to the intelligence agencies are now readily available online.'

Sir David Pepper, Director, GCHQ (2003-2008) speaking in 2011.

Interpretation

'Give me the facts, Ashley, and I will twist them the way I want to suit my argument.'

Sir Winston Churchill to the Oxford historian Maurice Ashley who assisted him with his biography of the first Duke of Marlborough. It is also thought to sum up Churchill's attitude to secret intelligence which he tended to use highly selectively, ignoring that which did not fit his point of view. Once when a naval officer pointed out that secret intelligence indicated the very reverse of the situation that Churchill believed did exist, Churchill did not thank him but had him instantly removed from his post and carried on regardless. Quoted in

Churchill and Secret Service by David Stafford (1995).

Interrogation

'If you want to get the truth out of a man, the important thing is to start him talking. Do not start shooting a lot of leading questions; let him do the talking. Do not at once attempt to take notes and if he says something of importance do not at once jot it down; remember it.''

Lt Col Meinerzthagen. Quoted in *Armour Against Fate* by Michael Occleshaw (1989). Meinerzthagen was a leading intelligence officer, although doubt has since been cast on many of his more outrageous claims. He was an exponent of garbology which means producing intelligence from trash. For instance, in East Africa during the First World War, he used to order his men to search the German officers' latrines as they often used old intelligence reports and coded messages as toilet paper. Not all of espionage work is glamorous.

'Of course, they always expected, to be badly treated, but our Intelligence officers were trained to treat them very pleasantly, gave them a cigarette to smoke and so on, and gradually drew them out and got very good information from them.'

General James Marshall-Cornwall highly experienced British intelligence figure who was a member of both military intelligence and MI6 where he was Deputy Chief. Quoted in *Armour Against Fate* by Michael Occleshaw (1989). If you want to see a good example of this interrogation technique in action then watch the movie *The One That Got Away* (1957). Several former British interrogators were advisers to the movie which accounts for its authenticity. It is the exact opposite of the approach usually shown in TV shows such as *"24"* where torture or violence is used to elicit information. That almost never works (for a variety of reasons). That is one reason that CIA intelligence was so poor in the wake of 9/11. People in pain will tell you anything you want to hear either deliberately or simply to make the pain stop.

'There was the examining officer who favoured terrorism. This gentleman would come into the torture chamber, clamp down a couple of revolvers, swill off a whisky and soda, scowl at the victim, and then start barking. This system rapidly fell into disuse.'

The Secret Corps by Captain Ferdinand Tuohy (1920) writing about the interrogation of German prisoners during the First World War.

Investigatory Powers Act 2016

'The UK has just legalised the most extreme surveillance in the history of western democracy.'

Edward Snowden, the NSA (US signals intelligence) whistleblower who absconded to Russia with a great deal of top secret information in 2013. It is thanks to him that we now know just how pervasive state surveillance is in the internet age. It is often thought that China is the nation that makes greatest use of the power to spy on the activities of its citizens. It isn't. It is the United Kingdom. The only real difference between the two is that this great store of intelligence will only be accessed if the authorities decide that you have become a problem – for whatever reason.

Iraq

Iraq is the incident which destroyed confidence in the modern intelligence services and made many commentators ask the reasonable question: "If our intelligence services cannot recruit a high-level source in a country run by one of the most hated dictators in the world, then what use are they?"

'Don't they know there is no nuclear programme? We don't have enough spare parts for our conventional military, we can't even shoot down an aeroplane, we don't have anything left!'

> An unnamed high-level Iraqi agent working for the CIA. Shortly after this statement and despite all the evidence to the contrary, the United States' National Intelligence Estimate said that Iraq was reconstituting its nuclear programme. This was used as a justification for the war. If a government is determined to go to war then it does not matter whether the intelligence is right or not. Quoted in James Risen's *State of War: The Secret History of the CIA and the Bush Administration* (2006).

'All intelligence, by its very nature, is incomplete.'

> Tony Blair, former British Prime Minister, quoted in *The Independent* newspaper 1 May 2005.

No it isn't. Not if your intelligence service is doing its job properly. This myth has been widely propagated in recent years as an excuse for poor performance by intelligence services.

'God would tell me: "George, go and fight those terrorists in Afghanistan" and I did. Then God would tell me: "George, go and end the tyranny in Iraq", and I did'.

> President George W. Bush speaking at an Israeli-Palestinian summit in 2003. It was this kind of lunatic thinking together with Tony Blair's arrogance which accurate intelligence might have challenged. But it did not because we did not have it. In fact, the secret services provided the intelligence that it thought the leaders wanted to hear. And that was the greatest failure of the intelligence agencies during the period that led to the Iraq War. A war that produced an entirely new wave of terrorism across the world and a boom time for intelligence services as their budgets ballooned because of that very renewal of the terrorist threat. It is no wonder that conspiracy theorists have a field day.

'Having been attacked by al Qaeda, for us now to go bombing Iraq in response would be like our invading Mexico after the Japanese attacked us at Pearl Harbour.'

> Richard Clarke, US Counter Terrorism Chief quoted in *The Truth with Jokes* by Al Frankel (2005). And yet that is exactly what happened.

'C [Richard Dearlove, then Chief of MI6] reported on his recent talks in Washington. There was a perceptible shift in attitude. Military action was now seen as inevitable. Bush wanted to remove Saddam, through military action, justified by the conjunction of terrorism and WMD. But the intelligence and the facts were being fixed around the policy. ... There was little discussion in Washington of the aftermath of military action.'

> Cabinet Office minutes released as part of the Butler Inquiry into the invasion of Iraq. From *The Truth with Jokes* by Al Franken (2005).

95

'I think there is a real risk that the [US] administration underestimates the difficulties. They may agree that failure is not an option, but this doesn't mean that they will avoid it.'

David Manning, foreign policy advisor to Tony Blair quoted in *The Truth with Jokes* by Al Franken (2005).

'When I heard him using those words, I could almost hear a collective raspberry going up around Whitehall.'

John Morrison, special investigator for the British Intelligence and Security Committee (ISC) describing his reaction to a Panorama reporter when Tony Blair described Iraq as a *"serious and current threat to the UK"*. In an apparent act of revenge, Downing Street had him sacked for daring to make these remarks even though he had cleared the interview with the chairman of the ISC. It was to be many years before the ISC regained its independent investigation capability. The ISC is the Parliamentary committee responsible for oversight of the British secret services. Established in 1994, results have shown that it is largely a waste of time and effort as it is unable to penetrate through the layers of secrecy surrounding the different organisations. For more about this committee see under "ISC".

'I have little choice but to conclude that some of the intelligence related to Iraq's nuclear weapons programme was twisted to exaggerate the Iraqi threat.'

Joe Wilson, American diplomat. He was correct about what had happened but such is the state of American politics that even this mild comment was enough to provoke supporters of President Bush into revenge: his wife, Valerie Plame, was a CIA officer and her identity was subsequently leaked to the Press. This potentially put her life in danger and ended her career. Furthermore, the false intelligence about Iraq sourcing uranium in Africa (which is what Wilson was referring to) was one of MI6's few independent contributions to the case for the war. And it was wrong, a point worth bearing in mind the next time someone repeats the old cliché that the UK has the best intelligence service in the world. Sadly, that myth is based on the James Bond image rather than reality. Quoted in *The Independent* newspaper 30 October 2005.

'It was intelligence that was crap and that we couldn't move on, but the Brits wanted to plant stories in England and around the world so we let them have it".

Unnamed US intelligence officer explaining why faulty MI6 intelligence on Iraq was not challenged. Quoted in *The Independent* newspaper (in turn quoting *The New Yorker* magazine) 12 April 2005.

'Not all the blandishments of the Turks, nor all the gold they have distributed, nor any German effort can undermine the influence among the tribes of one man: Leachman.'

A footnote from history. The recent Gulf War was not the first time that Iraq has been the centre of armed conflict. During the First World War, the secret services of Germany and Britain were locked in a struggle for this area which was then part of the Turkish Empire. These words were part of an entry found in the diary of Conrad Preusser when he was captured along with a number of other German prisoners in April 1918. Preusser was a German secret service officer in Iraq. When his group were forced to surrender, Preusser apparently clicked his heels, marched smartly forwards and presented himself to his captor. That captor was Lieutenant Colonel Gerard Leachman. Leachman was the British "super agent" in the area at the time and his exploits were a match even for those of the legendary T.E. Lawrence (Lawrence of Arabia). Interestingly, the Germans had their own "super agent" working in the area. His name was Wilhelm Wassmuss, referred to by some historians as "the German Lawrence" because of his ability to stir up the tribes against the British and his incredible adventures. Yet now, like so many of the great secret agents in history, both men are all but forgotten. Quoted in *OC Desert* by HVF Winstone (1982).

Israel

'A nation creates the intelligence community it needs. America relies on technical expertise because we are concerned to discover, rather than secretly rule. The Israelis operate differently. Mossad, in particular, equates its actions with the country's survival.'

William Casey, former Director of the CIA. Quoted in *'Gideon's Spies'* by Gordon Thomas (1999).

J

Journalists

'Spies and journalists go together like Marks and Spencer.'

> Espionage historian Philip Knightley from his book *The Second Oldest Profession* (1987).

'Much journalism is in fact little more than spying.'

> Brian Innes in *The Book of Spies: 4000 years of cloak and dagger* (1967).

'If spies pose as journalists, people will see journalists as legitimate targets.'

> John Foster, general secretary of the UK's National Union of Journalists, making a statement after *The Independent* newspaper revealed that MI6 officers were working undercover in Yugoslavia by forging press passes and pretending to be journalists. Although intelligence services often claim that news stories about spying may put their lives at risk, the truth is that more journalists have been killed because of the intelligence services than secret agents have been killed because of media stories. Quoted in *Spies, Spin and the Fourth Estate* by Paul Lashmar (2020).

'Spies are, after all, very like journalists in their methods – but merely less reliable.'

> The journalist David Leigh in an article published in 2000 uncovering the propaganda work of MI6.

'The truth is that they are very deliberately seeking to control us.'

> David Leigh again. He had worked as a "confidential contact" of the UK intelligence services. This use of certain trusted journalists has always existed and used to be seen as useful to both sides. However, in the modern age, the use of short-term employment contracts and intense competition caused by the rise of internet sources has meant that the power balance in these relationships now only goes one way: either print what you are told or the secret service will take their business elsewhere. David Leigh was one of those journalists who removed himself from the relationship because of this implied threat. Quoted in *Spies, Spin and the Fourth Estate* by Paul Lashmar (2020).

'Those very few journalists who do have some sort of access or privilege are so jealous and guard it so clearly that it's almost worthless. They're in the pocket of the person who's providing them with what information they can get.'

> Philip Knightley to the academic Justin Schlosberg. This is why the intelligence services find it much easier to control journalists these days: many of them are on short term contracts and they have to bring in good stories – regularly. It is tremendous pressure and once they have supped from the intelligence service tap it is hard to disconnect. Quoted in *Spies, Spin and the Fourth Estate* by Paul Lashmar (2020).

'Intelligence, if publicised, can be highly manipulated by intelligence elites, while civil society's ability to assess and verify claims is compromised by absence of independent evidence.'

Professor Vian Bakir. Quoted in *Spies, Spin and the Fourth Estate* by Paul Lashmar (2020).

'I got the distinct impression that part of the exercise was punishment. The State acts in these circumstances to send warning to all journalists that if you delve into these areas, if you take an interest in matters we consider no business at all of the public, then there will be a price to pay. At the very least, we will make your life uncomfortable for several months.'

Journalist Ed Moloney, Northern Ireland correspondent for *The Sunday Tribune* newspaper who was hounded for years in order to reveal who his sources were during the conflict there.

'There are more of them in Afghanistan than there are of us – and they are paid better.'

CIA officer Bill Harlow explaining how the TV news network CNN had been able to get hold of an Al-Qaeda video archive from Afghanistan and the CIA hadn't. Quoted in the *New York Times* 19 August 2002.

K

Karate

'The most it's good for is self-confidence.'

Elena Vavilova, an SVR (Russian foreign intelligence service) agent. She lived under cover in Boston as "Tracy Foley" for almost twenty years. Such deep cover agents are known in the trade as "Illegals". She had received intensive firearms and self-defence training before leaving Russia, but did not use any of it. This is true for most spies and contrary to what the movies and books would have you believe. Although all spies are trained in the use of firearms, most of the time spies do not carry guns for the simple reason that possession of a firearm is hard to explain in most cover roles. So, on the rare occasions when a spy brings a gun on a mission for self-protection, they spend almost as much time worrying about the damned thing as they do being reassured that they have it. The preferred solution for spies is to have military trained back-up nearby who can come to the rescue if things get out of hand. As for karate, most spies do not have time to regularly practice any martial art, at least not so that it becomes instinctive enough to use when under great pressure. Instead, spies are taught to improvise by using whatever comes to hand. It is astonishing how many common items can be turned into a weapon, especially when coupled with the element of surprise. Quoted in *The Guardian* newspaper 23 August 2019.

Knowledge

'When you know a thing, to hold that you know it and when you do not know a thing, to allow that you do not know it: this is knowledge.'

Attributed to Confucius.

'I am wiser to this small extent: that I do not think that I know what I do not know.'

Plato, *The Defence of Socrates.*

'News does not become knowledge by the mere process of gathering.'

Arthur B. Darling in his book *The CIA* (1990). Darling was the CIA's first official historian, appointed in 1952. He makes a very good point. Too often spies will send in gossip or half-truths disguised as intelligence. They want to look busy and besides really good intelligence is hard to collect. Reports officers, who sit in headquarters and review raw intelligence reports before issuing it to their customers, must constantly be on the lookout for this tendency.

Fictional characters know it:

'It is a capital mistake to theorise before you have all the evidence. It biases the judgement.'

Sir Arthur Conan Doyle's immortal detective Sherlock Holmes in *A Study in Scarlet*. The classic example would be the belief that there were Weapons of Mass Destruction (WMD) in Iraq. Western intelligence services did not have access to Iraq's most senior military inner circles and therefore did not have any real knowledge of the situation. They disbelieved the few "straws in the wind" that they did gather because the truth (that Iraq did not have WMD) seemed so unlikely.

And even the bad guys know it:

'Don't tell me what you think. Give me the facts and the source!'

Josef Stalin quoted in *The Mitrokhin Archive Vol 1* (1999). Vasili Mitrokhin was a KGB archivist who defected to the West in 1992 together with a valuable collection of secret documents. British intelligence set him up to work with the Cambridge historian Professor Christopher Andrew and together they produced two volumes that published the documents together with other ancillary works. They also make good door stops – they are huge!

'Before you become too entranced with gorgeous gadgets and mesmerising video displays, let me remind you that information is not knowledge, knowledge is not wisdom and wisdom is not foresight.'

Attributed to the science fiction author Arthur C. Clarke.

L

Languages

'Knowledge of languages is the doorway to wisdom.'

Roger Bacon from his *Opus Majus* (c1672). Students sometimes ask me what they should study if they are considering a career in the intelligence services. My answer is always the same: learn a foreign language. This is for several reasons: First, it is a good discipline and indicates a flexible mind; Second, if one is going to run foreign agents it is best done if you speak a common language – even through an interpreter one loses certain indications which can be vital in judging trustworthiness; Third; in truly learning another language one learns about the culture of other nations. This sort of cultural sensitivity is an important trait in successful agent runners. But if you have not learned another language, do not fret. As part of their recruitment process most intelligence services run linguistic aptitude tests to judge just how good the recruit may be at learning a new language. There will always be some language or dialect that the service needs but does not have so they need to be flexible. For more about Bacon see under "Codes and Ciphers."

Last Words

'Passion and levity have destroyed me. I pay with my life for my sins. Pray for me.'

The suicide note of the Austrian Colonel and Chief of Intelligence, Alfred Redl, one of the most talented intelligence officers of his time and a national hero, but who was caught spying for the French, Russians and the Italians. He shot himself in the head with a revolver in his hotel room shortly after writing these words. He seems to have worked only for money and it is now thought that he was suffering from some form of mental illness at the time of his betrayal. Quoted in *Fifty Amazing Secret Service Dramas* (1937).

'I will show them that a Belgian woman knows how to die.'

Gabrielle Petit, a Belgian agent working for British intelligence in the First World War. She was executed on 1st April 1916 aged just 23. Her story shows how a great spirit can emerge from the most unpromising of beginnings: she was a frail and timid person. Her mother died at an early age and she was raised in an orphanage. She became involved in espionage because she helped her wounded soldier boyfriend to safety in neutral Holland. There she came across the path of British Army intelligence who convinced her to go back and help other Allied soldiers find their way to safety. She ran agents and distributed an underground newspaper. She became such a problem that German intelligence sent out two agents especially to catch her. She refused to talk under torture and died defiant to the last.

'I only regret that I have but one life to lose for my country.'

Nathan Hale, one of the very first American spies who worked for General George Washington during the War of Independence. He was given no training and had no real idea how to maintain his cover as a Dutch school teacher. It is hardly surprising that he only lasted a few days before he was caught and hanged. He was so ill prepared that he was still carrying documents containing his real name. But he had been the only person to volunteer for the dangerous mission and both sides respected his courage. Today a statue of Hale stands outside CIA headquarters at Langley. Quoted in *Spies, Lies and Algorithms* by Amy B. Zegart (2020).

'I am reconciled to death but detest the mode.'

Major John André, British contact of the American traitor Benedict Arnold during the Revolutionary War. André had been captured behind American lines whilst in civilian dress. He was sentenced to be hanged rather than shot which he thought rather unfair as he saw himself as a soldier rather than a spy. On the other hand, Benedict Arnold escaped and lived to a ripe old age. A rare case of the agent runner rather than the agent paying the price for failure.

'The game is up. I am a German. I confess everything.'

Not quite the last words of German spy Robert Rosenthal but the words that sealed his fate. In 1914 he was sent to spy in England as a cigar dealer. He had a US passport in the name of Harry Berger and he was able to carry this off because he had spent some time in the United States before the war. He completed his mission and got away. The Germans were so impressed that they sent him back again – and again he completed his mission. It was on his third mission in 1915 that he was finally caught - and it was by a cruel twist of fate rather than poor tradecraft. He was sending intelligence back to his operational officer using invisible ink messages in letters which were posted to Norway (which was neutral and therefore, supposedly, letters were not censored). Quite by chance, one of these letters was placed in the mail bag for Berlin. This was far more suspicious and these letters were of course examined by the Post Office censor. The message was discovered and he was hunted down. Even so, he almost got away: he was arrested just as he was boarding the steamer for Bergen. Even then he nearly escaped the noose. At his trial he claimed that he was an innocent businessman and that some other person, the real spy, must have got to his letter and added the secret message implicating him. Seeing as he had made no admissions during interrogation, it was becoming difficult to prove beyond a reasonable doubt that he actually was guilty. But then, at a key point in the prosecution case, he suddenly stood up and made the statement above. It doomed him and he was hanged on the 15 July 1915. Even so, there were those who admired him. Herbert Fitch, the noted spycatcher, wrote in his diary: *"Hanged at Wandsworth. Kept his courage to the last."* Quoted in *Traitors Within* by Herbert Fitch (1933).

'My only regret is that I was not able to cause more damage to the Soviet Union and render more service to France.'

Vladimir Vetrov, whose codename was "Farewell", speaking shortly before he was shot in 1985. He was a KGB officer who spied for France. From *The Mitrokhin Archive Vol 1* by Vasili Mitrokhin and Professor Christopher Andrew (1999).

'The boys will have to fight the battles without me.'

Confederate spy Sam Davis who was hanged but earned the admiration of both sides for his courage. For more about Davis see under "Honour."

Laughter

'To survive the multiple hazards of espionage it is better not to be too serious. The trick, I believe, is to be light-hearted without being superficial. I never took life, myself, or other people too seriously. I was criticised for this ... by none other than Major General Stewart Menzies, the head of British Intelligence, who added that it was ideal for my job.'

Dusko Popov, the most successful MI6 double agent of World War Two. He was a Serb recruited by the Germans because he had good business contacts in London. In fact, he was working for the British and helped to deceive the Germans about key operations such as the D-Day landings. What did Menzies mean? Almost certainly that Popov's alcoholic and bed-hopping lifestyle was a liability, but also perfect cover - for who would think this frivolous playboy could also be a double agent? This sort of lifestyle has been cover for more than one successful agent in the annals of espionage so perhaps this is one of the few areas where the James Bond image does touch on the truth. Quoted in Popov's book *Spy, Counter Spy* (1974).

'The book must have seemed to the average reader as a fantastic Marx Brothers affair but during the Second World War many people discovered that those responsible for secret intelligence do, in very fact, as often as not, behave like characters created by the Marx Brothers.'

The author and MI6 officer Compton Mackenzie who wrote the comic novel *"Water On The Brain"* after he was prosecuted under the Official Secrets Act in 1933. It remains one of the most strangely accurate accounts of the life of a spy. Quoted in *Literary Agents* by Anthony Masters (1987).

'Hess or no Hess, I am going to see the Marx brothers!'

British Prime Minister Winston Churchill upon hearing unconfirmed reports that Nazi Germany's deputy leader, Rudolf Hess, had arrived in Scotland. It was such an extraordinary occurrence that at first even Churchill could not believe that it could be true. For many years, because certain papers were withheld from the National Archive, some conspiracy theorists proposed that MI6 was behind Hess' defection. It is now known that this is not true although Sir Ivone Kirkpatrick, a former military intelligence officer, was the first to interrogate Hess to try to determine if he was genuine (Kirkpatrick spoke fluent German and had met Hess in Germany). Poor mental health was the real reason behind Hess' extraordinary behaviour. Quoted in *Churchill and Secret Service* by David Stafford (1995).

'My God, your service thinks of everything!'

Unnamed Mossad officer to MI6 officer Nicholas Elliot. They were both at a nude swimming party (that raises a few questions in itself). The officer noticed that Elliot was circumcised and assumed that this was part of Elliot's cover. From Elliot's memoir *Never Judge a Man By His Umbrella* (1991).

'When each country was asked to say what was their top priority security concern, I said "Terrorism" and the Namibian delegate said "Cattle rustling."'

Dame Stella Rimington, former Director General of MI5, from her memoir *Open Secret* (2001).

'One thing that sticks in my mind about my first visit to the Soviet Trade Delegation is the profusion of squirrels.'

So begin the memoirs of Bill Graham, an MI6 agent who for about a year in the early 1980s was able to bug and burgle the Soviet Trade Delegation at will – despite the squirrels. *Break In* by Bill Graham (1987).

Leaks

'A tale-bearer revealeth secrets: but he of a faithful spirit concealeth the matter.'

The Book of Proverbs, Chapter 11, Verse 13.

'If a piece of news is divulged by a spy before the time is ripe, he must be put to death together with the person to whom the secret was told.'

Sun Tzu, *The Art of War*, Chapter 13, Paragraph 19.

Le Carré (The pen name of former MI6 officer David Cornwell)

'...what imbecilities are committed in the hallowed name of intelligence.'

Cover quote provided by Cornwell for *The Second Oldest Profession* by Phillip Knightley. (1987).

'That fellow knows something.'

Sir Stewart Menzies (1890-1968), Chief of MI6 1939 – 1952, when asked what he thought of Cornwell's work. This is important. You may hear former officers say that he created an inaccurate picture. But this is only their professional pride speaking. In fact, Cornwell wrote some very deep truths about the world of espionage - as Menzies knew. Quoted in *The Secret Servant* by Anthony Cave Brown (1988).

'John Le Carré I would gladly hang, draw and quarter.'

Daphne Park, former MI6 senior officer and member of the House of Lords. Quoted in *The Art of Betrayal* by Gordon Corera (2011). Park never married or had a family and dedicated her whole life to MI6 and the Conservative Party. She could not bear to hear anyone speak ill of either. Incidentally, MI6 did not agree with her: for many years it was the highlight of the training course for new MI6 intelligence officers to attend a lecture given by Cornwell. He stopped doing it when he fell out with the Service over its support for the Iraq War.

'I know who you are, you're a bloody Communist spy!'

Denis Healey approaching Cornwell at a dinner party. But this was not just a casual comment, Healy was a former Minister of State for Defence and knew just how hated Cornwell was by the intelligence community.

'We are definitely not as our host here describes us.'

Sir Maurice Oldfield, Chief of MI6, to the actor Sir Alec Guinness who was about to play the role of George Smiley. Cornwell had arranged for Guinness to meet "the real thing." The irony is that it was later revealed that Oldfield had betrayed his entire service. He had denied his own sexuality at a time when homosexuality was illegal, while supporting the expulsion from MI6 of any other homosexual who was caught. This secret double life enabled him to climb the ladder of promotion to the very top of the organisation. The scandal was so great that when the truth emerged in 1987, a statement had to be made in Parliament by the Prime Minister. On that evidence, it seems that the service is almost exactly as Cornwell portrayed it.

'By denigrating Jack's job he has undermined our country and let us become the laughing stock of the Soviets.'

Lady Clanmorris, wife of John "Jack" Bingham, senior MI5 officer. Bingham and Cornwell shared an office together and Bingham (who was also a thriller writer) helped Cornwell to get his first book published. Bingham never forgave him for not painting the intelligence world in a better light. Quoted in *Literary Agents* by Anthony Masters (1987). Incidentally, Cornwell never could remember how he made up his pen name of Le Carré. At one point he claimed that he had seen the name in an advertisement on the side of a bus. However, in later years, he said that the name had just come to him and he could not think where it had sprung from.

Lie Detectors (No, they are not! See Polygraphs)

Litvinenko (Alexander)

'There is a different scale of crime in the eyes of the Kremlin committed by me or Litvinenko. We can write a book together, but he is a former officer who is committing treason while I am just a writer. This is why he is dead and I am alive.'

Yuri Felshtinsky, who co-wrote the book *Blowing Up Russia* (2002) with Litvinenko. The basic rule in espionage is "Spies don't kill spies". (Sorry, James Bond fans). For Russia (under its current leadership) there is an exception to this rule which is that "Traitors do not count as spies." This has always been the case e.g. the assassination of GRU defector Walter Krivitsky, murdered in his New York hotel room in 1941. This rule is not followed in the West. No assassins were sent after Burgess, Philby or Blake.

      Of course, this does not mean that there is no death in espionage: thousands of agents have died (see the Preface for the difference between officers and agents). That is because in most cases it is the agents, not the officers, who run the risks. Also, remember another of the unwritten rules of espionage: "To every rule, there may always be an exception." Quoted in *The Observer* newspaper 2 August 2015.

Lock Picking

'I don't look at picking a lock, I look at the person whose job it is to keep the lock closed, then persuade them to open it.'

In general, spies do not pick locks. However, there is an immediate caveat to that: you can go onto the internet right now and find lots of guides on the principles of lock picking and how to pick the simplest locks. That's fine and spies are trained in those simple techniques. However, most locks and other security systems that spies encounter are a great deal more complicated than that. The quote above is from Jenny Radcliffe, a professional security tester. Her job is to get into premises that are guarded by security systems so that companies can see how their security needs to be improved. Although not a trained spy, she seems to have discovered the same principles that spies use; that *a security system is only as good as the people using it.* This principle applies not just to security systems but also to computer protection, message encryption and practically any other security device. In fact some security testers refer to themselves as "people hackers" in a similar way to "computer hackers". They learn how to persuade, trick and, sometimes just to simply ask people to help them bypass security systems and locks. Another term for this is "social engineering." That is why spies spend most of their training learning how to manipulate people not learning how to manipulate gadgets. Again, not very James Bond. There is one further caveat: every intelligence service will have a section that specialises in locks and security systems. This is for two purposes: first, to improve their own defences and second, to provide an extra option if "people hacking" does not work. But even then it is almost always the security team that goes in, not the intelligence officer – some skills just take too long to teach. Quoted in *The Guardian* newspaper 4 February 2023 in an interview to promote the book *People Hacker: Confessions of a Burglar for Hire* by Jenny Radcliffe (2023) (which I recommend buying if this area of the work interests you.)

Loneliness

'When you're working in MI5, it's hard to develop new relationships. You can't just go along to a dating agency or answer a personal ad, as it would be impossible to maintain the level of secrecy required.'

Stella Rimington, former head of MI5, explaining why she hadn't divorced her husband even though their relationship had been over for more than twenty years. The pressure put on spies and the high divorce rate in all of the intelligence services is another aspect of the life that rarely gets much attention. Quoted in *The Independent* newspaper 17 June 2004 from an interview Rimington gave in *Good Housekeeping* magazine.

'No one has a good word to say for spies except those who need their services.'

Professor Bernard Porter in his book *Plots and Paranoia* (1989).

Luxury

'Torrie approved, Jilling willing.'

A note in the diary of Major John Lawrence Baird (later Viscount Stonehaven), one of the original members of the British Army's Intelligence Corps in 1914. They were completely unprepared for gathering intelligence in France. They had been selected for the Corps as early as 1910, largely because they could speak foreign languages and because they could ride a motorcycle. It was thought that they would need to travel fast and independently around the battle area. It was thought that if you could ride a horse then you could ride a motorcycle so many officers were signed up from cavalry units. In fact, you can't, they couldn't and many promptly fell off or were involved in accidents. Upon hearing that war had been declared and that the Corps was to be activated, Baird raced off to buy a uniform and then thought that, as a spy, he might need the services of his butler – I can't imagine why. But he was unsure if his new Commanding Officer, Major Torrie, would agree. And would his butler (a man named Jilling who was at that time dismantling the family yacht to save it from the Germans) agree to join the army and go to war? Baird sent off a telegram asking permission and this diary entry records the outcome. Spying: It's alright for some. Quoted in *Spies of the First World War* by James Morton (2010).

Lying

'He that has eyes to see and ears to hear may convince himself that no mortal can keep a secret. If his lips are silent, he chatters with his fingertips; betrayal oozes out of him at every pore.'

Sigmund Freud, from his *Introductory Lectures on Psychoanalysis* (1920).

'A prudent man at the end of his life will have decided that most men are liars: a year's experience of the secret service will teach even the most imprudent that all men are liars. And that, in many moods, might be held the beginning and end of its utility.'

Author and MI6 officer Compton Mackenzie in *Extremes Meet* (1928).

'Sometimes when I'm in a fanciful mood, I enjoy devices such as brain scanning lie detectors and hi-tech sniffer dogs, because their appeal speaks to our desire for simple mechanical explanations in a complex world. But I enjoy them most because ... they show how much of security is about theatre rather than reality."

Professor Ben Goldacre in his *"Bad Science"* column in *The Guardian* newspaper 26 February 2011 explaining why brain scanning lie detectors and sniffer dogs don't work. Despite all the technological innovations of recent years, successful interrogations still rely on psychology rather than gadgets. The trick to surviving interrogations is to never give in - no matter what they tell you that the machines say.

'Once you decide to lie, the only problem is getting caught. Getting caught is often the result of guilt. Get over the guilt and lying with a straight face requires less skill than robbing a liquor store with a shotgun.'

The Las Vegas magicians Penn and Teller in their book *The Unpleasant Book of Penn and Teller* (1994). Magicians are often experts in lying and deception and their expertise has sometimes been used in espionage. The outstanding example is the work during the Second World War of stage magician Jasper Maskelyne who showed MI9, the section of Military Intelligence that helped POWs to escape, how to hide equipment in ordinary items such as chess pieces and bars of soap. He also contributed to the operation to mislead the Germans about the location of the D-Day landings by being part of the team that created inflatable tanks that looked convincing when photographed from the air by German reconnaissance.

'Any fool can tell the truth but it requires a man of some sense to know how to lie well.'

From the notebooks of the poet Samuel Butler (1613-1680).

'I am not the mysterious Third Man'.

Kim Philby, speaking to the Press during an infamous briefing in 1955. The first two Cambridge spies, Maclean and Burgess, had just escaped to the Soviet Union. Everyone was sure that they must have been tipped off by a mysterious spy known as "the Third Man". Philby had known them both and he was the prime suspect. He had been exonerated in Parliament by no less a figure than the Prime Minister but even this was not enough to quieten the spy hunters who were sure he *must* be the man. To try to to deflect attention, Philby agreed to give an interview to the Press (at his mother's London flat). His words are probably the greatest whopper in the history of espionage. (You can find recordings of the press conference on the internet and see for yourself just how cool he was under immense pressure.) Of course, he <u>was</u> the mysterious Third Man. The Press and the public would have been horrified if they had also known that there were at least <u>*five*</u> spies in the ring, not just three.

'Unless we all start to believe in conspiracy theories and that the officials are lying, that I am lying, ... there is simply no truth in the claims that the United Kingdom has been involved in rendition.'

This was Jack Straw, UK Foreign Secretary addressing the House of Commons Foreign Affairs Committee in answer to allegations that Britain's intelligence services were involved in the US policy of rendition and torture after the 9/11 attacks. In 2018, a report by the Intelligence and Security Committee issued after a three year investigation revealed the truth: The UK intelligence services had planned, agreed or financed at least thirty-one renditions and probably many more.

*'What readers don't get to see is another kind of to-and-fro. The direct appeal to editors and reporters. The insistence that our secret services "don't do this kind of thing", are bound by rules, by UK, EU and international law, are Crown Servants, and , in any case, are bound by a sense of decency. Except, as is now quite clear, it was all a **<u>bloody lie!</u>**'*

Peter Beaumont, journalist for *The Observer* newspaper for many years during which time he had the job of liaising with the intelligence services and deciding which stories to print and which to suppress. He was speaking in the wake of damning official reports in 2018 which revealed that the UK intelligence services had consistently lied about such issues as mass data collection from citizens and involvement in rendition and torture. Quoted in *Spies, Spin and the Fourth Estate* by Paul Lashmar (2020).

'But if I didn't dramatise in some manner the reader would go to sleep!'

Military cryptologist Herbert Yardley responding to criticism of his book *The Black Chamber* (1931) which was supposed to tell the true story of America's first codebreaking centre but which is notoriously, sometimes laughably, unreliable. Quoted in *The Literary Spy* by Charles E. Lathrop (2004).

'You get so used to lying that, after a while, it's hard to remember what the truth is.'

Former CIA officer Philip Agee in his book *Inside The Company* (1975) Agee has a point. The constant need to protect secrets by deception or to live a life under cover can lead to an increasing sense of unreality. It is one of the key factors that increases the strain on the mental health of many intelligence officers – and something that James Bond never has to deal with.

M

Mail

'This proceeding cannot be English any more than masks, poisons, sword-sticks, secret signs and associations and other such dark ventures.'

The "proceeding" to which this editorial in *The Times* was referring was the opening of private mail by the state, a practice which had been revealed during the Mazzini Affair in 1843. Mazzini was an Italian nationalist who was trying to promote Italian independence from his place of exile in London. The British government was opening his mail and passing the intelligence to the Austrians. This enabled them to crush several rebellions and set back Italian independence by many years. No Parliamentary authority for the practice had ever been sought. Many people were under the impression that this sort of thing was only done by "foreigners" (by which they were usually thinking of the French!). But they were in for a rude awakening, as the French knew...

'The English have tricks to open letters more skilfully than anywhere in the world.'

Phillip de Comminges, French diplomat. Quoted in *Espionage in the reign of Charles II* by Alan Marshall (1994).

'In the dark future, the development of the intelligence service will continue to investigate and to influence you. In the future, the secret power of the intelligence service will be larger than in the past and present.'

Colonel Walter Nicolai, Head of Department IIIb, the German foreign intelligence service during World War One. Quoted in *Spynest* by Edwin Ruis (2016).

Mata Hari

'Without scruples, accustomed to making use of men, she is the type of woman who was born to be a spy.'

Captain Pierre Bouchardon, prosecutor at the trial of the exotic dancer Mata Hari in July 1917. Her real name was Margarethe Zelle and she was Dutch.

'A fat old hag without attraction.'

Admiral Reginald "Blinker" Hall (not much of a looker himself!) who interrogated her in 1916 when she arrived in Britain. He had her deported to Spain with a warning not to become involved in further spying activities. If she had listened to him, she would have lived. By the time he met her, she was 40, overweight and her charms had faded considerably. But, by all accounts, she was never a great beauty, it was her manner that fascinated men. Quoted in *Spymaster* by David Ramsay (2008).

'There wasn't enough evidence to hang a cat.'

Mata Hari's defence attorney speaking after her trial. She was executed by firing squad on 15 October 1917. The prosecutor had claimed that: *"she sent ten thousand French soldiers to their deaths"* - which was nonsense. The documentary evidence is that she did agree to spy for Germany (largely because she was short of money) and was assigned a code number (H21) but that she produced almost no intelligence other than some idle gossip. Her death had more to do with misogyny and the political situation in France than it did with espionage. Yet because so few women were involved in espionage at this time she became a legend. Sadly, other, more deserving, women have been forgotten.

'Why had I remembered her name yet nothing of her story?'

Julie Wheelwright, biographer of Mata Hari, quoted in *Female Intelligence* by Tammy M. Proctor (2003). Most members of the public remember her name and her image but know nothing of the tragic reality.

'A courtesan? I admit it. A spy? Never!'

Mata Hari at her trial.

Maugham (W. Somerset)

'The work appealed both to my sense of adventure and my sense of the ridiculous.'

Maugham was one of the most famous spies of the early years of British intelligence. Already a famous writer, he was first hired by British Military Intelligence to work in Switzerland. That country was important as it bordered Germany and many agents were run from there. Also, a great deal of intelligence could be gleaned from German banking and insurance activities in the country which shone a light on economic conditions in the country. He later travelled to Russia for MI6 but the mission was overtaken by the events of the Russian Revolution of 1917.

'Fact is a poor storyteller.'

From the preface to Maugham's spy novel *Ashenden* (1927). A collection of short stories, the book contained so much fact that Churchill advised Maugham to destroy several chapters and change other material – which Maugham did. But it is still a valuable resource.

'If you do well, you'll get no thanks. If you get into trouble, you'll get no help.'

Major John Wallinger, head of British Military Intelligence, to Maugham just before sending him on his first mission. John had recruited Maugham because their mistresses knew each other and thought Maugham would make a good agent. Maugham needed to get out of the country because of a scandal so he took up the offer. Incidentally, John's brother Ernest "Peg Leg" Wallinger was also a spy and one of the great characters of the early years of British intelligence. Having been invalided out of the Army after he lost a foot in battle, he ran an extensive military intelligence organisation from his flat in London where he lived with his butler and housemaid. He came up with all sorts of hare-brained schemes, many of which were surprisingly successful – such as sending hot air balloons over the Front carrying baskets of pigeons along with a note asking French civilians to send back intelligence. It worked! But his brother John was not of the same quality, the intelligence his networks produced was poor, con men swindled him out of funds and Maugham himself described John as: *"A very ordinary man on the fringe."* Quoted in *Spies of the First World War* by James Morton (2010).

Memoirs

'I shall call them "The Indiscretions of a Secret Service Chief". It will be a splendid-looking publication bound in red with the title and my name embossed in gold and consisting of four hundred pages – every one of which will be blank!"

Mansfield Cumming, first chief of MI6, quoted in *The Secret Servant* by Anthony Cave Brown (1988). Cumming did not live to retire and write his memoirs. He died in June 1923 sitting on the sofa of his office having just briefed an agent about to depart on a mission. His operational diaries were kept locked in the MI6 archives and were long believed to be a treasure trove of fascinating information. MI6 finally gave permission for 'C's diaries to be studied and they were found to be disappointingly terse or even blank for large periods. Cumming's private papers which might have shed an invaluable light on the origins of MI6 were destroyed by his family after his death.

MI5 (UK Security Service)

'There are people inside MI5 who think that what has happened in the last ten years is absolutely disgusting and a betrayal of what they should be doing and a regrettable lurch into dishonourable activity.'

Sir David Hare, playwright, who spoke to several serving intelligence officers as part of his research for a new play for the BBC. Quoted in *The Guardian* newspaper 22 February 2014.

'...a professional backwater, suitable only for officers with a knowledge of foreign languages and for those who were not wanted for command'.

A description of the Service under Vernon Kell, its first Director General by F. Hinsley the official British intelligence historian. Quoted in *The Perfect English Spy* by Tom Bower (1995).

'Over almost a century MI5 has made five separate attempts – in 1914, 1921, 1931, 2004 and 2009 – to support its foundation myth with supposed facts, all of which have failed miserably. Five attempts to revive a corpse are surely enough...'

Nick Hiley, the intelligence historian *par excellence,* whose in-depth investigation of MI5's most long standing claim - that they wiped out a German intelligence network at the start of the First World War - exposed the story as *"a complete fabrication".* Quoted in *Spies, Spin and the Fourth Estate* by Paul Lashmar (2020).

'In case any of you should be tempted after the war to act up as a gentleman burglar, I think I should point out there is precious little in it for you. What you do for MI5 in wartime is strictly privileged. You may have to face risks because you are dealing with enemy agents who are potentially desperate. But there are positively no legal penalties – even if very occasionally you

shoot to kill.'

Inspector William Melville, former police officer responsible for training MI5 "housebreakers" during World War One. Quoted in *Defending the Realm* by Nick Hollingsworth and Nick Fielding (1999).

'In truth, since the war, MI5 has been one of the worst and most ridiculed security services in the Western alliance'.

Roy Hattersley, former British Labour Party shadow Home Secretary (responsible for MI5) speaking in 1988. Quoted in *UK Eyes Alpha* by Mark Urban (1997). And that view appears to be common in both of the UK's main political parties...

'The tone of MI5 is one of sound mediocrity ...'

Jonathan Aitken, former UK Conservative Party Cabinet Minister. Quoted in *UK Eyes Alpha* by Mark Urban (1997).

'MI5 officers display a notable incapacity for weighing evidence and a tendency to conceal this incapacity by unnecessary recourse to secrecy.'

Foreign Office memo 1940.

'You and your staff will maintain the well-established convention whereby Ministers do not concern themselves with the detailed information which by the Security Service in particular cases, but are furnished with such information only as may be necessary for the determination of any issue on which guidance is sought.'

Sir Maxwell Fyffe, Home Secretary, 1952. This directive has become notorious in intelligence circles since it effectively makes MI5 unaccountable. The organisation itself, and no one else, decides what it is "necessary" for Ministers to know. Even the creation of the Intelligence and Security Committee (ISC) has not changed this situation as the ISC must also rely on what the intelligence services choose to tell it. Quoted in *Defending The Realm* by Mark Hollingsworth and Nick Fielding (1999).

'I am convinced now that an organisation of people who live in the fevered world of espionage and counterespionage is entirely unfitted to judge between what is subversive and what is legitimate dissent.'

Roy Jenkins, former Home Secretary and therefore responsible for MI5 during his time in office. From *Hansard*, House of Lords, 16 March 1988, Column 1034.

[MI5 officers] *'...appeared to savour Sherlock Holmes, Richard Hannay, Bulldog Drummond or even James Bond and lived in a completely closed world whereby what really went on and what people actually thought and did, they just did not understand.'*

Lord Carver, Chief of Defence Staff 1973-1976. From *Hansard*, Lords, 16 March 1988, Column 1150-51.

'I gained the impression that it was employing people whose degree of political sensitivity was rather low.'

Lord Beloff, fellow of St Antony's College, Oxford, who was frequently asked to give references for MI5 recruits. Quoted in *Plots and Paranoia* by Professor Bernard Porter (1988).

'MI5 is a way of finding employment for muscular under-achievers from the ancient universities.'

Anonymous civil servant quoted in a report in *The Times* newspaper, 25 March 1981.

'MI5 tends to see dangerous men too freely and to lack that knowledge of the world and sense of perspective which a Home Secretary rightly considers essential.'

Sir Winston Churchill. Part of the problem is that MI5 officers are not really spies. They have more in common with police officers but they lack the necessary powers of arrest so their cases have to be passed to the police for action. They are more accurately described as "spooks" or "secret policemen" and are not really spies at all. Quoted in *MI6* by Stephen Dorril (2000).

"What do you mean, oh dear?" he asked in an even more chilly tone.
"Well, it's not very nice, is it, MI5? It's full of people spying."

Charlotte Bingham's reaction upon learning that her father was a senior MI5 officer and that he expected her to join. Quoted in *MI5 and Me* by Charlotte Bingham (2018).

'I'm just a girl at MI5
And heading for a virgin's grive.
My legs it was wot got me in,
I'm waiting for my bit of sin.'

Origin unknown but was once well known in intelligence circles as the "MI5 typist's lament". Officers of both MI5 and MI6 have been noted for marrying their secretaries. Quoted in *Literary Agents* by Anthony Masters (1987).

Mistakes

'I am more afraid of our own mistakes than of our enemies' designs.'

Pericles of Athens, 432 BC from Thucydides, *History of the Peloponnesian War.*

'Naval Intelligence places no credence in these rumours.... No move against Pearl Harbour appears imminent or planned for the foreseeable future.'

US Naval Intelligence assessment of the possibility of a Japanese attack on Pearl Harbour – just days before that attack happened. Quoted in *The Literary Spy* by Charles E. Lathrop (2004).

'One of the most serious intelligence breakdowns in British history.'

Roger Casement, the human rights activist, passionate Irish nationalist and German agent, was heading to Ireland on a German submarine to assist with the Easter Rising in 1916. A supply of arms was also heading to Ireland on a ship from Germany. Fortunately, the timing of the Rising and Casement's mission were known about from intelligence produced by radio interception by the Naval Intelligence Division (NID). But, incredibly, the British Cabinet refused to believe the intelligence. Fortunately, the Royal Navy intercepted the ship carrying the arms which, in part, led to the defeat of the Rising. Casement was also discovered, arrested and brought to trial. He was found guilty of treason and hanged at Pentonville Prison in London on 3 August 1916. From *Spymaster* by David Ramsay (2008).

'An anarchist and a crank who for some obscure reason is trying to get us into a war with Russia.'

CIA officer James Jesus Angleton upon receiving intelligence from Soviet agent Oleg Penkovsky. Penkovsky turned out to be one of the most valuable agents of the Cold War. Quoted in *The Literary Spy* by Charles E. Lathrop (2004).

'It was a major error.'

George Tenet, Director of the CIA, at a press conference called to explain how CIA intelligence had led to the bombing of the Chinese Embassy in Belgrade in May 1999. Even local tourist maps turned out to be more accurate than the intelligence provided by the CIA.

'The Dardanelles and the Bosphorus might as well be on the moon for all the military intelligence I have to go upon.'

General Sir Ian Hamilton commenting on the available intelligence before the Gallipoli landings. They became an infamous series of disasters. Once again MI6 (as it was to become) and the other British intelligence agencies had failed to do their job. Quoted in *Spies of the First World War* by James Morton (2010).

'All who knew Stewart at Eton, or who have known him in later years ... can state without fear of contradiction that he is absolutely incapable of a mean or dishonourable act and would <u>never</u> stoop to play the miserable role of a spy.'

A letter to The Times on 5 February 1912 written by leading barrister Reginald Arkwright to protest Bertrand Stewart's innocence against charges of spying. In fact, Stewart, who had been arrested in a public toilet in Germany, was indeed an MI6 agent. He had been sent to meet another agent codenamed "Agent U". This was Arsene Verrue, a Belgian conman who had been a British agent since 1910. In fact, he was working as a double agent for the Germans (he was also working for the French). Stewart was not supposed to enter Germany but he was lured in with the prospect of valuable intelligence. He was given incriminating documents during a meeting with Verrue at a restaurant and while he was checking the documents in the bathroom to see if they were genuine, the Germans moved in and arrested him. He was sentenced to three and a half years in prison for espionage but was released in May 1913 as part of a general amnesty to mark a visit to the UK by the Kaiser. Upon his return, Stewart sued Mansfield Cumming, the head of MI6, for £10,000 because Stewart believed that he had been put in danger by the poor preparation of MI6 (or "the Secret Service Bureau" as it was known in those days). The start of the First World War interrupted the court case. Stewart joined the newly-formed Army Intelligence Corps and was killed in action on 16 September 1914. His widow received a payment of £10,000 in final settlement of the case. The letter also shows the strong disapproval for spying that many people held in the early days. This disapproval was common in most parts of the world. It was far from the heroic, "James Bond" image that would later prevail.

'Police work is becoming so highly organised and so aided by mechanical and scientific devices that a spy would not really have much chance. Thinking the matter over, I should say that serious spying is rapidly going the way of bows and arrows.'

Special Branch detective and expert spycatcher Herbert Fitch from his book *Traitors Within* (1933). He was so wrong...

'To compromise an agent through carelessness, or worse, is to sin against the Holy Ghost of espionage. No service can forgive it.'

Alan Judd in *The Quest for C* (1999). For more about Judd see under "Agent Handling."

'If in normal life an arrangement is made to meet in a pub a red-haired stranger carrying a copy of Gibbon's Decline and Fall, then this unusual encounter would generally take place without hindrance. If, however, an intelligence officer arranges to meet the same man as his agent, then the chances of the pub burning down, or of there being a police raid, or of the agent's ex-wife and mother-in-law turning up, or of there being a convocation of red-haired Gibbonians that evening, are surprisingly high.'

Alan Judd in *The Quest for C* (1999). See above re: Judd.

'The human story does not always unfold like an arithmetical calculation on the principle that two and two make four. Sometimes in life they make five or minus three; and sometimes the blackboard topples down in the middle of the sum and leaves the class in disorder and the pedagogue with a black eye. The element of the unexpected and the unforeseeable is what gives some of its relish to life and saves us from falling into the mechanical thralldom of the logicians.'

Sir Winston Churchill quoted in *The Irrepressible Churchill* by Kay Halle (2005).

'...a failure of imagination...'

From the US Congressional 9/11 Commission Report describing the inability of US intelligence agencies to prevent the 9/11 attacks.

'On the evening of 21 August 1968 I read highly classified British intelligence reports which stated "there would be no invasion" [of Czechoslovakia by the Soviet Union]. I was woken a few hours later to be told that the Russians were invading'.

David Owen who was Foreign Secretary in 1968. Quoted in *UK Eyes Alpha* by Mark Urban (1987).

'A slam-dunk'.

CIA Director George Tenet describing how certain he thought it was that weapons of mass destruction were present in Iraq. They weren't. Quoted in *The Economist* magazine 19 March 2005.

'The earliest possible date by which the USSR might be expected to produce an atomic bomb is mid-1950 and the most probable date is mid-1953.'

CIA intelligence briefing issued on 20 September 1949 – three days *after* the first Soviet atomic bomb was actually tested. Quoted in *CIA Under Truman* by Michael Warner (1994).

"I had no idea your billet was such a good one .... I doubt its being worth your while to take this appointment – but you must decide this for yourself".

Rear Admiral Bethell, Director of British Naval Intelligence in 1909, offering the post of Chief of the Secret Intelligence Service to Mansfield Cumming. At the time Cumming was in charge of the very dull and highly technical task of designing a boom defence for Portsmouth Harbour. Cumming was highly reluctant to lead the Secret Service and could only be persuaded to take the job provided he could keep his boom defence work as well. Quoted in *The Quest for C* by Alan Judd (1999).

'I am now placing my life in your hands. Please don't screw up.'

Russian UN delegate Sergei Fedorenko agreeing to work for CIA officer Aldrich Ames. But Ames was a Soviet double agent, quite possibly the most deadly in American history - and Fedorenko was betrayed in 1985. Quoted in *The Literary Spy* by Charles E. Lathrop (2004).

'Good intelligence does not necessarily win battles.'

Frequently quoted in military and intelligence circles but the originator is unknown. However compare it with this:

'It was a most fortunate error, for if Halsey had steamed to the north and encountered six Japanese aircraft carriers, probably neither the Enterprise nor Halsey would have survived the first day of the war.'

This is the perceptive analysis of W. J. Holmes a former US naval intelligence officer, in his book *Double-Edged Secrets* (1979). Holmes was referring to the fact that Halsey, commanding America's most powerful aircraft carrier *Enterprise* and hearing of the attack on Pearl Harbour, demanded to know where the attackers were so that he could bring them to battle. However, direction-finding equipment was so primitive in those early days of the war that it was difficult to tell what was a signal from enemy vessels and what was the reciprocal (i.e. the echo of the signal). The Japanese fleet was, in fact, to the north, but the signals were interpreted as coming from the south. Halsey was so advised and sent his aircraft in that direction – thus saving him, the *Enterprise* and quite possibly America - as Holmes correctly surmises.

This is not the only example of where poor intelligence has won a battle. Another example is the US Civil War battle of Gettysburg. All the intelligence led Union General Hooker to believe that Lee was far from the town so he sent units in and occupied Cemetery Ridge. In fact, Lee was close by, battle was joined and the Union army won a famous victory. The tide of the entire war turned at that point.

And finally:

'Without further words I plunged into the night. As luck would have it, I ran across a suspect that very evening. He was dressed in army khaki, but my sharp eye noted that the insignia was not that of any Army outfit. I trailed him for three days, and his actions were most suspicious. Every day he would sneak out into the woods around the town and meet up with a band of midgets. Then they would all go about setting fires.

I determined to bring my quarry to bay. So, one evening as he trudged along the road with his midget band, I sprang from the bushes and confronted him. 'I am Marx, the Master Spy,' I snarled.

"Glad to meet you Mr Marx, he said. 'I am Clarence Snood, Scoutmaster of the Beaver Troop.'

Of course it was a bitter pill for me to swallow, but in a way I did not regret it – we all toasted marshmallows and became firm friends.

Groucho Marx in *'How To Be a Spy'* from *This Week*, 16 February 1946 cited in *'The Essential Groucho'* edited by Stephen Kanfer (2000). In fact, the only one of the Marx Brothers to work as a real spy was Harpo. In the 1950s his silent antics were a great hit in Soviet Russia where the wordplay of Groucho's gags was not understood. Harpo was invited by the Communist Party to make a tour of the Soviet Union. Harpo was not keen, but the CIA urged him to accept the invitation - and to collect some top secret documents from an agent while he was there. He returned with the documents taped to his leg as he was the only member of the party who would not be searched at the airport.

Mobile Phones

'Cellphones are the great betrayers of people.'

Robert Baer, former CIA officer and author. Baer was referring to the fact that mobile phones are often used to pinpoint a location for assassination by drone. But given the use of spyware which can turn your mobile phone into an audio and video bugging device that spies on you without a foreign agent even having physical access to it, he could have been speaking more generally. Spies certainly understand this risk: visitors to any top secret facility, such as Vauxhall Cross in London, the HQ of MI6, have to leave all mobile devices at the door and this practice has spread to many areas of the commercial world that have secrets to keep. Quoted in *See No Evil* by Robert Baer (2002).

Money

'I am the master of money, not its slave!'

Paul Bolo, yet another con man who found success in the world of espionage. He was a former Marseilles lobster salesman who married a rich widow. She died under mysterious circumstances and left him a fortune. He used this to con his way into wealthy society and eventually into the circle of the Khedive of Egypt (essentially, the ruler of Egypt but under British control). The Khedive wanted to be rid of the British and Bolo suggested that, with a suitable supply of funds, he could buy up certain newspapers and persuade public opinion in France to favour the Khedive against Britain. The Khedive fell for this and handed over a great deal of money but then the First World War began and scuppered that plan.

Not to be deterred, by 1915 Bolo had a new version of his newspaper plan. He contacted the German secret service and told them that for £10 million - an astonishing sum at the time - he would place German propaganda in the French newspapers that he would control. The Germans agreed, although they would not hand over all the money at once. Bolo bought the newspapers and soon became quite a public figure in France - he was even invited to meet the US Undersecretary of State in Paris at a gala dinner. But the French secret service was already aware of the large sums that were passing through Bolo's hands and that seemed to originate mysteriously from Switzerland. Eventually a French agent was able to reveal what was going on and Bolo was arrested in his luxury suite at the Grand Hotel. Several French politicians had become involved in his schemes and the whole case became a national scandal but in the end, as tends to be the way when politicians become involved, only Bolo suffered for the crime. He was charged with treason and when the case came to trial it took the jury just 15 minutes to find him guilty because Room 40, the codebreaking section of British Naval Intelligence, had supplied key information from their intercepts of German communications. Bolo was shot at dawn on 17 April 1918. And if you are wondering why the German secret service was prepared to pay so much money to get stories into the French newspapers, remember that there was no radio or television in those days. This case mirrors many modern "agent of influence" espionage cases – money, media and politicians are always at the heart of them.

'Americans have a great love of money and a desire for financial gain. This American trait can be exploited by paying an agent for his work in order to increase his personal interest in working for us.'

From a GRU (Russian military intelligence) training lecture in 1961. But this approach to agent recruitment tended to work against the Russians. One of the keystones of counter-intelligence is to watch out for those who are eager to advance gifts or money (especially if they are diplomats coming from a country as normally hard up as Soviet Russia). KGB and GRU officers could often be spotted by their readiness to part with champagne, caviar or, in one memorable case, a speed boat. This psychological tactic is known in intelligence circles as "give to get" i.e. "I help you and then you will feel more like helping me." But it requires considerable subtlety to use with any prospect of success. However, the GRU were right in thinking that, in a country based on capitalism, money was a good way into certain American circles of power. Several recent cases in the USA have shown that this is still true. Quoted in *The Literary Spy* by Charles E. Lathrop (2004).

'I had forty agents in London, but the sum total of their remuneration was hardly worth worrying about.'

Gustav Steinhauer, former Pinkerton detective, bodyguard to the Kaiser and controller of many of the German agents in the UK in the years before the First World War. What he says would seem to be true. For instance, one of his key agents in London was Karl Gustav Ernst, a hairdresser living in Islington. He acted as a "letter box" or "cut-out" for other agents i.e. they would send coded letters to his address and he would arrange for the intelligence to be forwarded to Germany. Even a key man such as this was only paid £1 a week by Steinhauer – not exactly riches, especially when one considers that Ernst was given seven years in prison when he was arrested at the outbreak of the war. Quoted in *Spies of the First World War* by James Morton (2010).

'American intelligence has always been characterised by huge expenditures of money and a dependency on quantity rather than quality.'

John Ranelagh in his book *The Agency* (1986). There is a lot of truth in this observation and it is certainly also true that many other services have to make do with whatever budget they can scrape together and this can actually make them more efficient and even creative. However, there are some occasions when just throwing money at a problem does work – so this aspect of American espionage is not the whole story.

'The life of a spy is difficult. He is reliant on his master sending him money and this is often only paid by results.'

Herbert Fitch, UK Special Branch officer and spycatcher, from his book *Traitors Within* (1933).

'Among agents there are some whose only interest is in acquiring wealth without obtaining the true situation of the enemy, and they only meet requirements with empty words. In such a case, a spymaster must be cunning.'

Not Sun Tzu's *The Art of War* but a similar tract – possibly by Sun Bin. But it is correct in any case.

'I have seen a good many secret spy letters, and a good twenty-five per cent of them included really frantic appeals for money.'

Herbert Fitch again (see above), *Traitors Within* (1933).

'What? This is my money. Where are your references?!'

The retort by Ernst Fetterlein to a clerk at the Bank of England. Fetterlein was the greatest of the UK's Russian code breakers during the inter-war period. After the Russian Revolution, he fled across Europe and, after a number of hair-raising adventures, arrived in London. He was quickly snapped up by Room 40, Britain's code breaking centre. With his thick-lensed glasses and professorial manner he was quite a character. He had arrived without a penny to his name, so it was a proud moment when he received his first pay cheque and went to the Bank to deposit it. He could not believe that someone would question who he was. He worked as one of Britain's greatest code breakers for many years and went on to become one of the key members of Bletchley Park. Quoted in *Spymaster* by David Ramsay (2008).

'An intelligence service thrives on threat. Its continued existence and its funding depends on its ability to convince its political masters that the nation is in danger ...'

Phillip Knightley in his book *The Second Oldest Profession* (1988). Knightley, who died in 2016, was one of the world's leading experts on intelligence - although viewed as overly sceptical by some. Yet there is some truth in what he says: intelligence budgets only go up when there is a disaster somewhere. Winning the Cold War led to the greatest slashing of intelligence budgets in fifty years and calls by some to get rid of the agencies altogether.

Morality

'This is a war. It's graphic and unpleasant because it's fought on a tiny scale, at close range; fought with a wastage of innocent life sometimes, I admit. But it's nothing, nothing at all besides other wars – the last or the next.'

> Alec Leamas, the fictional MI6 anti-hero of *The Spy Who Came In From The Cold* (1963). The novel is by John Le Carré, the pseudonym of David Cornwell, a former MI6 officer so he knew what he was talking about.

'There are great occasions in which some men are called to great services, in the doing of which they are excused from the common rule of morality.'

> Attributed to Oliver Cromwell.

'You wanted an eleventh Commandment that would match your rare soul! Well, here you have it ... We sent him because we needed to; we abandon him because we must. This is the discipline you so admired.'

> *The Looking Glass War* by John Le Carré (MI6 officer David Cornwell) (1965).

'Sire, State policy is not the same as private morality. A king who alone wished to be absolutely just among the wicked and to remain good among the wolves would soon be devoured along with his flock.'

> Pierre-Augustin Caron de Beaumarchais, French spymaster justifying his methods to King Louis XVI in 1775. Quoted in *The Literary Spy* by Charles E. Lathrop (2004).

'I should think he was working all he knew for his country during the war, and I do not think I should blame him for that.'

> Earl of Lucan answering questions in the House of Lords in the 1930s about the notorious German spy Franz von Rintelen. He had settled in the UK and some people were upset by that. During the war von Rintelen had arranged for bombs to be planted on British merchant ships which was seen by some as an unforgivable crime. But those who had been his greatest enemies, including British spymaster Admiral "Blinker" Hall, became his friends and supported him. Quoted in *Spies of the First World War* by James Morton (2010).

'I would not authorise my men being used as spies. Officers must act straightforwardly and as Englishmen. Espionage was hateful to us Army men.'

> Field Marshall Douglas Haig, commander of British forces in WWI. Quoted in *The Spying Game* by Michael Smith (1996).

'The accomplished spy of today is invariably a man of at least quasi-criminal proclivities, a being entirely lacking in moral sense, a degenerate.'

> Hamil Grant from "The Ethos of the Spy" in *Spies and Secret Service* (1915).

'Our work does imply getting dirty hands from time to time, but we do it for a cause that is not dirty in any way.'

Kim Philby, the MI6 traitor, in a speech to young Stasi officers in 1981.

'We can see now why they were so reluctant to disclose them (the internal guidance documents). They highlight how the security services instruct their staff to flout important principles in a cavalier way.'

Richard Stein, partner at Leigh Day solicitors, after the Investigatory Powers Tribunal discovered that all three UK intelligence services had been allowing their staff to intercept privileged communications between lawyers and clients even in cases where the agencies themselves were being sued. Quoted on the BBC News Website 6 November 2014.

'In the war against terror forget about morality.'

Avraham Shalom, Director of Shin Bet 1980-86. Shin Bet is the Israeli security service.

'There is something fatal to most natures in Secret Service work, especially to those whose first consideration is how to advance their own careers and enhance their reputations. Starting from that is only a small step to jealousy, suspicion and underhand doing, until one gets to putting the Almighty Double Cross on a pedestal to be bowed down to every day. Everything else is put away and trampled down – honour, duty, friendship, self-respect.'

Col. R J Drake of British Military Intelligence quoted in *Armour Against Fate* by Michael Occleshaw (1989). As Occleshaw points out, there were other officers of the same view and these were not men with chips on their shoulders but men who had been very successful in the world of intelligence.

'I do not think that Secret Service work breeds an altruistic spirit.'

Sigismund Payne Best, a long-standing officer of MI6, commenting on why there is so much vicious gossip in secret service work. Quoted in *Armour Against Fate* by Michael Occleshaw (1989).

'In war you do not have to be nice – you only have to be right.'

Sir Winston Churchill quoted in *The Irrepressible Churchill* edited by Kay Halle (1987). And spies are always at war…

'… he should be a gentleman, and a capable one, absolutely honest with considerable tact and at the same time force of character … experience shows that any amount of brilliance or low cunning will not make up for scrupulous personal honesty. In the long run it is only the honest man who can defeat the ruffian'.

Mansfield Cumming, the first chief of MI6. Quoted in *The Quest for C* by Alan Judd (1999).

'I abhor this dirty work, but when one is employed to sweep chimneys one must black one's fingers'.

Sir James Harris, British ambassador to the Hague in the eighteenth century, reflecting on the fact that diplomats were expected to run secret overseas informants as well as undertake their normal diplomatic duties, since there was no organised British secret service at this time. Quoted in *Secret Service* by Professor Christopher Andrew (1985).

'We repudiated entirely customary morals, conventions and traditional wisdom. We were, that is to say, in the strict sense of the term, immoralists. The consequences of being found out had, of course, to be considered for what they were worth. But we recognised no moral obligation on us, no inner sanction, to conform or obey'.

John Maynard Keynes, leading economist and member of the Apostles, the Cambridge society that spawned the Cambridge Spy Ring. Quoted in *The Secret Servant* by Anthony Cave Brown (1988).

'Wars are not won by respectable methods.'

Amy Elizabeth Thorpe, an MI6 agent in the Second World War when asked whether she was ashamed that she had to use casual sex as a weapon. Known for her beauty, in one case she seduced a French naval attaché, broke into the embassy and then answered the office door wearing only high heels and a necklace in order to allay the suspicions of a guard. It wouldn't have worked for me. Quoted in *Cast No Shadow* by Mary S Lovell (2017).

The Mossad (the Israeli Foreign intelligence service)

'The Mossad is opening up. Not to everyone. Not to many. Maybe to you.'

Like almost every other secret service in the world, the Mossad now advertises openly for new recruits rather than relying on the classic "tap on the shoulder". This was their first advert in the press in August 2000.

Motivation

'For as long as there are bullies and liars and madmen in the world, we shall spy.'

Former MI6 officer David Cornwell writing as John Le Carré in *The Secret Pilgrim* (2011).

Movies

'If you rely on spy movies to provide your tradecraft, you had better be really good, or very lucky.'

Former senior CIA operations officer Jack Devine. Quoted on the BBC News website on 20 October 2021. He was commenting on the Jonathan Toebbe spy case. Toebbe was a US Navy engineer who tried to sell secret intelligence about US nuclear submarines to the Russians. He had no training in espionage but used methods such as dead letter boxes (a remote or disguised location in which messages are left for the contact to collect) for his communications with the Russians. He got caught.

Myths

'In the higher ranges of Secret Service work the actual facts in many cases were in every respect equal to the most fantastic inventions of romance and melodrama. Tangle within tangle, plot and counter-plot, ruse and treachery, cross and double-cross, true agent, false agent, double agent, gold and steel, the bomb, the dagger, and the firing party were interwoven in many a texture so intricate as to be incredible and yet true. The Chief and the high officers of the Secret Service revelled in these subterranean labyrinths, and amid the crash of war pursued their task with cold and silent passion.'

Sir Winston Churchill quoted in *Special Intelligence Agent* by former MI6 officer Montgomery Hyde (1982). For once, what Churchill says is over romanticised bunk. But thanks to movies and thrillers this is what most people believe.

<u>N</u>

Napoleon

'Bonaparte was an avid user of spies, both militarily and politically. His handling of secret intelligence was brilliant and one of the cornerstones of his success (something nineteenth-century writers wrongly downplayed because of the dishonour associated with espionage).'

> Terry Crowdy, expert in espionage and Napoleonic history, in *Marengo* (2018).

'The word of a spy, at the right moment and in the right place, is worth an army corps.'

> Attributed to Napoleon.

'Gold is the only suitable reward for spies.'

> Also attributed to Napoleon.

'I have given you vast sums of money in return for your services in the past. You may have another half a million francs. But I cannot honour a spy.'

> This time we may be more certain of since this is from an official document in which Napoleon refuses to award his intelligence chief with the Legion d'Honneur medal.

Nature of the Work

'[Espionage] began as a triangle and developed into a pentagon. A and B might have mutual interests unfriendly to C, who, suspecting them, would employ D to find out such contriving and planning; then they in their turn would send E to guard their secret schemes.'

> Margaret Richings in *Espionage* (1934). One of the best definitions of the work that you will find.

'You are spies. You have come to see the weakness of the land.'

> The Book of Genesis, Chapter 42, Verse 8

'The spy is the greatest of soldiers. If he is the most detested by the enemy, it is only because he is the most feared.'

> King George V upon knighting Sir Paul Dukes in 1920. Dukes remains the only MI6 officer ever knighted for his work in the field. Quoted in *Operation Kronstadt* by Harry Ferguson (2008).

'There is nothing more necessary than good intelligence to frustrate a designing enemy, and nothing that requires greater pains to obtain.'

> George Washington. Quoted in *Spies, Lies and Algorithms* by Amy B. Zegart (2022).

'People spy because other people want to know something.'

Alan Judd, former "Foreign service" officer in his book *The Quest for C* (1999).

'Anyone who spends more than ten years in the secret service must be either weird or mad.'

Harold Macmillan, UK Prime Minister. Quoted in *MI6* by Stephen Dorril (2000).

'I can't tell you what sort of job it would be. All I can say is that if you join us, you mustn't be afraid of forgery and you mustn't be afraid of murder.'

This was the introduction to the world of espionage for Bickham Sweet-Escott, an officer of both MI6 and SOE (wartime special operations). In a "you couldn't make it up" moment (of which there are many in espionage) he was being interviewed in Baker Street by a man dressed very like Sherlock Holmes. Quoted in *Literary Agents* by Anthony Masters (1987).

'I was never at risk in my secret work; I was frequently bored stiff by it.'

Former MI6 officer David Cornwell (John Le Carré) reflecting on his career at MI6. Quoted in *The Guardian* newspaper 13 April 2013.

'To perceive things in the germ is intelligence.'

The Chinese philosopher Lao Tzu in the *Tao Te Ching* (c.400 BC).

'What the hell do you think spies are? Moral philosophers measuring everything they do against the word of God or Karl Marx? They're not! They're just a bunch of seedy, squalid bastards like me: little men, drunkards, queers, hen-pecked husbands, civil servants playing cowboys and indians to brighten their rotten little lives.'

Alec Leamas, hero of *The Spy Who Came in from the Cold* (1963) by former MI6 officer David Cornwell, writing as John Le Carré.

'If people think that being attached to 'Secret Service' means a life of continual hair's breadth escapes let me tell them at once that they are sadly mistaken. It means hours of infinite drudgery in which, only very rarely, there occur moments approaching the dramatic.'

Edward Knoblock, MI6 officer during World War One. Quoted in *Spies of the First World War* by James Morton (2010). Knoblock was also the officer who, in his memoir *Around the Room*, revealed Mansfield Cumming's interest in fast cars, pretty secretaries and French pornography (which he kept in his desk at work). Mansfield was the first chief of MI6. Some espionage traditions are determined very early.

'The gathering of knowledge by clandestine means is repulsive to the feelings of an English gentleman.'

A British officer writing during the Crimean War. It was the complete absence of intelligence during that conflict (officers had to use maps from tourist guide books) that led to the establishment of the very first Military Intelligence Department in Britain.

'It is not a pleasant profession, being a spy. But it is not a mistake that I did it: it was my duty.'

Paul-Auguste Erhardt, German spy and army reserve captain, caught by the Belgians in Ostend where he had been sent to spy on British troop movements in the very first weeks of the war. He was executed by firing squad on 7 November 1914. Quoted in *Spynest* by Edwin Ruis (2016).

'People think it's always on the edge, but actually most of it is very routine and very boring.'

Elena Vavilova, KGB illegal who lived under cover in Boston as "Tracy Foley" for almost twenty years. Quoted in *The Guardian* newspaper 24 August 2019.

'And you know what they say about a spy in the field? That he's like a test pilot or a professional boxer – after seven years he's burnt out.'

Alan Williams in *Gentleman Traitor (1974)*. Williams was a journalist who specialised in work behind the Iron Curtain and in various war zones. He knew many spies, British, Russian and American and was sometimes accused of being one himself.

'This type of work appeals to the disordered mind.'

Rear-Admiral Sir Barry Domville, Director of Naval Intelligence 1927-1930. Domville may not have been the best person to judge about disordered minds: he was a fascist who found Adolf Hitler to be *"absolutely terrific; absolutely A1"*. He was imprisoned in 1940 as a threat to the safety of the country when he was found to be a member of a secret pro-Nazi organisation. Quoted in *Secret Service* by Professor Christopher Andrew (1985).

'...The uncertainty and irregularity of the duties ... are...no doubt in many cases very distasteful and repugnant to the better class of men in the service, as their duties constantly bring them into contact with the worst classes, frequently cause unnecessary drinking, and compel them at times to resort to trickey [sic] practices which they dislike'.

Superintendent Adolphus Williamson, first head of the Met's CID in a memo dated 22 October 1880, PRO MEPO 2/134 from Porter *'Origins of Britain's Political Police.'* Williamson was speaking about the work of police detectives who were used to track terrorists in Britain before the creation of MI5 in 1909.

'The very term "spy" conveys to our mind something dishonourable and disloyal. A spy, in the general acceptance of the term, is a low sneak who, from unworthy motives, dodges the actions of his fellow beings, to turn the knowledge he acquires to his personal account. His underhand dealings inspire us with such horror that we would blush at the very idea of having to avail ourselves of any information obtained through such an agency.'

Colonel A. G. Furse writing in 1895 in *Information in War*, one of the first ever text books on military intelligence. For more about Furse see under "Agent Selection."

'We desire to live on terms of amity with every neighbouring nation and the practice of spying can but tend to inflame hostile feelings ... Spying upon one another gives rise to such ill-feeling that if it could be stamped out, it should be.'

Mr Justice Darling during his sentencing of German spy Heinrich Grosse in February 1912. Grosse was a convicted forger – he was jailed for forgery in Singapore in 1898, served ten years, returned to Europe and was promptly arrested for forgery again, this time in Hamburg. He was released by the Germans on condition that he agree to go on a spying mission to England (as his spoken English was near flawless). He travelled to England under cover as a merchant sea captain named "Hugh Grant." He was so successful in this ruse that he even started dating the daughter of his landlady. (This didn't please his real fiancée when she turned up at his trial.) Unfortunately, his espionage work was clumsy, he was quickly spotted by the authorities and MI5 let him run for a while just to see what the German secret service was interested in. Grosse has the distinction of being the first spy tried under the Official Secrets Act (OSA). He was sentenced to just three years imprisonment. He was lucky: if he had been arrested a few years later the sentence would have been death. Or maybe not so lucky: he was released in August 1914 but by then the war had started so he was promptly re-arrested and sentenced to be held in an internment camp. He died shortly afterwards. Quoted in *The Times* 10 February 1912.

'For anyone who is tired of life, the thrilling life of a spy should be the very finest recuperation. When one recognises also that it may have valuable results for one's country in time of war, one feels that even though it is a time largely spent in enjoyment, it is not by any means time thrown idly away; and though the 'agent', if caught, may 'go under', unhonoured and unsung, he knows in his heart of hearts that he has done his 'bit' for his country as fully as his comrade who falls in battle.'

Lord Baden-Powell in *My Adventures as a Spy* (1915). Like Churchill, Baden-Powell occasionally let his prose get the better of him.

'As in the case of ghosts, any phenomenon which people don't understand, from a sudden crash on a quiet day to a midnight creak of a cupboard, has an affect of alarm upon nervous minds. So also a spy is spoken of with undue alarm and abhorrence, because he is somewhat of a bogey'.

Lord Baden-Powell in *My Adventures as a Spy* (1915). And in this he is right. The secrecy of the profession leads to a proliferation of myths, many of which intelligence services turn to their advantage.

'Undoubtedly spying would be an intensely interesting sport even if no great results were obtainable from it. There is a fascination which gets hold of anyone who has tried the art.'

Lord Baden-Powell in *My Adventures as a Spy* (1915). He is right in this as well although possibly not in the way he intended. He was trying to convey the idea that espionage is thrilling fun. But the real truth is that, while the work has its moments of excitement, there is a greater cost and dealing in the secret world can undermine the mental health of exponents for the rest of their lives.

'The problem is that you boys have placed your fingers against the fabric of the State – and you have felt it move.'

An unnamed Catholic priest speaking to the author and summing up one of the reasons why secret service has such a long-lasting, and often damaging, effect on the mental health of spies.

'The ordinary public has no conception of Secret Service. The beautiful female spy is not essential to every Secret Service coup – she rarely figured in our wartime services – for every Gabrielle Petit or Louise de Bettignies, the two brave Allied agents who paid the supreme penalty for their devotion to duty, there were a hundred male spies, less glamorous but just as efficient; nor is drugging or the rifling of safes and strongboxes a common practice. Physical violence is an exception, and so also is the carrying of firearms or any other weapon, even as a means of defence'.

MI6 officer Henry Landau in *All's Fair* (1934). He is right except that Petit and de Bettignies were not "beautiful female spies", they were professional intelligence agents, every bit as capable as (in fact probably more than) their male counterparts – as so many women working in the world of espionage today. The use of feminine wiles has its place, but it is far less than the movie goers and thriller readers believe. For more about Landau see under "Agent Selection."

'...the agent-case officer relationship is not only often close but rather more two way than we case officers like to admit.'

Alan Judd, former MI6 officer in his novel *Legacy* (2001).

'From time to time, God causes men to be born – and thou art one of them – who have a lust to go abroad at the risk of their lives and discover news – to-day it may be of far-off things, tomorrow of some hidden mountain, and the next day of some near-by men who have done a foolishness against the State. These souls are very few; and of these few, not more than ten are of the best...'

Kim by Rudyard Kipling (1900). Still the best novel written about espionage.

'...secret intelligence is one of the more potent aphrodisiacs of power.'

David Stafford, historian and intelligence expert in *Churchill and Secret Service* (1987). This aphrodisiac is potent both for those who practice it and for those who receive the product of it. Churchill could not be without it, whether he was in or out of office. He made sure that it was leaked to him if he could not get it through official channels. Tony Blair never seemed to understand how the intelligence world works and believed in it so much that he went to war. But an exception to this fascination is UK Prime Minister Margaret Thatcher: she was always sceptical of what she received and was loath to see intelligence budgets become bloated. Her approach certainly surprised me.

'The besetting sin of all intelligence work is that, in the last analysis it is all too often profoundly frivolous. Any espionage operation, no matter how ingenious or how skilfully conducted, has no value unless it performs a specific function or is part of a larger strategy. The game of foxes can too easily become just that – a game. Intrigue for intrigue's sake, with no object other than to demonstrate the intriguer's own brilliance. The history of espionage is littered with the bones of white elephants – schemes of mind boggling deviousness which achieved little more than wasting the time of the various secret services involved.'

Anthony Read and David Fisher in *Colonel Z* (1985) the biography of Claude Dansey, vice-Chief of MI6 in the 1940s. Exactly right.

'...a field not notable for either truth or humour.'

Malcolm Muggeridge, author, broadcaster and former MI6 officer. From the introduction to *British Agent* by John Whitwell - the pseudonym of MI6 officer Leslie Nicholson. (1966).

'The story of many a spy is commonplace and drab. It would not pass muster in fiction. The subject is a failure in life. The motive is sordid. Fear is present. Patriotism is absent. Silence is not the equipment of a brave man, rather it is the reaction to a dread of consequence. High adventure just means nothing at all.'

Colonel Robin "Tin Eye" Stephens of the Second World War, the best breaker of spies in the business – perhaps because he really understood them. Quoted in *Agent Zigzag* by Ben MacIntyre (2007).

'The only excitement which can compare with the trade of a spy is that of the life of the gambler.'

Honore de Balzac. Quoted in *The Spy's Bedside Book* by Hugh and Graham Greene (1957). Graham Greene worked for MI6. There was a third brother Herbert who was also a spy – for the Japanese. He had been recruited in the 1930s by Japanese Intelligence and had the codename Midorikawa which means *Green River*. He also spied for the fascists during the Spanish Civil War.

'We have the assets... but they are all in hock to America.'

Geoffrey Robertson QC. Quoted *The Establishment* by Owen Jones (2014).

'The work of an agent in the Intelligence Department is on the whole monotonous. A lot of it is uncommonly useless.'

Former Military Intelligence and MI6 agent the author Somerset Maugham in his foreword to *Ashenden* (1927).

'Espionage is an odd profession – for some it is a vocation, with an unscrupulous purity, untouched by mercenary or even patriotic considerations – spying for spying's sake.'

Graham Greene, novelist and MI6 officer during the Second World War. Quoted in *Literary Agents* by Anthony Masters (1987).

'There are currently two schools of thought about our intelligence services. One school is convinced that they are staffed by murderous, powerful, double-crossing cynics, the other that the taxpayer is supporting a collection of bumbling, broken-down layabouts.'

John Bingham, the 7th Baron Clanmorris and MI5 officer. He believed that the intelligence services got a bad press especially from John Le Carré. This particularly upset him as he worked in the same room as Le Carré when they were both at MI5 and helped him to get his first book published.

'The belief encouraged by many spy writers that intelligence officers consist of moles, morons, shits and homosexuals makes the intelligence job no easier.'

John Bingham again (see above). He was not only an MI5 officer, he was also a spy writer in his own right although he believed in only writing "patriotic" thrillers. In this quote he was referring to his old colleague John Le Carré (David Cornwell) whose view was rather different. Quoted in *Literary Agents* by Anthony Masters (1987).

'The closed style of management in the service means that the junior ranks are not involved in any way in the overall operation of the service. The bright young recruit often feels the work is futile. There is no outlet for initiative.'

Miranda Ingram, former MI5 officer. Quoted in *The Observer* newspaper 12 May 1985.

'Peel away the claptrap of espionage and the spy's job is to betray trust.'

Former CIA operations officer William Hood in his book *Mole* (1993).

Need to Know

'So much depended on it that the knowledge tortured me. I was sometimes haunted by the insane fear which grips one on the giddy edge of cliffs and tempts one to jump over – the fear that I might go mad and shriek it from the housetops.'

Violet Bonham Carter (née Asquith), daughter of British Prime Minister Herbert Asquith. Winston Churchill had told her father the secret of Room 40, the top secret signals decryption centre which was a vital weapon in the war against Germany. But Asquith could not keep the secret and amongst those that he told was his daughter. She then had to carry the terrible burden herself. From her memoir *Winston Churchill As I Knew Him* (1965).

'It is wonderful how well men can keep secrets they have not been told.'

Sir Winston Churchill quoted in *The Irrepressible Churchill* edited by Kay Halle (1987).

Novelists

'I suppose that every novelist has something in common with a spy; he watches, he overhears, he seeks motives and he analyses character, and, in his attempt to serve literature, he is unscrupulous.'

Graham Greene, novelist and MI6 officer in his memoir *A Sort of Life* (1971).

'Successful novelists may be bad news for the secret world, but they are not half as dangerous as the failed ones.'

John Le Carré (David Cornwell) who served in both MI5 and MI6. By "failed novelists" he meant some of the officers who serve in the intelligence services who he described as *"unfulfilled fiction-writers"* and whose interference with the lives of their agents sometimes proved deadly. Quoted in *Literary Agents* by Anthony Masters (1987).

O

Observation

'One of the attractive features of the life as a spy is that he has, on occasion, to be a veritable Sherlock Holmes. He has to notice the smallest details, points which would probably escape the untrained eye, and then he has to put this and that together and deduce a meaning from them'.

Lord Baden-Powell in *My Adventures as a Spy* (1915). This is quite right. I remember an old officer once saying that once an intelligence officer is fully trained, they walk down the street and see things quite differently from other people: number plates, faces, buildings. Another officer described the ability as rather like having *"a radar that is hard to switch off"* and the point she was making was that this level of alertness, sometimes bordering on paranoia, can be debilitating to an officer's mental health. On the BBC TV series *Spy* we only subjected the entrants to a few months of this discipline and we had already had one incident by the time we finished the training. Once again, it is a hidden cost to a spy that thriller writers, with the possible exception of Le Carré, rarely talk about.

Official Secrets Act

'It's so long ago I don't think it matters any more. And if I'm in trouble then John Le Carré is in terrible trouble.'

Charlotte Bingham, former MI5 secretary and author, speaking about her book *MI5 and Me* (2018) which gives away a lot of details and why she doesn't fear prosecution under the Official Secrets Act.

This application ... *'is the most iniquitous, outrageous and dangerous I have ever heard in all my career at the Bar.'*

Counsel for *The Observer* newspaper which was trying to publish information from whistleblower Cathy Massiter that MI5 was acting solely in the interests of the Conservative Party. The government tried to gag the newspaper but soon gave up when the weakness of its position became obvious. Quoted in *Spies, Spin and the Fourth Estate* by Paul Lashmar (2020).

Old Boys Network

'The unrecorded nature of things fixed, acquired or carried through in this way (the Old Boys network) is one reason why there could be no fully satisfactory history of MI6.'

Former "Foreign Service officer" Alan Judd in *The Quest for C* (1999).

'For me, Elliott represented the worst kind of Old Etonian, full of his own importance and superior social standing.,

"Elliot" was Nicholas Elliot, MI6 officer and friend of Kim Philby. He used to boast that he had been recruited to MI6 over a glass of champagne at Ascot by the head of the Foreign

Office. He was a member of White's (the private dining club) and therefore had access to senior MI6 officers on a regular basis. So, he owed his selection to his connections in the Old Boys Network. As a spy, he was a disaster: he was responsible for the Crabb affair (when a British diver was found dead having tried to bug a Russian warship). He had described Crabb as the best frogman in England even though he was overweight, unfit and a heavy smoker and drinker. He was also the man who allowed his old friend and Russian spy, Kim Philby, to escape justice – either through incompetence or design. Quoted in *A Spy Called Cynthia* by Anonymous (2021).

'MI5 and MI6 seemed oblivious to the possibility that subversion and treachery could be found within their own ranks and the upper classes. This was largely because they recruited from people like themselves: upper-middle class, public school-educated men with same political and social prejudices and narrow world view.'

Alan Hollingsworth and Nick Fielding in *Defending The Realm* (1999).

'The people at the top all suffered from the extraordinary belief that the upper classes were trustworthy in matters of security and the lower classes were not ... the received wisdom was that their own sort was loyal and that everybody else was potentially disloyal.'

Peter Wright, MI5 officer, 1955 – 1975. From his memoir *Spycatcher* (1987).

'The image of MI6 affairs being arranged behind the polished doors of London clubs, beloved of spy books and films, was, from the earliest days, always at least partly true.'

Former "Foreign Service officer" Alan Judd in *The Quest for C* (1999).

Hence this account of a dandy trying to get hired during the 1920s:

'I was in White's billiard rooms when Stewart (Stewart Menzies, then 'C' of SIS) *came in. I asked him if I might have a word with him and we went and sat by the fireplace. He told me to say nothing for the moment and I noticed that the man with the chalk on the table left the room. Then I said to Stewart that I wanted a job in the secret service. He said he would see what he could do for me and told me to be at White's at 5:00 p.m. the next day.* (White's was, and still is, an exclusive London dining club). *At that hour I waited and a man came up to me and asked me if I was Guy Vansittart and when I said that I was no other he asked me to accompany him. He got into the back of a car which had blinds drawn. He then drove for about an hour or so and then I found myself outside a large Victorian house but in a district I had not visited before.*
    We then went up to the front door and a burly man opened it and I was shown into a room that was bare except for a table and three chairs. I heard a great deal of clumping about on bare boards and then two men came in. I had not met either before, although I think I saw one of them later at Boodle's (another exclusive London club). *They asked me a lot of questions about my politics, money, whether I was "queer", and said they would get in touch with me and then I found myself back in the car being driven round London until, presently, I found myself back at White's'.*

Guy Vansittart, brother of Sir Robert Vansittart who was permanent head of the Foreign Office quoted in *The Secret Servant* by Anthony Cave Brown (1988). MI6 couldn't find a place for Vansittart because of budget cuts so he joined General Motors instead. Interestingly, Sir Robert ran his own intelligence network separate from that of MI6. The *"wilderness of mirrors"* is sometimes just as confusing as the phrase implies. Sir Stewart

Menzies, chief of MI6, treated White's, the oldest and most exclusive "gentleman's" club in London, as an extension of his office. He was there almost every day, even having his Top Secret papers forwarded there. Everyone at the club, including the staff, knew what he did and the billiards room was where he conducted much of his secret service business. Women were never admitted to the club. Today another club has taken over that mantle – but I am not allowed to say which one.

'What I call "the Establishment" is today more powerful than ever before.'

"The Establishment" is an aspect of British society that means you must come from a particular privileged section of society. The term was first coined by journalist Henry Fairlie in 1955 – he was writing about the British intelligence services as the prime example of this problem. It is also referred to as the "Old Boy Network" and "the Chumocracy". Quoted in *The Establishment* by Owen Jones (2014). And just in case you thought that might have changed:

'I thought they're not really called Foxy and Percy any more, they don't really talk in ridiculous accents and all got to clubs. But actually, when I went in in 2000, they had toffee accents, accents from years ago, and Le Carré was entirely accurate about how public school, white and posh and archaic it all was.'

Playwright Sir David Hare who was invited in by MI5 in 2000 as part of a programme of presentations and who claims very close but secret contacts with serving MI5 officers. Quoted in *The Guardian* newspaper 22 February 2014. The reason that this has remained true is because secrecy means that secret service organisations are not subjected to the same scrutiny and social changes that affects other parts of society. They remain closed to most people - rather like the private members dining clubs so popular with their senior managers.

'In the spring of 1939, a telegram arrived from Warsaw, announcing the arrival of a senior colleague ... whom I had not met ... the telegram ended "Will be wearing Old Etonian tie"... I felt sorely tempted to cable back "Regret unfamiliar with OE colours"...'

Leslie Nicholson, MI6 head of station in Riga in 1939. Quoted in *SIX* by Michael Smith (2010).

'To know anything one only had to go out to lunch, and I am bound to say that at such houses as the late Lady Paget's and Mrs J. J. Astor's the information was generally up to date and accurate. The well-fed oracle from the War Office, carefully waiting until the servants had left the room, with a peach and a glass of port before him and his "Well, I can soon tell you the little I know," remains a type of those days. He would be so deep in the imparting of his information that the return of the domestics with the coffee and cigarettes was never allowed to interrupt it.'

Filson Young, an intelligence officer in the Royal Navy during World War One, explaining how leaky the intelligence world was if you moved in the "right" circles. Sadly, this is still true today. I once had to stop a Colonel (who shall remain nameless) from telling all about a certain secret operation simply because he assumed that I was one of those "in the know". A similar problem of "the right people" exists in the United States. This is one of the reasons that Russian Illegals (deep cover agents) have started targeting these elite social circles. Two notable examples are Maria Butina, who was deported from the United States in October 2019. She had been using her looks to infiltrate the right-wing US gun lobby knowing that it was one of the ways into the extremist lobby around President Trump. Another is the Russian Illegal using the name Maria Rivera, she was an attractive brunette who claimed to be a South American jewellery designer. She settled in Naples in 2013 and set up a shop there. Naples also happens to be the home of NATO's Allied Joint Force Command. She partied with NATO staff and even had an affair with a NATO officer. She became the secretary of the Naples branch of the International Lions club (a group that raises money for charity) and this enabled her to meet even more NATO staff. In September 2018, the citizen activist group Bellingcat exposed a ruse whereby Russian GRU (military intelligence) officers working undercover were using passports from a certain numerical range. Rivera had one such passport. Before she could be arrested she disappeared back to Russia and has never been seen again - although a final Facebook message claimed that she left because she needed treatment for cancer. Who knows how much intelligence she picked up during those five years simply by mixing with "the right sort of people"? Not all spying is high tech and gadgets. Sometimes a pretty face is enough.

Thanks to some superb internet detective work, Belllingcat were subsequently able to prove that Rivera was in fact a Russian woman named Olga Kilobova. This is another way in which the espionage game is changing – citizen journalists can now carry out very effective investigations of their own – sometimes for good, sometimes for ill. But it is something that intelligence officers must always be aware of. Quoted in *Inside Room 40* by Paul Gannon (2010) and *The Observer* newspaper 27 August 2022.

Oneupmanship

'Oh yes, I know you, I read your reports.'

> Soviet leader Nikita Khruschev to Allen Dulles, head of the CIA, at a White House dinner 15 September 1959. Quoted in *The Literary Spy* by Charles E. Lathrop (2004). Although Khruschev did not always have the last word: at another dinner he was introduced to a British diplomat. He asked what the diplomat did at the embassy and the man replied *"I am the local British spy"*. Khruschev laughed because he had never heard of the man but in fact he was indeed the MI6 head of station.

Oppression

'The most rabid demagogue can say in this free country what he chooses ... He speaks not under the terror of an organised spy system'.

> The novelist Charles Dickens in *Household Words*. Quoted in *Secret Service* by Professor Christopher Andrew (1985). One of the reasons that Britain did not have an organised intelligence system until 1909 was this fear that a "secret police" was against the interests of democracy. It is also one of the reasons that the CIA did not emerge until 1947. The FBI existed far earlier of course, but Hoover had twisted it into something that its creators never envisaged.

'They have an admirable secret police in Paris, but they pay for it dear enough. I had rather half a dozen people's throats should be cut in Radcliffe's Highway every three years than be subject to domiciliary visits by spies and all the rest of Fouché's contrivances.'

> Earl Dudley quoted in *Plots and Paranoia* by Professor Bernard Porter (1988). Joseph Fouché was the infamous leader of Napoleon' security service.

O.S.S. (Office of Strategic Services – the wartime forerunner to the CIA).

'Actually, despite the Official Secrets Act, practically everything there is to know about MI6's operations during the war years has, in one way or another, already been divulged. Its close wartime liaison with its American opposite number, the Office of Strategic Services, whatever other advantages may have accrued, was to prove ruinous to its security. Deception and double-agent techniques, for instance, have been written up in great detail in American novels, memoirs and magazine articles. So have the methods and uses of cipher cracking. Every OSS man has a best seller in his knapsack, and the FBI's of course is strewn with film rights.'

Malcolm Muggeridge, author and former MI6 officer in *Tread Softly For You Tread on My Jokes* (1968).

'This set-up has been incredibly wasteful in manpower and, except for a few spotty accomplishments, has been a national failure.'

An OSS officer writing to "Wild Bill" Donovan, the head of OSS in 1943. Quoted in the *New Yorker* magazine 10 October 2022.

'His escapades often risked too much and gained too little.'

Historian Amy Davidson Sorkin summing up the view of many historians about "Wild Bill" Donovan, the first head of OSS. For many years he was seen as an intelligence "hero" but now his reputation is being re-assessed. A former Wall Street lawyer, Donovan was personally ordered by Roosevelt to create a national intelligence service following the shock of the Pearl Harbour attack. But Donovan concentrated on military capabilities and has been accused by some historians of, in effect, running a private army. Its achievements were often dramatic but quite possibly not what America really needed. Quoted in the *New Yorker* magazine 10 October 2022.

Overt sources (known in espionage as OSINT)

'It has happened that intelligence services have risked gathering in secret what a little effort on their part or on the part of their taskers would have discovered overtly.'

Former "Foreign Service officer" Alan Judd in his book *The Quest for C* (1999).

'It is a fallacy to think that countries get all their information through their Secret Service. Occasionally they buy information from certain international organisations, which make a regular business of spying, and profit by being able to sell the same information to several different countries. As a rule, these organisations have their headquarters in Switzerland, and are run by spies who have gained their experience in one of the national Secret Services. It is, however, from sources entirely extraneous to any system of espionage that by far the greatest bulk of information is obtained.'

Former MI6 officer Henry Landau in his book *All's Fair* (1934). One of the greatest changes in espionage in the past forty years has been the rise in the use of private intelligence and security organisations by state intelligence services. This is for a number of reasons: one is flexibility, in an age when it is becoming harder and harder to maintain a cover story, private companies can introduce fresh faces, often with legitimate backgrounds. Another reason is that it introduces yet another layer of deniability (the key reason for having a secret service in the first place) and governments always like to be as far from the dirty end of intelligence activities as possible. A third reason is cost: it is often cheaper to bring a company in for a one-off operation than for a service to maintain a capability for many years. This is one reason why, if you follow such things, you will notice a great many former senior intelligence officers joining big international security companies (often on huge salaries) when they retire. As always, David Cornwell (John Le Carré) had his finger on the pulse of the intelligence world and if you would like to get a taste of how this modern espionage world feels then his thriller *A Delicate Truth* (2013) pretty much nails it.

P

Paperwork

'Any intelligence service is only as good as its records.'

Alan Judd, former "Foreign Service officer" in *The Quest for C* (1999).

Paranoia

'The worst of spying is that it makes you always suspicious - even of your best friends'.

Lord Baden-Powell in *My Adventures as a Spy* (1915).

'After a while an intelligence-agent tended to see spies everywhere, rather as certain lunatics saw references to themselves in every newspaper.'

Patrick O'Brien in his novel *Treason's Harbour*. O'Brien created one of the greatest spies of English literature, the naval surgeon Stephen Maturin. O'Brien lived a life of secrecy, so much so that many thought that he had been a spy himself. It is now known that although he wasn't Irish and O'Brien wasn't his real name, he never was a spy. But he was a friend of certain spies and perhaps knew rather more about the world of intelligence than he should have done.

'Broadly speaking no highly intelligent, sensitive, counter-intelligence expert should be involved in this fascinating specialisation for more than about twelve years. After that the "Wilderness of Mirrors" starts to take over from common sense.'

John Bruce Lockhart, MI6 officer. He was the nephew of the famous Robert Bruce Lockhart who was the diplomat who made the con man Sidney Reilly famous as "the Ace of Spies." John joined MI6 during World War Two and rose to a senior rank. He was the MI6 officer who succeeded Kim Philby in Washington. That must have been a difficult posting. Quoted in *The Literary Spy* by Charles E. Lathrop (2004).

'There is less danger in fearing too much than too little.'

Attributed to Sir Francis Walsingham, spymaster to Queen Elizabeth I.

Patriotism

'Patriotism or any other version of the herd instinct seems to me an entirely inadequate basis of virtue.'

Robert Cecil (1864-1958). He wasn't a spy but his family have long had a close association with espionage and he was the Foreign Office advisor to MI6 during the Second World War. This quote often comes to mind when one meets a certain "gung-ho" type of intelligence officer. Patriotism is an important quality but in a spy it needs to be leavened by something more: an understanding that your nation is not always right. Without it you cannot be a good agent runner. It is this realisation that may account for the bitterness of many former spies in their subsequent writings (Cornwell, Muggeridge, et al.). Quoted in *Gilbert Murray: An Unfinished Autobiography* edited by Jean Smith and Arnold Toynbee (1960).

Philby (Kim)

'I do not agree with several writers who have stated that Kim was essentially an ordinary man in an extraordinary situation; rather, I would say, he was an unusual man who sought and found an unusual situation.'

Ian Innes "Tim" Milne in his memoir *Kim Philby: The Unknown Story* (2014). He was a former MI6 officer who had known Philby well. But his memoir was banned by MI6 and only published after Milne's death. Milne was a nephew of the famous A.A.Milne, author of *Winnie the Pooh*. Tim, as he was known by his family for reasons long forgotten, had been Philby's best friend since they went to boarding school together. They went on hiking holidays in Europe and it was Philby who helped Milne to join MI6 during the Second World War. Milne served in Iran, Germany, Switzerland, Japan and Hong Kong and rose to become a senior officer in MI6. When he retired in 1968, he became a clerk to the House of Commons. No-one knew Philby better.

'Perhaps if in a drunken moment he had let slip a hint, I would have given him twenty-four hours to get clear and then reported it.'

Graham Greene, novelist and former MI6 officer, who worked for Philby and knew him well. Quoted in *Literary Agents* by Anthony Masters (1987).

'I got to know Kim Philby as well as any man I have ever known and I'll be damned if I believe that he is a traitor.'

James Jesus Angleton, head of counterintelligence for the CIA 1954-1974. Showing that even the professionals can be fooled. Quoted in *A Spy Called Cynthia* by Anonymous (2021).

Polygraphs

'The federal government may as well put its faith in Wonder Woman's magic lasso than rely on the accuracy of the polygraph.'

Mark Zaid, US attorney who specialises in representing people who have fallen foul of polygraph tests. American institutions appear to love polygraphs but in reality intelligence services don't trust them and only use them because people tend to be intimidated into telling the truth if they think an "infallible machine" is monitoring them. Detainees in Guantanamo Bay prison facility frequently asked to take polygraph tests to prove their innocence but these requests were refused by the US authorities on the grounds that the results are unreliable. It is essentially a con trick. Once you know that, anyone can beat them. Quoted in *The Literary Spy* by Charles E. Lathrop (2004).

'A polygraph test measures fear: the idea is that you can tell when someone is lying because they are afraid of detection....'

Polygraph examiner Tristram Burgess quoted in *The Guardian* newspaper 20 October 2009. This principle is quite an ancient one: certain tribes in Africa would try to determine who was lying by placing a red hot knife on the tongue of the suspect, the idea being that a nervous liar will have a dry mouth, will not be able to summon up the saliva to protect himself, and will be burned. In ancient China, a similar technique was used: the suspect had to fill their mouth with dry rice. After some time the rice was inspected and if it was still dry then they were guilty as they were clearly too nervous to salivate.

The truth is that "lie detectors" don't work. Tests have shown that their accuracy in predicting a lie is no better than tossing a coin. Further evidence of this is that numerous traitors have been subjected to polygraphs and passed with flying colours. The CIA has a particular trick with some applicants: they are asked to take a polygraph test and are asked questions about their past such as "have you ever been drunk?" or "have you ever taken drugs?". At the end of the test the examiner (chosen to be as threatening as possible) will say something like: *"We have detected that you have not told the whole truth in some of your answers, but don't worry, that happens. We will run the test again and this time try to give more truthful answers."* Apparently it is astonishing what some applicants then admit to and all because they assume that a machine can know whether or not they are telling the truth. It is always a scary thing to undergo any kind of "lie detector" test but even brain imaging machines cannot do it, so there is no need to panic just yet.

'There's no special magic. Confidence is what does it. Confidence and a friendly relationship with the examiner: rapport, where you smile and that you make him think you like him.'

Aldrich Ames, the infamous CIA traitor. He took a polygraph test every year and yet it never detected that he had been working for the Russians for almost ten of those years. It is thought that at least ten American agents were executed as a result of his betrayal.

'Some cultures polygraph more effectively than others. Arabs and Iranians, for example, are notoriously difficult because lying under certain circumstances is culturally acceptable. The polygraph is device initially devised by Westerners for use on other Westerners.'

Former CIA officer Duane Clarridge in *A Spy For All Seasons.* (2002). This understanding of the importance of cultural differences is one of the espionage skills that you never hear about in spy thrillers. Take for instance, proxemics. This is the study of the effect of distance on people in human interaction and how it varies between different cultures. For instance, in Mediterranean societies an arm around the shoulder, a slap on the back or other friendly physical contact may be acceptable and seen as a sign of trust. However, in many Asian cultures this would not be the case and uncalled for physical contact is frowned upon. It may even have the opposite effect. When you really get into the subject you find that this awareness can even affect such things as rate of eye contact or the distance that you stand from someone during a conversation. These are the real skills of a spy – influencing people without them realising what you are doing, not abseiling down the side of a building with a box of chocolates in your backpack. Although you never know...

Preparation

'A nation which starves its armed forces, and also starves its intelligence service, deserves the fate it will get'.

> Admiral Reginald "Blinker" Hall from a 1930s lecture. Quoted in *The Quest for C* by Alan Judd (1999).

'Nothing would more contribute to make a man wise than to always have an enemy in his view.'

> Attributed to Lord Halifax but there are many more ancient versions. Such as:

'The superior man, whilst resting in security, does not forget that danger may come.'

> Confucius.

'Success [in war] *depends on sound deductions from a mass of intelligence, often specialised and highly technical, on every aspect of the enemy's national life, and much of this information has to be gathered in peace-time.'*

> Sir Winston Churchill from his book *Triumph and Tragedy* (1953).

'No war can be conducted successfully without early and good intelligence.'

> Attributed to John Churchill, First Duke of Marlborough.

Privacy

'Privacy has never been an absolute right.'

> Robert Hannigan, Director of GCHQ. Quoted in *The Guardian* newspaper 5 November 2014. This is a rather worrying statement coming from a man whose organisation has the power to spy on anyone of us. He may well have qualified these words later but it illustrates that the political views of those who are appointed to senior intelligence positions have the potential to affect all of our lives. Fortunately, when politicians who might seek to use the intelligence services to their own ends have taken power (Donald Trump comes to mind) the intelligence services have thus far, been pretty resilient. But that could change.

Propaganda

'Say nothing. Let the story rip.'

> Orders to Lt. Col. Alexander Scotland. It had been alleged in the Press that he had been a secret agent in Hitler's General Staff during WWII. In fact, he had only been attached to German forces as a supply officer between 1904 and 1907. Scotland wanted to hold a press conference to set the record straight, but it suited the intelligence services to let everybody believe that they were a good deal more powerful than they actually are. Quoted in *The London Cage* by Alexander Scotland (1957). For more about Scotland's career see under "Boredom."

143

'For a lie to be believed, make the truth unbelievable.'

Attributed to Napoleon.

'I fear three newspapers more than one hundred thousand bayonets.'

Also attributed to Napoleon. I don't know, one hundred thousand bayonets sounds like a lot especially if they are coming towards you. However, you can find the same quote in similar forms e.g.:

'Four hostile newspapers are more to be feared than a thousand bayonets.'

Also attributed to Napoleon, so he probably said something like this. It is certainly true that propaganda and the planting of misinformation has always been a key espionage skill. In the modern age, it is an important part of hybrid warfare – the art of hurting your enemy without actually declaring war. Computer based communication such as social media allows an enemy to create false narratives, sway public opinion on foreign policy issues and even to influence elections (Russia's efforts towards Donald Trump's election as US President are now well known). This threat has become so acute that in 2016 NATO set up a centre especially to study this aspect of espionage: the European Centre of Excellence for Countering Hybrid Threats (aka Hybrid CoE) based in Helsinki. It is a good example of how the espionage war is "hot" even when the public are unaware of the fact.

Purpose of Intelligence

'All Sovereign Princes and States ought, like cunning gamesters, to use all endeavours to know what cards are in their neighbours hands, so that they may play their own to their best advantage.'

Samuel Morland, right hand man to John Thurloe, Oliver Cromwell's chief of intelligence and also a Royalist double agent. Quoted in *Espionage in the reign of Charles II* by Alan Marshall (1994).

Q

Qualities of a good spy

'He must be cool, courageous and adroit, patient and imperturbable, discreet and trustworthy. He must have the resolution to continue unceasingly his search for information, even in the most disheartening of circumstances and after repeated failures.'

> Colonel David Henderson, former Director of Military Intelligence, describing his ideal agent. Quoted in *Spymaster* by David Ramsay (2008). Note the part about repeated failures – it is reflected by espionage history.

'Clever and effective spies seldom get caught, but the very best ones are not even suspected.'

> George Hill, MI6 officer during World War One from his memoir *Go Spy the Land* (1932). He was a notable embellisher of his reputation and there is a suspicion that Hill may have been a double agent for the Russians – although nothing has ever been proved. If it was true that would make him a very good spy indeed.

'To be a really effective spy, a man has to be endowed with a strong spirit of self-sacrifice, courage, and self-control, with the power of acting a part, quick at observation and deduction, and blessed with good health, and nerve of exceptional quality'.

> Lord Baden-Powell in *My Adventures as a Spy* (1915).

'Physical attractiveness is a far better recommendation than any letter of introduction'.

> Aristotle. He may be right but the problem is that although physical beauty may get you a target's attention (whether you are male or female), convincing the target that you are not romantically interested in them while you are trying to get close enough to them to recruit them as an agent, can become a major battle of wits (and wandering hands).

'The ideal spy is a man of keen intellect, though in outward appearance a fool.'

> Not Sun Tzu although it sounds like him. It is nevertheless true.

'The best spies are unpaid men who are doing it for the love of the thing.'

> Lord Baden Powell. He may well have been right: consider the case of Sir Paul Dukes, England's greatest spy of the modern era. He was a concert pianist with no espionage training who could not get into the army because of a congenital heart condition. But he was able to penetrate to the heart of the Russian government, escape a manhunt designed especially to catch him and lived to tell the tale. Yet he was never paid a dime for his work.

'Successful Field Officers will be generally found to have three important characteristics: they will be personalities in their own right; they will have humanity and a capacity for friendship; and they will have a sense of humour which will enable them to avoid the ridiculous mumbo-jumbo of over-secrecy.'

Nick Elliott, MI6 officer and good friend of Kim Philby in his memoir *With My Little Eye* (1994). As stated elsewhere under "Cambridge Spies", Nick Elliot was sent to Beirut to get Philby to confess but he let Philby slip through his fingers. Deliberately? We will never know.

R

Racial Discrimination

'It must be assumed that the communist intelligence services are fully aware of the possibilities of recruiting agents from among disaffected coloured people.' This disaffection resulted: *'...simply from the colour of a man's skin, which gave him a chip on his shoulder. It will be a long time before this chip is removed.'*

> Martin Furnival Jones – the Director General of MI5 (1965-72) speaking at a Cabinet Office meeting in 1967 to explain why MI5 did not employ black people and was also uneasy about new racial equality legislation that the Labour Government of the time planned to introduce. Quoted in *The Guardian* newspaper 15 October 2018.

Incidentally, in yet another "you could not make it up" moment, the very first person of colour to serve with MI6 was actually a white man. No, really. In 1939, when Montgomery Hyde joined MI6, at headquarters he met another officer called Maurice Jeffes:

' ... a nice, but peculiar looking man, with a dark office on the ground floor which matched his complexion. ... Jeffes was a jolly, good-natured fellow who always gave me a friendly greeting when I entered the building. The curious gunmetal colour of his face was due to a doctor having inoculated him with the wrong serum which turned it a kind of purple-blue that could not be changed. Once the manager of an American hotel where he had booked in wished to turn him out on the ground that he was coloured .... Jeffes had considerable difficulty in convincing him that he was white.'

> Quoted in *Secret Intelligence Agent* by Montgomery Hyde (1982). Jeffes had a very successful career becoming head of station in Paris and New York. Sometimes truth is not just stranger than fiction, it blows it clean out of the water. MI6 has never said when it recruited its first black officer but you can bet that it was a long time in coming.

Records

'It also means that we cannot rely on the evidence we are able to see. The reason for this is that all spies and secret agents are liars, trained in techniques of deception and dissimulation, who are just as likely to fake the historical record as anything else.'

> Professor Bernard Porter, distinguished historian of the secret services. Quoted in *Spies, Spin and the Fourth Estate* by Paul Lashmar (2020).

Recruitment

'...there's some truth in the service's [MI6's] dictum that no agent should be considered properly recruited unless he or she accepts handover to a new case officer, demonstrating that the relationship is by then with the service rather than with the individual.'

> Alan Judd, former "Foreign Service officer" in his spy novel *Legacy* (2001). For more about Judd and why his views are worth listening to, see under "Agent Handling."

'There is a growing tendency in this service to count the conscious provision of intelligence as a recruitment. It isn't.'

> Alan Judd also from *Legacy* (2001). See above. What Judd is highlighting is that a target may give you valuable intelligence but until the target has, in so many words, said: "Yes, I understand who you represent and I am willing to work for you, understanding all the risks that this entails," he is not recruited. This is a damned sight harder than it might sound. For someone to step over that invisible line into outright betrayal of their country is a massive obstacle – even for those who think they have good reason. Only the most skilled intelligence officers can handle the crisis that often arises at this point in the relationship.

'To the Jews I became as a Jew, in order to win the Jews, to those under the law I became as one under the law – though not being myself under the law – that I might win those under the law. To those outside the law I became as one outside the law ... To the weak I became weak, that I might win the weak. I have become all things to all men that I might be all means recruit some.'

> Saint Paul in 1 Corinthians, Chapter 9, Verses 20-22.

'How to work with foreigners? You promise a favour for a favour. You get documents from him and tell him to fuck himself. But say "not to upset you, I will take you to a restaurant and give you an expensive gift. You just need to sign for it." That is the ideal working method.'

> Victor Podobny, SVR intelligence officer (Russian foreign intelligence, the successor organisation to the KGB Foreign Directorate) talking to a colleague and not realising that the call is being monitored by an FBI wiretap. Quoted in *Collusion* by Luke Harding (2017). This approach might explain why Podobny was not a very successful agent runner.

Reform

'Our intelligence effort has to generate better results. That's my mandate pure and simple.'

> John Negroponte, the first director of all US intelligence speaking before the Senate Intelligence Committee in April 2005 of the need for a complete overhaul of the agencies.

'... triplication of management, triplication of bureaucracy and triplication of turf battles.'

> David Bickford, former Legal Director for both the Security Service and MI6, speaking of the need for a single unified intelligence agency. Quoted in *MI6* by Stephen Dorril (2000). He was right, in particular no-one has ever really explained why we have a separate police and security service – there is a massive amount of duplication and MI5 cannot act without police assistance as they cannot arrest anyone. But, sadly, the three agencies have too much influence in the corridors of Whitehall for there to be any meaningful change.

Relations with other government departments

'Today the old type of Secret Service has disappeared and melodrama has given place to a more sober style of enquiry from which the diplomat need no longer, as he was very properly required to do before, withdraw the hem of his garment'.

> Instruction to Heads of Mission from the British Foreign Office in 1922 recognising the new 'respectable' status of espionage. Quoted in *The Quest for C* by Alan Judd (1999).

The War Office *'...have constantly injured my Service. From the day of my appointment I have been disgracefully treated, my authority has been deliberately undermined and my influence even among my own staff damaged by the constant slights and humiliations ... They have made many promises to secure my submission to their scheme of spoliation, but have never kept one of them and in all my dealings with queer people in my strange and unique service I have met no one who was so thoroughly unscrupulous and untrustworthy as the author of the proposal* [for amalgamation of all the intelligence services under War Office control] *put forward'*.

Mansfield Cumming, the founder of MI6, writing in 1919. Quoted in *The Quest for C* by Alan Judd (1999).

Reliability

'We had to invent, exaggerate and write those reports. It was very silly...'

KGB defector Oleg Gordievsky speaking about the quality of Soviet intelligence. Quoted in *Private Eye* Issue No. 1480.

Rendition

'Beyond any shadow of a doubt, the ugliest phrase to enter the English language in 2005 was "extraordinary rendition"'.

The author Salman Rushdie quoted in the *Independent on Sunday* newspaper 22 January 2006. It is still ugly but in fact rendition has been used since at least the Tudor period. Consider the case of Dr John Story (1504-1571). He had been the Regius Professor in Civil Law at Oxford and a prominent supporter of the Catholic Queen Mary. At first under the Protestant Queen Elizabeth, he was left in peace. But when he refused to comply with the Act of Supremacy in May 1560, he was imprisoned. In 1563, he escaped and sought sanctuary with the Spanish Ambassador. He was then smuggled to Flanders. There he took Spanish citizenship and became an advisor to the Duke of Alva (the commander of Spanish occupation forces in the Low Countries). A British intelligence agent named John Prestall made contact with Dr Story and pretended to be a Catholic but in fact he was an *agent provocateur* whose mission was to trap Story. Together he and Story developed two plots to murder the Queen and a plan for the Spanish to invade England. Sir Robert Cecil, who was in charge of the British secret service at this time, decided that he must act. He put together a team of twelve men. In July 1570, they hired a ship and crew under a Dutch captain. They sailed across the Channel and docked in Bergen. Story was lured to the ship because part of his work for the Spanish was to search ships that had arrived from England for Protestant literature.

He was transported back to England and lodged in the Tower of London to await trial. Now the problem for Elizabeth's government was that he was a Spanish citizen and they had clearly abducted him. The government got round this by appointing judges who simply ignored that fact. Story would not even plead on the grounds that the court had no right to try a foreign national, but it did not save him. He was found guilty and hanged, drawn and quartered a few days later, on 1 June 1571 at Tyburn - the first recorded use of the infamous triangular gallows there (the "Tyburn Tree.") The mission was supposed to demonstrate to Catholic plotters on the Continent that they were not beyond the reach of retribution. But, as

149

with other rendition operations, the mission actually had the opposite effect. Story became a martyr and the manner of his death seemed to confirm to the Catholics the evil of the Elizabethan reign. The number of plots increased rather than decreased. Meanwhile, the team were never fully paid for the job and most of the money for the operation had to come out of their own pockets. That was not the end of it: several of them suffered for their involvement when the Spanish hunted them down and took revenge. Rendition has always been a dirty business.

'If you want a serious interrogation you send a prisoner to Jordan. If you want them to be tortured you send them to Syria. If you want a prisoner to disappear then you send them to Egypt.'

Former CIA officer Bob Baer. Quoted in *Spies, Spin and the Fourth Estate* by Paul Lashmar (2020).

'... if the UK intelligence agencies and the UK government were involved, this is not only contrary to the policy the British government has pursued for a long number of years, but also to the assurances that were given to the Intelligence and Security Committee (ISC) and to Parliament as a whole.'

Malcolm Rifkind, Chairman of the ISC, commenting on the Abdul Belhaj rendition case. But the UK intelligence agencies really were involved. Belhaj was a Libyan rebel commander who, in 2004, was rendered from Thailand by the CIA and then placed in the custody of Colonel Gaddafi. Belhaj was then tortured. He somehow survived and was freed as part of an amnesty in 2010. He then became one of the key figures in the overthrow of Colonel Gaddafi in 2011. Files were later found showing that, despite their earlier denials, MI6 had been involved in his rendition. The UK government apologised for his treatment and paid compensation. Quoted in *The Guardian* newspaper 11 April 2012.

'I don't have any recollection of it at all.'

Tony Blair speaking about the Belhaj rendition, quoted on the BBC News website on 12 April 2012. It is not believable that the Prime Minister would not be consulted in a decision of this sensitivity involving the UK intelligence services. It is quite possible that in 2012 he did not remember giving the order - but that only shows how easy it is for some people to condemn a suspect to horrendous torture and then to walk away and forget about it.

'There is simply no truth in the claims that the United Kingdom has been involved in rendition full stop, because we never have been. We were opposed to any use of torture. Not only did we not agree to it, we were not compliant in it and nor did we turn a blind eye to it.'

Former Foreign Secretary Jack Straw addressing the House of Commons in 2005 after allegations that MI6 was involved in rendition and torture. Quoted in Private Eye magazine on 13 July 2018.

And ...

'No Foreign Secretary can know all the details of what its intelligence agencies are doing at any one time.'

Former Foreign Secretary Jack Straw speaking in 2018 after it had been proved by the

Intelligence and Security Committee that he had given oral approval for numerous MI6 rendition operations and acceptance of "intelligence" gained under torture. Also quoted in Private Eye magazine on 13 July 2018. What he says is true about the mass of day to day operations, but with operations of this gravity, it is simply not believable that the UK Foreign Secretary (who has responsibility for MI6) would not be consulted.

'An abduction is a high-risk operation and needs a superpower to do it. Thailand is not a superpower.'

Former deputy director of Thailand's National Security Agency (TNSA) Nantiwat Samart, trying to deny that the TNSA was involved in abducting and murdering political opponents of the regime of retired general Prayuth Chanocha. But it doesn't need to be a superpower, you just need a car and a couple of thugs. When these abductions were recorded or reported, the Thai government simply called them "fake news." One victim was Wanchalearm Satsaksit, a Thai pro-democracy activist who had fled the country to Pnohm Penh capital of Cambodia. He was forced into a black Toyota by three men. As well as this, eight Thai dissidents were abducted from Laos between 2016 and 2018. In Jan 2019, Surachai Danwattananusorn and two aides, Phu Chana and Kasalong, were taken from Vientiane, the capital of Laos. The bodies of the aides were found weighted down with concrete at the bottom of the Mekong with their faces smashed in to try to prevent identification. In May 2019, Thai pro-democracy activists Siam Theerawut, Chucheep Chivasut and Kristana Thapthai were abducted from Hanoi and disappeared. The Asian Human Rights Commission detailed 82 similar disappearances since 1980 involving Thai families. Sometimes all a government has to do is to deny an operation - it is very hard to get proof and that is why governments have secret services. Monitoring how they are used is crucially important because they have so much power. The situation in Thailand at this time is a good example of what happens when that independent oversight is missing.

Requirements (In espionage, this means the intelligence that the government wants.)

'Bring me back reliable information.'

Inscription on Hittite clay tablet with instructions (now in the British Museum) from an unnamed monarch to one of his emissaries bound for Egypt in 1370 BC. This must be one of the earliest surviving intelligence requirements.

'[Intelligence Services] tend to be as good, or as bad, as the requirements placed upon them. If the requirements are precise, clear and important the response of both case officers and agents tends to be better, ... than if the requirements are woolly, general and not obviously relevant, producing answers as unsatisfactory as the questions'.

Former "Foreign Service officer" Alan Judd in *The Quest for C* (1999).

'Know everything.'

Motto of the Stasi (the East German security service in the Soviet era).

'The chief value of a Secret Service to a country is not the volume of information that comes through but the means which it affords for employing direct action in obtaining specific information required. Country X has a new engine of war, details of which are vitally important to Country Y. Country Y cannot sit and wait until chance brings her the information; she tells the Secret Service to go and get it.'

Former MI6 officer Henry Landau in his book *All's Fair* (1934). For more about Landau see under "Agent Handling."

'Generally, in the case of armies you wish to strike, cities you wish to attack and people you wish to assassinate, it is necessary to find out the names of the garrison commander, the aides-de-camp, the ushers, the gatekeepers and the bodyguards. You must instruct your spies to ascertain these matters in minute detail'.

Sun Tzu, *The Art of War*, Chapter 13, Paragraph 20. It sounds simple, but this quote just goes to show that the rules never change. What Sun Tzu is saying is that your intelligence about these key factors must be detailed. Consider the war in Iraq and the supposed "intelligence" about the non-existent weapons of mass destruction – Sun Tzu's point still holds true. Vague intelligence is not enough and requirements placed on intelligence services must be detailed and specific.

'Go back over everything. See if Saddam did this. See if he's linked in any way.'
'But, Mr President, al Qaeda did this.'
'I know, I know. But – see if Saddam was involved. Just look. I want to know any shred.'
'Absolutely, we will look – again. But you know, we have looked, several times, for state sponsorship of al Qaeda and not found any real linkages to Iraq. Iran pays a little, as does Pakistan, and Saudi Arabia, Yemen.'
'Look into Iraq and Saddam'.

A transcript of President George Bush talking to Richard Clarke, the US counter terrorism chief, after the 9/11 attack by al Qaeda on the World Trade Centre. Clarke was horrified at how determined Bush was to pin the blame on Iraq in the face of all the evidence. This reminds us that, ultimately, intelligence chiefs are at the mercy of their political masters. Quoted in *The Truth with Jokes* by Al Franken (2005).

Resistance to Interrogation

'Always speak slowly, this enables hesitation to be covered when necessary; create the impression of being vague; give the impression of being bewildered, frightened or stupid; feign drunkenness or tiredness long before they actually occur. Above all stick to your cover story.'

Major Thomas "Tar" Robertson of MI5, master of interrogation, speaking to an SOE training course (National Archives KV4 172). He was known to many as "Tar" after his initials (his middle name was Argyll). But he also tended to wear the tartan trousers of the Seaforth regiment and because of his way with the secretaries at MI5 (one described him as "monstrously good-looking") he was consequently known in some quarters as "Passion Pants".

Revenge

[If you criticise them...] *'the intelligence community has six ways to Sunday to get back at you.'*

US Senator Chuck Schumer – although when the intelligence services came under attack during the Trump administration Schumer defended them by saying that the Republican party had *"devolved into delusional, self-serving paranoia"* so he is aware that the power dynamic can run both ways.

'A discarded spy, like a discarded mistress, is dangerous for any man.'

Gustav Steinhauer, German spy chief before the First World War. Quoted in *Spies of the First World War* by James Morton (2010). This is one reason why the intelligence services are careful about how they recruit, you do not want a high "churn" rate with lots of disaffected ex-spies wandering the streets having learned all the secrets. When a TV drama series about the UK intelligence services led to an increase in applications, the services were initially pleased. However, when the mundane reality did not match the excitement of the TV show, the churn rate went through the roof and service chiefs were much less happy. Recruitment publicity for the intelligence services is fine but you have to be careful how it is done.

Risk

'... intelligence services need people, just as armies do, who will occasionally turn Nelsonic blind eyes. If what you do works, you are congratulated; if it doesn't, you are never forgiven.'

Former "Foreign Service officer" Alan Judd in *The Quest for C* (1999).

Romance

'Pillow talk can have its dangers. From comments by fellow prisoners while I was in custody, I had learned that most had been ratted out by their most significant others. I wasn't going to make the same mistake.'

Kevin Mitnick, once the world's most wanted computer hackers, who managed to evade the FBI for years until he was finally caught – not by them – but by a fellow IT professional. Quoted in *Ghost in the Wires* by Kevin Mitnick (2011).

Room 40 (The British Navy codebreaking centre in World War One).

'Can I count on a quiet night, gentlemen?'

Admiral Jellicoe, First Sea Lord. Quoted by David Ramsay in *Spymaster* (2008). In the First World War, some German codes were changed at midnight. The race was then on to break the new codes. Sometimes this meant that in the early hours of the morning, there would be dramatic news for Jellicoe as a key piece of intelligence was broken. On other days, Room 40 did not manage to crack the code at all and at midnight the whole game would start again. The impact of Room 40 on British fortunes in the First World War was massive and has tended to be forgotten in the shadow of Bletchley Park in the Second World War. It should be remembered.

Russia

'The Russian bear is sick, ... but this bear is still armed to the teeth and very, very proud.'

> The author John Le Carré (MI6 officer David Cornwell) in a 1990 speech when asked if the end of the Cold War meant an end to the threat from Russia.

'Russia is a semi-Asiatic child who has now grown up, and to this child security work and espionage is the essence of living.'

> John Bingham, MI5 officer and author. Quoted in *Literary Agents* by Anthony Masters (1987).

'Nobody recruits a Russian ... they recruit themselves.'

> Former CIA operations officer Philip Agee from his book *Inside the Company* (1975). You could say this about all agents. Most of them are "looking for something" in their lives. The trick is to spot them (known in the trade as "targeting") and then to turn their vulnerability into a recruitment.

S

Satellites

'...it was as if an enormous floodlight had been turned on in a darkened warehouse.'

Albert Wheelon, the CIA's first deputy director of science and technology, describing the success of CORONA, the very first US spy satellite. In just one mission it gathered more photographic intelligence than every flight by all the U-2 spy planes combined. Quoted in *Spies, Lies and Algorithms* by Amy B. Zegart (2022).

Secrecy

'The life of a spy is to know, not to be known.'

George Herbert in his poem *Jacula Prudentum*.

'Secrecy can only be maintained by deception.'

Sir Winston Churchill to President Roosevelt shortly before Operation TORCH (the Allied landing in North Africa in the Second World War). Quoted in *Churchill and Secret Service* by David Stafford (1987).

'The fox barks not when he would steal the lamb.'

Shakespeare, King Henry VI Part II Act III Scene I.

'Three may keep a secret - if two of them are dead.'

Benjamin Franklin writing in his annual collection of witty phrases and other information *Poor Richard's Almanac* (1732-1758).

'The urge to discover secrets is deeply ingrained in human nature; even the least curious mind is roused by the promise of sharing knowledge withheld from others.'

John Chadwick in his book *The Decipherment of Linear B* (1958).

'As my father always told me, never write it down.'

Bobby Kennedy quoted in the biography *Robert Kennedy: His Life* by Evan Thomas (2002). This is so true. If you want to be a spy, live by it. There is perhaps one proviso: today the sentence should read "never write it on an electronic device." If you do, it is no longer a secret – no matter what you may think.

'Secrecy: the first, last and most necessary essential of a Secret Service'.

Mansfield Cumming. Quoted in *The Quest for C* by Alan Judd (1999).

Which leads us to:-

'If Great Britain employs spies, I know nothing of them ...'

The Special Branch officer and First World War spycatcher, Herbert Fitch in his book *Traitors Within* (1933). Of course, when Fitch was writing, the British intelligence services were "unavowed" i.e. if challenged the UK government would deny their existence. Fitch, Cumming and all the early figures of twentieth century intelligence would probably be gobsmacked if they knew that in 1993 the UK intelligence services would go public, have well-known headquarters buildings in London (or Cheltenham in the case of GCHQ) and advertise openly for staff in the media. Indeed, these days can they be called "secret" services at all? "Intelligence services" is probably more correct.

'The necessity of procuring good intelligence is apparent and need not be further urged. All that remains for me to add is that you keep the whole matter as secret as possible. For upon Secrecy, success depends in most enterprises of the kind, and for want of it, they are generally defeated, however well planned and promising a favourable issue.'

George Washington to Elias, the head of his secret service on 26 July 1777. A copy of this phrase hung on the wall of Maurice Oldfield, Chief of MI6, 1983-1988. Quoted in *C: A biography of Sir Maurice Oldfield* by Richard Deacon (1985).

'Even the whereabouts of Cumming's headquarters was a secret, although the average taxi driver knew well that they were at Whitehall Court...'

Anthony Cave Brown in his book *The Secret Servant* (1988). The same problem occurred when MI6 moved to Century House, a Lambeth tower block, in 1964. It was so well-known that officers had to take cabs to addresses several streets away to avoid attention from the cab drivers. Eventually, MI6 took on a fleet of cars and drivers to ferry officers around London. In 1994, SIS finally stopped hiding and moved into a "cream and green" headquarters on the banks of the River Thames that was so ugly that no one could possibly ignore it. It is known in some quarters as 'Legoland' because of its blocky appearance. When it was struck by a Russian-made Mark 22 anti-tank missile on 20 September 2000 there was a rumour that disaffected members of the National Institute of Architects were responsible. In fact, it was an Irish terrorist group. Sadly, there was only superficial damage.

'Half the secrecy that we are maintaining is of no practical good.'

Mansfield Cumming. Quoted in *The Official History of MI6* by Professor Keith Jeffery (2010).

And finally, when an SIS officer is enciphering her secret messages to HQ, each country is referred to not by name but by an ultra top secret number. During the Second World War, the secret SIS number for Germany was twelve (Zwölf in German)....

'In Istanbul, in the war, when the German national anthem was played at a night club, a party from the German Embassy jumped to their feet and sang "Zwölfte-land, zwölfte-land, über alles!"'

Clearly someone had been leaking the top secret British codes.... From the memoir *Tread Softly For You Tread On My Jokes* (1968) by former MI6 officer Malcolm Muggeridge.

'In the darkness of secrecy all sorts of things can go wrong.'

Attributed to the philosopher Jeremy Bentham.

'Where secrecy or mystery begins vice and roguery are not far off.'

Attributed to Samuel Johnson.

'The habits and language of clandestinity can intoxicate even its own practitioners.'

Former Director of the CIA William Colby in his book *Honorable Men* (1978). Some spies love the secrecy. It makes them feel about six inches taller.

'If I thought my coat knew my plans I would take if off and burn it.'

Attributed to Frederick II. Sometimes also attributed to Wellington and that if he thought his hair knew what his brain was thinking he would shave it all off.

'An agency whose servants are obliged forever to keep everything secret will never develop an objective view of the world.'

Aubrey Jones, former MI6 officer. Before he joined MI6 during the Second World War he was a journalist for *The Times*. Quoted in *The Literary Spy* by Charles E. Lathrop (2004).

'Secrecy is poison.'

David Shayler, the MI5 renegade (I don't believe "whistleblower" is the correct term). To be clear, I have little sympathy for Shayler: he betrayed secrets and he paid the price. But, that having been said, I do feel for a man who appears to have had mental health issues and who clearly felt increasingly cornered. I heard him say this phrase once during an interview, I can't remember exactly where, but it is worth recording because, over the years, this comment has come back to me and it has always rung true. This is not to say that all secrecy is bad – Lithium is poisonous yet can be vital to a patient's survival. Rather, it seems to me that secrecy can be used for good but it is astonishingly potent and that can have all sorts of bad side effects: secrecy for secrecy's sake, a misplaced sense of self-importance, imperviousness to much needed change, undue influence and more. Shayler was right on this and secrecy needs to be handled judiciously by intelligence agencies.

'Of course, I know you've all got to pretend that what you are doing is secret. You're like film stars the other way round. They live by publicity, and you live by secrecy.'

Author and MI6 officer Compton Mackenzie in *Water On The Brain* (1933). The point that Mackenzie often liked to make is that the activities of the intelligence service have to be kept secret because if they were not people would realise how useless it all is and demand some changes. As he says later in the book, his reasons for writing the book as a comic novel were so that the British intelligence service:

'... should not run the slightest risk of the unpleasant experience that the Emperor underwent in Hans Andersen's tale, in which, it will be remembered, a small child among the spectators called

out that the Emperor, so far from wearing a beautiful new suit, was walking in the procession with nothing on at all.'

In other words, he wanted to the public to be ready when they found out that secret service really achieves very little. (But then the secret service had just sued him for breach of the Official Secrets Act so he wasn't in a very good mood.)

[The main reason that people join the intelligence services is the secrecy] *'... as a means of outgunning people we would otherwise be scared of; of feeling superior to life rather than engaging in it; as a place of escape, attracting not the strong in search of danger but us timid fellows who couldn't cope with reality for one calendar day without the structures of conspiracy to get us by.'*

John Le Carré (David Cornwell) former MI5 and MI6 officer. Quoted in *Literary Agents* by Anthony Masters (1987).

More than four million people now have access to Top Secret material in the United States. The number is also growing in the UK. Is that really secret? The question is not "should there be secrecy in espionage" but "how much and when?" as Richard Moore, head of MI6, discussed recently:

'There is a paradox at play here: to stay secret, we are going to have to become more open.'

On 30 November 2021, the Chief of MI6, Richard Moore gave a speech to the International Institute for Strategic Studies. This was his first public speech since becoming Chief in October 2020. One theme of his speech was that MI6 will need to become more open and that there will have to be a *'sea change'* in MI6's *'culture.'* Only those who have worked in the secret world know what a dramatic statement this was from the head of the Service. To attract the right sort of candidates, to engage (and hopefully win) the PR war, and to better the deceive the country's enemies out and out denial is no longer enough. This was just one of several recent signs that the very nature of secrecy in espionage is changing.

Secret Messages

'They were rolled up into pellets and pressed into a small hole bored in a walking-stick, the hole being then plugged with clay or soap. Or they were put into the bowl of a pipe underneath the tobacco, and could thus be burnt without suspicion if necessary...'.

Lord Baden-Powell in *My Adventures as a Spy* (1915). Of course there are all sorts of electronic devices available these days. Also, messages can be sent instantly over the internet, encrypted and disguised in all sorts of ways e.g. as a message hidden in the data file of a digital photograph – this is known as "steganography." However, one thing that has been learned in recent years – especially by terrorist groups – is that anything transferred electronically is vulnerable to interception. MI6 learned this lesson in 2006 when a rock in a Moscow park was discovered by the Russians to be made of plastic and concealing a communications device. It was being used as a "download station" by MI6 – their agents would walk through the park and transmit their intelligence to be picked up by the hidden download station hidden in the rock. Later, an MI6 officer from the British embassy would come along with a different device in his pocket which would receive the stored intelligence from the base station hidden in the rock. The idea seems perfect as the agent and the intelligence officer never have to meet - they do not even have to be in the park on the same day. But, having discovered the download station hidden in the rock, the Russian security teams watched the location, noted who passed close by and subsequently wiped out almost the entire MI6 station (in the sense that they were sent packing, not that they were shot.) So, some of the old techniques, such as Lord Baden-Powell might have used, are coming back into use because they may be more secure.

The use of some of these techniques can even get you a job as a spy: this is Monty Chidson, a pilot who had become a POW during the First World War:

'During his months in a prisoner of war camp, he had developed a method of communicating with England. He took up carving wood and secreted an intelligence message into each item mailed home. His family had been mystified by the arrival of the carvings, all labelled to fictitious relatives and had consulted the War Office. In due course MI5 had examined the wood-work and discovered the hidden messages. After the war, the head of MI5, Captain Vernon Kell, offered Chidson a job.'

Chidson worked for MI5 in Gibraltar and later went on to work for MI6 eventually becoming head of station at The Hague in the Netherlands. Quoted in *MI6* by Nigel West (1983).

'I did receive a fascinating course of instruction in the use of invisible ink from a large, rather sombre man, who explained to me the relative merits of various solutions ... In the last resort, he told me, bird shit (known in the trade as B.S.) would suffice. It had the advantage of being almost universally obtainable, though he personally had found town birds to be tantalisingly incalculable in providing supplies. For instance, one might put crumbs out on one's window-sill, and the birds would eat them without any B.S. being left behind. A more reliable method, he said, was to take a stroll through a park, and then, on seeing a good deposit of B.S., drop one's handkerchief as though by accident, and, in recovering it, scoop up the B.S.'

Author and former MI6 officer Malcolm Muggeridge in his memoir *Tread Softly For You Tread On My Jokes* (1968).

And you wondered what spies spent their time doing didn't you? Finally one reminiscence which should probably be filed under 'You couldn't make it up...'

'I shall never forget 'C's delight when the Chief Censor, Worthington, came one day with the announcement that one of his staff had found that semen would not respond to iodine vapour [commonly used for developing secret writing], *and told the Old Man that he had to remove the discoverer from the office immediately, as his colleagues were making life intolerable by accusations of masturbation. The Old Man at once asked Colney Hatch* [scientific research department] *to send the female equivalent for testing – and the slogan went round 'Every man his own stylo'. We thought we had solved a great problem. Then our man in Copenhagen, Major Holme, evidently stored it in a bottle, for his letters stank to high heaven, and we had to tell him that a fresh operation was necessary for each letter.'*

Frank Stagg, MI6 officer quoted in *The Quest for C* by Alan Judd. Stagg only served with MI6 for two years (1915-1917) but he had a fascinating career. He initially served in Copenhagen with the above-named Major Holme and the two of them came up with a scheme to smuggle intelligence out of Germany using cows. The cattle were allowed to cross the German/Danish border for grazing and travel to market and the cowherds escorted them were never searched. This scheme worked well for a while, but someone must have talked because the Germans discovered the scheme and suddenly replaced all the Danish cowherds with trustworthy German ones. Stagg also had a wicked sense of humour (as the extract above illustrates): he found that Germany was smuggling tins of sardines from Norway as a way of evading the British naval blockade. Rather than blocking that operation as some might have done, Stagg arranged a way to put croton oil (a strong laxative) into the tins of sardines.

Stagg then began travelling around the Baltic on a variety of missions but the interesting thing is that he travelled using *an American passport*. America was neutral at this time and if this ruse had been discovered there could have been a hell of a scandal. No-one has been able to find if the US government gave permission for this but if they had that would be significant. German spies were travelling on US passports so perhaps MI6 figured that they might as well do the same. Finally, Stagg got into a fight with the Foreign Office when he alleged that certain diplomats were making money by allowing certain goods to beat the German blockade. The Foreign Office investigated, could find no evidence and demanded that he be sacked. Stagg returned to the Navy soon afterwards. But even then his career in espionage was not over. His work in the Baltic for MI6 meant that he established a lifelong relationship with Norway and in the Second World War he worked there for SOE (secret military operations). He also broke all the rules and left a memoir of his time in MI6 (this, as today, was strictly forbidden). Thank goodness he did because this has become a rare and valuable historical resource – although Major Holme may have wished that he had stayed silent.

Sex

'I was forever amazed at how much trouble people got into over sex.'

> Former KGB General Oleg Kalugin in his book *The First Directorate* (1994). Kalugin was referring to how much success the Russian services have enjoyed by using honey traps and Romeo spies.

'On the sexual espionage front, we usually got the better of the CIA and hostile intelligence agencies for the simple reason that we were far more willing to use sex as a weapon and generally had fewer scruples.'

> Oleg Kalugin again. He's right. This is not because Western intelligence services are more moral than others but because because they tend to feel that the situation is akin to blackmail and will only produce resentful and unreliable agents. But then, remember the first rule of espionage: "there can be an exception to any rule."

'By gum, you fellows certainly see life!'

> Percy "Pay" Sykes, the paymaster of MI6 (1915-1945), during one of his rare visits into the field. Sykes was the monocle-wearing paymaster of MI6 for thirty years – an astonishing length of time to continue in such a sensitive post. He was a tiny, bookish man who almost never left the office. On one rare visit to the field, he was taken to a strip club in Prague by Leslie Nicholson, the head of station. He was apparently astonished by the sexual abilities demonstrated on stage by a pair of female Hungarian twins. A bar room brawl broke out and he said the words above as he and Nicholson hid under a table as the beer glasses smashed all around them. By gum indeed! Quoted in *SIX* by Michael Smith (2010).

SIS (MI6)

'The documents clearly show that MI5's and GCHQ's policies on snooping on lawyers have major loopholes. And MI6's policies are so hopeless that they appear to have been jotted down on the back of a beermat.'

Cori Crider from the human rights charity *Reprieve* speaking after it was revealed during the Investigatory Powers Tribunal hearing into the Abdul Belhaj rendition that all three British intelligence agencies were gathering and using legally privileged material. Quoted in *The Guardian* newspaper 7 November 2014. The reason that this quote is significant is because it is true that when officers work in the secret world it is very easy for a culture to emerge that the rules don't apply to you. The history of espionage is littered with such examples.

'Semper Occultis' (lit. 'Always secret'.)

Motto on the MI6 coat of arms. In view of the poor record of the Service and its failure to anticipate any of the major conflicts of the past 100 years, some have suggested it should be translated as: *"Always in the dark".*

'Governments come and go, but we go on for ever.'

MI6 officer to Philip Knightley quoted in his book *The Second Oldest Profession* (1986). This is a key point: most ministers only have five years or less to get to grips with the intelligence service for which they are responsible. Most of them will have never worked with the secret services before. Meanwhile, the services have seen ministers come and go and know how to play the game to their advantage. There is an imbalance of power.

'...part-time stockbrokers and retired Indian policemen, the agreeable epicureans from the bars of Whites and Boodles, the jolly, conventional ex-naval officers and the robust adventurers from the bucket-shop'.

Hugh Trevor Roper, historian and MI6 officer describing the quality of staff at the end of the Second World War. Quoted in *MI6* by Stephen Dorril (2000). He was a figure firmly on the right of the political spectrum so his criticisms are significant – you would expect him to be happy that MI6 officers were "the right sort."

'Went to the office and remained there all day, but saw no-one, nor was there anything to do.'

The entry from the personal diary of Mansfield Cumming for 7 October 1909. This was his first day as co-Chief of the newly formed Secret Service Bureau (SSB). His diary for the end of the month said much the same thing including the plaintive note *"Have only had one letter – and that included my pay."* This may sound surprising but it was never the intention that there should be a large, powerful and independent intelligence service – the Army and the Navy already had their own extensive intelligence organisations. The formation of the SSB was only ever really a "funding grab" by the Army and it was assumed that Cumming, who had no experience of espionage, would pack his bags in a couple of months. He had even kept his previous job in a part-time capacity so that he could go back to it. But from Cumming's lonely existence in an empty back room in Victoria Street, a series of historical accidents produced one of the most powerful intelligence agencies in the world. Sometimes history is strange.

'Ivory from the neck up!'

Description of the typical MI6 officer by 'Klop' Ustinov, father of the actor Peter Ustinov who was a British agent against Nazi Germany in the 1930s. He refused to deal with MI6 if he could avoid it and instead worked for a private Foreign Office network. He was sent to Lisbon in 1944 by MI6 to try to make contact with anti-Hitler elements that he had known in the past. It was a fairly successful mission although he still didn't like them. Quoted in *The Perfect English Spy* by Tom Bower (1995).

'...second rate men with second rate minds.'

Author and former MI6 officer Malcolm Muggeridge describing the senior management of MI6 as he knew them. Quoted in *Colonel Z* by Anthony Read and David Fisher (1985). Similar criticisms have been levelled at the more recent senior managers, most of whom appear to have been former public schoolboys whose university degrees suggest that they were not destined for greatness. It is an image that dogs the Service and which the Service is working hard to change in order to attract a wider range of recruits.

'The whole thing is a Pantomime.'

General Henry Wilson, Director of Military operations for the Army commenting on events surrounding the capture of Captain Bertrand Stewart in 1910 in a toilet on one of the very first MI6 operations. This is a little unfair – the double agent, Frederick Verrue, who betrayed Stewart had been recruited by the Army! Quoted in *The Official History of MI6* by Professor Keith Jeffery (2010).

'Qui custodiet ipsos custodes?' (lit. Who watches the Watchmen?")

Ancient Roman proverb. And the truth is that no-one can really know what happens in the British intelligence services as proper oversight simply does not exist. This has benefits such as allowing maximum security but also maximum incompetence.

'When I looked coolly at the world in which I found myself, I sometimes thought that, if this was our intelligence system, we were doomed to defeat. Sometimes I encouraged myself by saying that such an organisation could not possibly survive, unchanged, the strain of war: it would have to be reformed. In fact I was wrong both times. We won the war, and MI6, at the end of it, remained totally unreformed'.

Former MI6 officer Professor Hugh Trevor-Roper (Lord Dacre) quoted in *The Secret Servant* by Anthony Cave Brown (1988).

'...he had joined expecting Jesuitical devotion and had been mildly disappointed when Gerry told them that most people in Head Office clocked off at six.'

Alan Judd, former "Foreign Service officer" describing the disappointment of a new recruit to MI6 in his thriller *Legacy (*2001).

'MI6's interwar period was one of penny-pinching, muddling through, being ignored and bypassed. It grew in upon itself, its officers running it like a gentleman's club, contemptuous of the outside world...'

Philip Knightly in *The Second Oldest Profession* (1988). Some would say that it is little changed today...

'I realised how glad I was not to be surrounded by their crass inefficiency any longer. It reminded me of how often agents had been sent into the field wearing English clothes with the labels still attached, and the agent in Algiers whom they were sending to Italy with an ID photograph showing him wearing a specifically English shirt. No wonder the Americans had lost faith; so had I.'

Desmond Bristow, former MI6 officer, in his memoir *A Game of Moles* (2003).

'The upper echelons of MI6 at that time [World War Two] *consisted largely of service personnel most of whom had been thankfully unloaded, and miscellaneous eccentrics who could not have hoped to earn much of a living in competitive circumstances.'*

Author and former MI6 officer Malcolm Muggeridge in *Tread Softly For You Tread On My Jokes* (1968).

'It seemed that somewhere, lurking in deep shadow, there must be another service, really secret and really powerful.'

Kim Philby talking about how ineffective MI6 was. Quoted in *Kim Philby: The Unknown Story* by Ian ("Tim") Milne (2014).

As Milne recalls: *"I think that many on joining SIS had something of the same feeling."*

Quoted in *Kim Philby: The Unknown Story* by Ian ("Tim") Milne (2014).

And so did other officers:

'My first impression of this strange and diverse collection of human beings was that they must constitute a sort of false front or façade. When I had been fully vetted and tried out, I thought, I should be taken off to some other place and there make contact with the real Secret Service. It took me quite a time to realise that this was not so at all, and that what I had assumed to be a false front was, in fact, the genuine article.'

Author and former MI6 officer Malcolm Muggeridge in *Tread Softly For You Tread On My Jokes* (1968).

And just in case you thought Muggeridge was an isolated and embittered example:

'For a while you wondered whether the fools were pretending to be fools, as some kind of deception; or whether there was a real efficient secret service somewhere else. Later, in my fiction, I invented one. But alas the reality was mediocrity'.

David Cornwell (John Le Carré), novelist and former MI6 officer quoted in *UK Eyes Alpha* by Mark Urban (1987).

'You can't imagine how disgusting our world has become.'

Sir David Spedding, Chief of MI6 (1994-1999) to John Le Carré just before his retirement and quoted by him in *The Guardian* newspaper 12 October 2008.

Following a number of scandals such as involvement in rendition, MI6 engagement with two oversight investigations was ... *"wholly inadequate and extremely unsatisfactory ... they demonstrated a troubling tendency to be defensive and unhelpful, it provided inaccurate and incomplete information and generally sought to fence with and close down lines of enquiry rather than engage constructively"*.

Sir Mark Waller, Intelligence Services Commissioner, quoted in *The Guardian* newspaper16 September 2016.

'Their system was to include every rumour that was going and every tall story retailed to them without further examination. Eventually some story would turn out to be true, but at the time no-one could possibly weed out the grains of truth from the vast mass of falsehood!'

Captain Sigismund Payne Best of British Military Intelligence and MI6 quoted in *Armour Against Fate* by Michael Occleshaw (1989). Payne Best was another of those fascinating characters scattered throughout the history of espionage. In the First World War he ran one of his networks by supplying his agents with illegal drugs. Then he had a nervous breakdown after two of his agents were killed trying to get across the border from Germany. He was then recalled to the UK when it was discovered that he was having an affair with the wife of a leading figure in the Belgian Resistance. He left intelligence work, married a famous Dutch painter and became a notorious figure, frequently appearing in the Dutch press. He was of mixed Anglo-Indian heritage and described as "more English than the English". And for those who think that successful spies must be "grey men," Payne Best's life conveys an espionage truth: that sometimes being in the spotlight is the best way to hide. He wore spats and a monocle, he and his wife held riotous parties and were known for their ostentatious lifestyle. Thanks to a personal friendship with Claude Dansey, deputy chief of MI6, he was part of MI6's ultra secret "Z Organisation" in the late 1930s but was captured at the start of the Second World War and "sang like a bird" during his interrogation (he confessed in his memoir that he knew that he would not be able to endure pain). He ended up bankrupt and later tried to sue MI6. He claimed afterwards that he was given a briefcase full of cash by MI6 during a meeting in a restaurant to bring an end to the matter but then he was a notorious embellisher. For instance, many of the agents for whom he claimed lavish expenses were later found never to have existed.

Snowden (Edward)

'My sole motivation is to inform the public as to that which is done in their name and that which is done against them.'

Snowden quoted in *Spies, Spin and the Fourth Estate* by Paul Lashmar (2020).

'Snowden has done incalculable damage.'

Anonymous UK senior intelligence official commenting on the rumour that the Chinese and Russians had finally broken the encryption on Snowden's files and confirming that agents had been moved as a result. Quoted in *The Sunday Times* newspaper 14 June 2015.

This was probably an attempt to smear Snowden but the truth had already been told by one of those in a position to know:

164

'I sense that most of those interested in the activities of the NSA and GCHQ have not been told very much they didn't already know or could have inferred.'

Former MI6 Deputy Director Nigel Inkster quoted in *The Guardian* newspaper 13 September 2013.

'I do not want to live in a world where everything I do and say is recorded.'

Snowden.

SOE (British secret military operations during the Second World War)

'They all just wanted us scrubbed off the face of the earth.'

SOE veteran describing MI6's attitude in the scramble for survival by the intelligence services at the end of World War Two. MI6's performance during the war had been so weak that it seemed as if SOE, Churchill's organisation which had enjoyed an outstanding record during the war, would replace it. In the end, politicians who were old Etonian friends of the MI6 chief Stewart Menzies ensured that MI6 survived and SOE was scrapped. Quoted in *A Life in Secrets* by Vera Atkins (2006).

Spy fiction

'The lies that have been distributed are so many and so persistent that arguably fiction is the only way to tell the truth.

John Le Carré quoted in *The Guardian* newspaper 24 October 2015.

State Surveillance

'If you have nothing to hide, you have nothing to fear.'

Attributed to Joseph Goebbels, the Nazi minister for Propaganda.

Surveillance

'He alone is an acute observer who can observe minutely without being observed.'

Attributed to Johann Kaspar Lavater.

'Nondigital surveillance is weaponised boredom.'

William Gibson in his novel *Agency* (2020). As far as I know, Gibson has no experience of espionage. However, this quote accurately sums up what it is like to carry out "old-style" surveillance. No-one who has not been in an observation post for days on end can imagine just how life destroying that boredom can be. The ability today to review remotely-recorded footage using the fast-forward button has been a wonderful development.

Swordsticks

'I drew back the rapier-like blade with a jerk and with a forward lunge ran it through the gentleman's side. He gave a scream and collapsed to the pavement. His comrade, seeing that I had put up a fight and was not unarmed, took to his heels while I withdrew and fumbled for my revolver. Meanwhile the man I had run through staggered off, leaving my scabbard on the pavement. The swordstick thereafter had a value in my eyes.'

MI6 officer George Hill recounting how he defeated German Secret Service officers who ambushed him in Russia in 1919. But Hill was a notorious embellisher and may even have been a double agent himself. Quoted in his memoir *Go Spy the Land* (1932). The author Compton Mackenzie claimed that Mansfield Cumming, the very first chief of MI6, carried a swordstick, although he never had occasion to use it and later gave it to Mackenzie as a souvenir.

T

Taliban

'You can have either a carpet of gold or a carpet of bombs.'

In Berlin in July 2001, there was a final regional security conference about Afghanistan. This is what the CIA told the Taliban. Sometimes you have to be direct.

Technology

'We cannot hope to replicate the global tech industry, so we must tap into it.'

On 30 November 2021, the Chief of MI6, Richard Moore gave a speech to the International Institute for Strategic Studies. This was his first public speech since becoming Chief in October 2020. we have already noted one of the themes of his speech (see under "Secret.") But another theme, almost as ground-breaking, concerned technology. The spy wars of the future will still be fought between human assets but there will be a new dimension; technology. Already, computerised communication has transformed the way that intelligence is transmitted - and stolen. Soon other innovations such as facial recognition technology and artificial intelligence will further transform the playing field. MI6, as with other intelligence agencies, must stay ahead of the game. It does not have the money and resources to do this – it is beyond even a 'Q' Department (known in MI6 as 'TOS – Technical Operations Section). As Moore said in his speech: *"An intelligence service needs to be at the vanguard of what is technologically possible."* MI6 must now *"join forces with the private sector"* in order to succeed in the new world of *"AI, quantum computing and synthetic biology"*. He described this technological change as *"a white hot focus for MI6."* The "Great Game" (as Rudyard Kipling described it) is changing.

Terrorism

'We compound the problem of terrorism if we use it to erode the freedom of us all.'

Eliza Manningham-Buller, former Director General of MI5 quoted in *The Guardian* newspaper 5 September 2012.

Thriller writers

'Thriller writers seem to settle in secret service as easily as the mentally unstable become psychiatrists, or the impotent become pornographers.'

Author and MI6 officer Malcolm Muggeridge quoted in *Literary Agents* by Anthony Masters (1987). As well as authors such as John Le Carré, Graham Greene, Compton Mackenzie and W. Somerset Laugham there are a host of others who you may well never heard of, such as Ted Allebeury, John Bingham, Phil Atkey, Francis Warwick, Peter Ward to name but a few. It is a very long list.

Timeliness

'The good effect of intelligence may be lost if it is not speedily transmitted.'

George Washington to his chief of intelligence during the War of Independence, Major Benjamin Tallmadge.

Torture

'Without torture I know we shall not prevail.'

Attributed to Sir Francis Walsingham, one of Queen Elizabeth I's spymasters. His use of torture is one of the reasons that he is not England's greatest ever spymaster.

'We are going to bring back a hell of a lot worse than waterboarding.'

US President Donald Trump speaking during his Presidential election campaign. However, once in office he claimed that Defence Secretary, Jim Mattis, convinced him that torture was ineffective. But the CIA's use of torture keeps the country on a slippery path. Quoted in *The Guardian* newspaper 17 March 2018.

'The effect is... to destroy tenderness or excite revenge ... they have sense enough to feel that they are the objects aimed at; and they inflict in their turn the examples of terror they have been instructed to practise.'

Thomas Paine, citing the torture and execution of Robert-François Damiens in *The Rights of Man* (1791). Seeing as America has used torture, the evidence is that many of America's allies feel justified in using it too.

'Torture demonstrates weakness, not strength. It does not show understanding, power or magnanimity. It is not leadership. It is a reaction of government officials overwhelmed by fear who succumb to conduct unworthy of them...'

Dr Burton J. Lee III, George Bush's personal physician who served in the US Army Medical Corps. Quoted in *'The Truth with Jokes'* by Al Franken (2005).

'Torture sometimes works.'

Eliza Manningham-Buller, then Director General of MI5 to a House of Lords Committee in October 2005. The committee was considering whether to allow evidence gained by torture. But consider this:

'I am confident that I know the answer to the question of whether torture has made the world a safer place. It hasn't.'

Eliza Manningham-Buller (see above) quoted in the *The Guardian* newspaper 5 September 2012.

'...we also have to work...sort of on the dark side...A lot of what needs to be done here will have to be done quietly, without any discussion.'

US Vice-President Dick Cheney. Quoted in *Time* magazine 12 December 2005.

'You have to torture. Without torture how can you fight terrorism?'

Senior Chechen security source to Vladislav Sadykov, the lawyer who heads the Joint Mobile Group investigating human rights abuses in the country including torture, kidnappings and murder of those who oppose the Russian backed rule of Ramzan Kadyrov. They had learned from the American example. Quoted in *The New York Times* newspaper 2 October 2011.

Torture victims *"...speak upon the rack. Where men enforced do speak anything."*

William Shakespeare, *The Merchant of Venice,* Act Three, Scene Two.

"I don't know MI6 as well as I know MI5, but I would be very surprised if there have not been agents for MI6 in the room while torturing was going on. I would be very, very surprised."

Playwright Sir David Hare who was invited in by MI5 in 2000 as part of a programme of presentations and who claims very close but secret contacts with serving MI5 officers. Quoted in *The Guardian* newspaper 22 February 2014.

'We tortured some folks. We did some things that were contrary to our values.'

President Barack Obama finally admits the truth after a Senate report on CIA interrogation techniques concluded that torture was used despite years of US government denials. The Senate also concluded that none of the information gained by torture was useful and often it was false, uttered simply to make the torture stop. One suspect was waterboarded more than 150 times. You do not do that if you want intelligence. If someone isn't telling you what you want to know after two or three times then the chances are that you are on the wrong track. The only reason to waterboard someone that many times is out of a sense of sadism or a desire for revenge. It was the CIA's darkest hour. Quoted in *The Observer* newspaper 3 August 2014.

"You can always make someone talk ... the problem is what they say."

Former torturer for Saddam Hussein when interviewed in prison in 2003. Quoted in *The Guardian* newspaper 27 January 2017.

'When they are in pain, people will say anything to get the pain to stop. Most of the time, they will lie, make up anything to make you stop hurting them. That means the information you are getting is useless."

Ali Soufan, former FBI officer who interrogated some al-Qaida suspects (without torture) in CIA secret prisons in the wake of the 9/11 attacks. He was horrified by what was being done by people who clearly had no training in proper interrogation.

'In interrogation ... the use of force is a poor technique as it .. can induce the source to say whatever he thinks the interrogator wants to hear.'

US Army Training Manual from the Second World War. Interestingly, the techniques used by the CIA in their secret torture prisons after 9/11 were from material issued by the Gestapo.

'I'm just a guy who got asked to do something for his country by people at the highest level of government and I did the best that I could."

James Mitchell, one of the psychologists who helped to design the CIA torture programme used after 9/11. This is remarkably similar to the Nuremburg defence used by Nazi torturers in the Second World War. He was never prosecuted. Quoted in *The Guardian* newspaper 19 April 2014.

' ... inhuman brutality that stands in stark contrast to our values as a nation and a stain on our history that must never again be allowed to happen.'

US Senator Dianne Feinstein, chair of the Senate Intelligence Committee talking about the programme that Mitchell devised. Quoted in *The Guardian* newspaper 19 April 2014.

'Is any of this stuff legal?

CIA Director to CIA Counsel John Rizzo (1976-2009) when being told what sort of torture methods the interrogation team in Thailand proposed to use. (From an undated interview with John Rizzo).

'We were at war and bad things happen in wars.'

CIA Deputy Director McLoughlin trying to justify the CIA's torture programme.

This is not about who <u>they</u> are, this is about who <u>we</u> are.'

Senator John McCain speaking in 2004 as details of the US torture programme began to leak. McCain was what one of the few Americans who knew what he was talking about. He had been captured by the Vietnamese during the Vietnam War and was tortured repeatedly over a number of years.

'It's all torture.'

Senator John McCain's only words as he walked out of a top secret CIA briefing at which they tried to convince him that waterboarding, drowning in freezing water, electric shocks to genitals, sleep deprivation, confinement for days in the tiniest of spaces, deafeningly loud music played directly into the ears for hours on end and all the other methods that the CIA were using were not torture and that he shouldn't interfere. McCain, a rare man of honour, was not having any of it.

'Persuant to HQ instructions, all the videotapes have been destroyed.'

Cable from the CIA black site in Thailand (Codename: SITE GREEN) where the first prisoners had been tortured. The US government was trying to make up its mind what to do about the tapes as destroying them would be a criminal act. The head of the CIA station who carried out these orders, Gina Haspel, later became head of the CIA almost as if it was a deliberate sign that the Agency didn't care what its critics thought.

'After 25 years with the CIA, I didn't think too much could flabbergast me, but reading that cable did.'

CIA Legal Counsel James Rizzo describing his reaction to seeing the cable that ordered all recordings of CIA torture sessions to be destroyed. He was not consulted before the cable was sent as the CIA knew that he would say no.

The Enhanced Interrogation Programme was *"brutal"*, *"mismanaged"* and *"not an effective means of obtaining intelligence"*.

Conclusion of the Panetta Review, the CIA's secret internal review of the torture programme. The CIA tried to keep this review from the wider public because of its damning conclusions.

Tradecraft

'Letting the cover fall, Mary steps back and again surveys the arrangement on the desk. As she does so his bit of tradecraft becomes apparent to her. Each of the three books, lying seemingly haphazardly across the papers, is aligned to the point of the scissors at their centre. Going to the kitchen Mary grabs the tablecloth, comes back and lays it on the floor beside the desk, then measures the distances between each object on the desk with her gloved hand. As gently as if she is lifting bandages from a wound she lays them in the same pattern on the tablecloth. The papers on the desk now lie free for her inspection.'

A *Perfect Spy* by John Le Carré (1986).

'Like a glove!'

MI6 officer Compton Mackenzie upon meeting one of his new staff and comparing the two halves of the security paper that they had been given. In World War One, because of the great distances and difficulties in communication, new agents carried a torn sheet of paper with them either a letter or page from a book. The other half of the page was sent by post or diplomatic bag (depending what was available) to the officer at the other end. When the two first met they would compare the two pieces of paper to ensure that they matched. From his novel *Extremes Meet* (1928).

Training

'Day after day, week after week, I was grounded in subjects that were essential to efficient Secret Service work. Broadly, they could be divided into four classes: topography, trigonometry, naval construction and drawing.'

Dr Karl Graves, German spy in the period before World War One in *Secrets of the German War Office* (1915). For more about Graves see under "Agent Selection".

Treason

'I don't know why you are telling me all this. Only people with foreign names commit treason!'

Reaction of Stewart Menzies, Chief of MI6, when confronted by an officer who had flirted with Communism whilst at Cambridge. Unfortunately Menzies' views on treason were dead wrong - he was 'C' whilst Kim Philby and the rest of the Cambridge Spy Ring wreaked havoc amidst Western intelligence agencies. Menzies received much of the blame. Quoted in *The Secret Servant* by Anthony Cave Brown (1988).

'Espionage for England is a commendable deed but espionage for Germany is a crime; an English spy is a man of honour, a German spy is a felon.'

Frank Greite, an American sailor who spied for Germany during World War One and who was arrested and imprisoned. He was petitioning for early release from his sentence. Quoted in *The Second Oldest Profession* by Phillip Knightley (1987).

'...who among us has not committed treason to something or someone more important than a country?'

The novelist and MI6 officer Graham Greene writing in the foreword to Kim Philby's memoirs.

'So this is how it ends.'

First words of the FBI traitor Robert Hanssen as he was finally arrested, having been a traitor for ten years.

'What inward, angry, over-controlled little Bettaneys will be getting on their secret bikes then?'

The novelist and former MI6 officer David Cornwell (John Le Carré) when asked whether he thought the collapse of the Soviet Union meant that the age of traitors like Kim Philby and Michael Bettaney was over. (Bettaney was an MI5 officer who tried to work for the Russians but was caught). Cornwell's point was that the new generation had plenty of other things to be unhappy about. Quoted in *Literary Agents* by Anthony Masters (1987).

'The whole affair was extremely painful to me and I only embarked on it because I felt this was a contribution to the safety of mankind'

The British nuclear spy Alan Nunn May confessing to his treachery. He was caught and was very lucky that he was British. He was only sentenced to ten years imprisonment in 1946. Ethel and Julius Rosenberg, who were American nuclear spies were sentenced to death in the electric chair. After serving just over six years of his sentence, he lived out the rest of his life quietly, continuing to work as a scientist in the UK and in Africa. He died in 2003.

'NO! Nobody tortured me! Nobody blackmailed me! I myself approached the Soviets and offered my services to them of my own accord!'

The moment when MI6 traitor George Blake suddenly confessed to his crime during his interrogation, just when he seemed that he might get away with it. He had joined MI6 soon after World War Two having worked for the Dutch Resistance. In 1950, he was captured during the Korean War while he was working under cover as a diplomat. He was held under brutal conditions in a prison camp. It was at about this time that he appears to have decided to work for Communism. He worked as a double agent for almost ten years and was finally given away by a Russian defector in 1961. He made the statement above when reacting to the suggestion by his interrogators that brain-washing in the camp had caused him to make his betrayal decision. Such was Blake's ego that he could not resist blurting out the truth. He was sentenced to 42 years imprisonment on the grounds that many of the agents he betrayed had been executed. This was later found to be untrue – nowhere near that number had been killed. It did not matter: in 1966 he escaped from prison with the help of two peace activists and an IRA supporter. He lived out the rest of his life in Russia and died in 2020, the last survivor of the great age of British traitors.

'How much time do you think I'll get?'

One of the first questions asked by USAF airman Bruce Ott when he was arrested by the FBI in January 1986. He had been trying to sell information on the SR-71 Blackbird spyplane to the Russians. The answer to his question was 25 years. Quoted in *The Literary Spy* by Charles E. Lathrop (2004).

'I wasn't enjoying myself.'

US Army intelligence officer Michael Peri who was arrested in 1989 for trying to sell classified material to the East German secret service. He also got 25 years in prison. He probably didn't enjoy that either.

'I'm glad it's over.'

NSA (US communications intelligence) analyst David Sheldon Boone when he was arrested in October 1998 for spying for Russia. He was sentenced to 25 years. It may seem odd but this reaction is fairly typical when someone is caught. I have worked in both espionage and law enforcement and when suspects are finally caught it almost seems to come as a relief to them – they have been living in fear of discovery for so long and now there is nothing to fear any more (although there are a large number of new problems to worry about.)

'In general, I do not agree with spying against one's country.'

Melita Norwood, the "grandma spy". Well, that was nice of her. See under "Agent Selection" for more about Norwood.

'They go to church every Sunday … if that means anything.'

Neighbour of the Hanssen's speaking to a representative of the Associated Press on 20 February 2001. FBI agent Hanssen had been spying for Russia for fifteen years. Which goes to show that, like spies, you will never know what a traitor looks like.

And finally:

'Though those that are betrayed
Do feel the treason sharply, yet the traitor

Stands in worse case of woe.'

William Shakespeare, *Cymbeline* Act Three, Scene Four. I could have picked any number of quotes about treason from the works of Shakespeare but I have met several "traitors", both theirs and ours, and this is the quote that seems right to me. They always seem to have a great sadness about them.

Trust

'In this Service, always be 100 per cent sure, and if possible 150 per cent, before you trust anybody.'

Claude Dansey, Deputy Chief of MI6 1939-1945, from his biography Colonel Z *by Anthony Read and David Fisher (1985).*

'We cannot really trust any foreign country.'

Malcolm Woollcombe, Head of MI6's political section who wrote the pro-appeasement paper *"What is to be Done?"* in September 1938. The paper recommended giving in to German demands including handing over the Sudetenland and creating a token nation where the Jews could be sent on the grounds that Hitler was too strong to oppose. MI6 intelligence on Germany in the 1930s is widely agreed to have been a disaster. German strength was always overestimated or underestimated and left the British government blind as to Hitler's true intentions.

'The very low esteem in which we hold spies should always make us distrustful of them.'

Colonel George Furse in the first British army handbook on espionage. For more about Furse see under "Agent Selection".

Truth

'Truth is like poetry. Most people fucking hate poetry.'

From the movie *The Big Short* (2015) written by Adam McKay and Charles Randolph.

'Hell is truth seen too late.'

Attributed to the philosopher Thomas Hobbes.

'It is not necessary to bury the truth. It is sufficient merely to delay it until nobody cares.'

Attributed to Napoleon.

'In wartime Truth is so precious she is best protected by a bodyguard of lies.'

Sir Winston Churchill.

However:

'... but it is a nice question how far this weapon should actually be used in times of peace.'

Sir Winston Churchill again. He knew from his wartime experience how valuable deception by the intelligence services could be. But in 1952 when the *Sunday Express* newspaper co-operated in a deception operation about Operation Hurricane, one of the first British atom bomb tests, even he could see the dangers of allowing the intelligence services to continue to use this method unmonitored. Quoted in *Spies, Spin and the Fourth Estate* by Paul Lashmar (2020).

'I am indeed sorry that you are compelled to make so unfavourable a report, but the knowledge of the whole truth is one element of security.'

Sir Robert Peel to Lyon Playfair. Quoted in *Most Secret War* by British intelligence services scientific advisor R.V. Jones (1978).

U

ULTRA (codename for the intelligence reports produced by breaking German codes during World War Two).

'It has simplified my task as a commander enormously.'

> Dwight D. Eisenhower quoted in *For the President's Eyes Only* by Christopher Andrew (1995).

'Cracked cipher material was, indeed, as things turned out, the staple product of MI6 and provided the basis for most of its effective activities.'

> Author and former MI6 officer Malcolm Muggeridge in his book *Chronicles of Wasted Time: The Infernal Grove* (1973). To hide the fact the German codes had been broken, ULTRA reports were issued by MI6 as if they had been produced by human agents working behind the Lines. This led many to assume that MI6 had enjoyed a brilliantly successful war. In fact, the German secret service had gutted MI6 at the very start of the war in a kidnapping known as "the Venlo Incident." The Germans had lured two MI6 officers, Sigismund Payne Best and Richard Stevens, to a meeting at a cafe just across the German border in Holland. The officers thought they were meeting German dissidents. Instead, the Germans raced across the border, captured the officers at gunpoint and took them back to Germany. Unknowingly, they had hit the jackpot, for while Stevens was a regular MI6 officer, Payne Best worked for MI6's ultra-secret "Z Organisation." Both men talked under interrogation and gave away valuable information about personnel and operating procedures. This undermined MI6 for the rest of the war. Meanwhile, Special Operations Executive (SOE) was a new covert unit formed by Churchill at the start of the war and their operations far outstripped anything MI6 was able to achieve. However, thanks to political influence and because so many people were unaware of the true origin of the ULTRA material, at the end of the war, MI6 survived and SOE was scrapped.

Understatement

'The Burgess and Maclean affair is certainly the gravest scandal to hit my old department, the Foreign Office. It may be that our security services haven't always quite made the grade.'

> Lord Vansittart, an old intelligence hand and Secretary at the Foreign Office 1930-1938 speaking in London on 20 January 1953. He trusted MI6 so little that he ran his own intelligence sources. Quoted in *The Great Spy Scandal* by Donald Seaman and John Mather (1955).

Unnecessary secrecy

'If you wanted to see one ticked-off Air Force Major General, you should have seen this guy!'

> Leo Geary, a USAF General who worked closely with the CIA, relating how USAF secrecy in the 1950s was so tight that the General in charge of USAF research and development was

not told about the development of the new U-2 spy planes until they were already in the air and operational. Quoted in *The Literary Spy* by Charles E. Lathrop (2004).

But how times change...

'We recognise that in a changing world we have to change too. We have a responsibility to talk about our work and explain it.'

Andrew Parker, Director-General MI5, in an interview with *The Guardian* newspaper on 1 November 2016.

'[In the 1970s] the CIA, it seemed to me, was in very real danger of ultimately being crippled as an effective weapon in the defense of the nation's security if not in fact threatened with being destroyed outright – unless something was done to reverse this trend. And that something, in my view, was to lift as much as possible that thick cloak of secrecy that had traditionally veiled the Agency and its operations from scrutiny.'

Former Director of the CIA William Colby in his book *Honourable Men* (1978). A long quote but worth quoting in full I think. Colby was no shrinking liberal violet, he was a spy of the old school. But if even *he* thought that the lid needed to be lifted so that the intelligence services could function effectively then it is a view worth weighing carefully.

'The American people have to trust us and in order to trust us they have to know about us.'

General Michael Hayden, former head of both the CIA and NSA. Another man who is no "weak-knee'd liberal." Quoted in *Spies, Lies and Algorithms* by Amy B. Zegart (2022). He even repeated this thought more graphically:

'My community has to show a lot more leg or we won't get to do any of what we want to do because the public support is so withdrawn that politically nobody is going to give us the authorisation.'

General Michael Hayden, speaking to the Henry Jackson Society and quoted by *The Guardian* newspaper 1 October 2013.

'Security, as applied retrospectively to intelligence matters, is a superb device for fitting locks onto empty stables.'

Author and former MI6 officer Malcolm Muggeridge from the Introduction to *British Agent* by John Whitwell (1966). Whitwell was the pen-name of MI6 officer Leslie Nicholson and his book was banned for many years.

'Security is like armour. You can pile on the armour until the man inside is absolutely safe and absolutely useless.'

Sherman Kent writing in *Strategic Intelligence* (1949).

'When we try to make a mystery out of everything related to intelligence, we tend to dissipate our effort to maintain the security of operations where secrecy is essential to success.'

Former Director of the CIA Allen Dulles in his book *The Craft of Intelligence* (1963).

'Not all official secrets need protection.'

Hugh Trevor-Roper, former MI6 officer.

'The ease with which public servants protected by the Official Secrets Act can now hide the proofs of their incompetence is completely destructive of true democracy, and until bills of impeachment have become once more a feature of our political life true democracy will not revive.'

Author and former MI6 officer Compton MacKenzie in his memoir *Greek Memories* (1939). Mackenzie was prosecuted under the Official Secrets Act for writing the book. He retaliated by writing the brilliant comic novel about espionage *Water On The Brain* – which possibly proves that suppression is not always the best course of action when secrecy is threatened.

'"Water on the Brain" was "must" reading in the wartime OSS. It is actually a useful casebook of do's and don'ts in intelligence work.'

Former CIA Director Allen Dulles in his book *Great Spy Stories from Fiction* (1969).

'The taboos remain so strong that even the tenuous justification for them is usually considered too secret for public discussion".

Professor Christopher Andrew, sometimes regarded as the unofficial historian of the British intelligence services, in *Secret Service* (1985).

'It is true that field-grade officers in intelligence are never officially terminated and are only placed on leave. But that is so that they may be kept under thumb. Occasionally though, one of us does manage to bend back a finger.'

Dusko Popov, MI6's most successful double agent of World War Two who had to fight for years for the right to publish his story, even after the official papers had been released. From his memoir *Spy, Counter Spy* (1974). He made it in the end.

'... the Official Secrets Act is a convenient weapon for tyranny.'

Sir Compton MacKenzie in *Greek Memories* (1939). It is hardly surprising that he was bitter as he was the first officer to be sued under its rather draconian terms.

'Secrecy is as essential to intelligence as vestments to a Mass, or darkness to a spiritualist séance, and must at all costs be maintained, quite irrespective of whether or not it serves any purpose.'

Author and former MI6 officer Malcolm Muggeridge in *Chronicles of Wasted Time* (1973).

'In many respects, the British Secret Service is still the most passionately secretive in the world. This ultra-secrecy is a symptom of the hypocrisy which periodically besots the British race, the pretence that one must not admit the existence of a Secret Service because its activities hardly conform with polite behaviour.'

Richard Deacon in *'C': A biography of Sir Maurice Oldfield* (1985).

'Not so much hush-hush, as what does it all mean?'

> Sir Maurice Oldfield himself commenting on the secrecy surrounding MI6 after his appointment as 'C'. Quoted in *'C': A biography of Sir Maurice Oldfield* by Richard Deacon (1985).

'Never was so much time wasted by so many people keeping non-secrets secret from their own people.'

> Former senior MI6 officer Desmond Bristow (1940-1954) from his memoir *A Game of Moles* (1993).

'The efficiency of our security services can only be reduced by publicity given to their organisation, personnel and techniques.'

> This was Point Three of a statement issued by Kim Philby, MI6 officer and traitor, and handed to the Press during his infamous briefing at his mother's flat after he had been accused of being "the Third Man". Of course, he was worried that if the Press were allowed investigate then he would be spotted. Traitors do not wish the efficiency of the intelligence services to be scrutinised because it allows inefficiencies to continue and makes the traitor's work easier. Quoted in *The Great Spy Scandal* by Donald Seaman and John Mather (1955).

'Certainly one of the many besetting sins of intelligence officers is the overuse of secrecy, ostensibly in the name of security, but actually to preserve some private empire.'

> Quoted in *Kim Philby: The Unknown Story* by former senior MI6 officer Ian ("Tim") Milne (2014).

'Secrecy keeps mistakes secret. Secrecy is a disease. It causes a hardening of the arteries of the mind.'

> Senator Daniel Moynihan of New York introducing a bill entitled *The Abolition of the Central Intelligence Agency Act* on 4 January 1995. Aldrich Ames had been convicted the year before and Moynihan argued that the CIA had largely failed. It was not the type of organisation that its creators had intended. It had not predicted the end of the Soviet Union or done much to achieve that. It could not even spot Ames in its ranks despite all the clues. Moynihan said the CIA should be disbanded and the State Department could do the work more effectively. He pointed out that the State Department already had the Bureau of Intelligence and Research which has been described as a mini secret service. He also pointed out the many other intelligence agencies which have espionage capabilities including the Treasury and even the Department of Energy. Moynihan was to a certain extent being disingenuous and trying to make a point about inefficiency as there was never a realistic chance that the bill would succeed. Quoted in *The New Yorker* magazine 10 October 2022.

V

Value

'When Waterlow thought of the risk of life that the collection of such information meant, of the labour involved in extracting it from the lucky agents who managed to get back, of the trouble and expense of telegraphing a digest of it to headquarters, of its probable lack of utility and almost certain lack of use, he was inclined to think that blowing bubbles would mean a more conspicuous but by no means necessarily a more actual waste of time and energy and ingenuity.'

Author and MI6 officer Compton Mackenzie in *Extremes Meet* (1928). Mackenzie was running agents into Bulgaria and Turkey during the First World War. His agents were under no illusion about the fate they would face if caught. It was in London, upon seeing the casual way that his intelligence was handled, that Mackenzie's disillusionment with espionage first began.

'You ought to know that intelligence is the most powerful means to undertake brave designs and to avoid great ruins.'

General George Monck (1608-1670), Oliver Cromwell's spy chief in Scotland from his book *Observations on Military and Political Affairs* (1670). See under "Agent Handling" for more about Monck.

'An agent in the right place is hard to find, but when he is found he should be regarded as a pearl beyond price – like a good wife!'

David Nelligan in *The Spy in the Castle* (1968). For more about Nelligan see under "In more than four words."

'What a spy adds in such a case is always ambiguous, because honour and truth are rarely the virtues of those who get themselves hanged for money.'

General Francois Philippe de Foissac-Latour, one of Napoleon's commanders in Italy. For all his caution he was eventually tricked by a spy and lost the city of Mantua. Napoleon never forgave him. Quoted in *Marengo* by Terry Crowdy (2018).

[The leadership in Moscow didn't realise] *'...how frequently the London Residency sought to pass off information from open sources as coming from confidential contacts or agents in order to disguise its failure to obtain secret intelligence.'*

Oleg Gordievsky, defector and former KGB Resident in London. Quoted in *Instructions from the Centre* by Professor Christopher Andrew (1991).

'Secret operations are essential in war; upon them the army relies to make its every move.'

Sun Tzu, *Art of War*, Chapter 13, paragraph 27.

'One spy in the right place is worth one hundred thousand men.'

Commonly attributed to Napoleon. It would have to be a good spy but then, consider the effects of ULTRA.

'Secret services are a measure of a nation's political health and the only real expression of its subconscious.'

Former MI6 officer John Le Carré.

'Intelligence is like health: we seldom or never have it perfect.'

Future Secretary of State, Henry Coventry MP 1667 during Parliament's examination of the Dutch assault on the Medway. Quoted in *Espionage in the Reign of Charles II* by Alan Marshall (1994).

'An army without secret agents is like a man without eyes and ears'.

A Chinese script. I have forgotten which. Not Sun Tzu's *The Art of War* but still correct.

'The fighting arms are always thirsting for an intellectual tonic. That is what the secret service is intended to provide. That, and a little mild mental recreation from the stern realities of war.'

Author and former MI6 officer Compton MacKenzie in *Extremes Meet* (1928).

'The intelligence community in any government has the task of preventing harmful surprises.'

Dan Raviv and Yossi Melman in *Every Spy a Prince* (1990).

'The most that spies can provide is cats' eyes in the dark'.

Colin McColl, former Chief of MI6 (1988-1994) quoted in *The Economist* magazine 19 March 2005. In England "cats' eyes" are those tiny coloured reflectors which mark the middle and the edges of the road.

'...they are not even straws in the wind, they are cornflakes in the wind.'

Foreign Secretary Sir Geoffrey Howe commenting on the value of reports from MI6. Quoted in *MI6* by Stephen Dorril (1999).

'When Marshal Subise goes to war, he is followed by a hundred cooks, but when I take the field I am preceded by a hundred spies'.

Attributed to Frederick the Great.

'It gets depressing. You start to wonder whether we can do anything good at all'.

Lindsay Moran, former CIA field officer, in her memoir *Blowing My Cover* (2005).

'Very rarely were those reports [from British intelligence] *telling us something better than one could read in the quality newspapers'.*

David Mellor, former Minister of State at the Home Office. Quoted in *UK Eyes Alpha* by Mark Urban (1987).

'I think there's no question that [MI6] is the finest intelligence service in the world. Even though the Americans had all the resources, certainly all the financial resources, their network of agents wasn't all that great, and they were very accident prone. Quite a few of them ended up getting caught and a lot of cells that they ran were busted, with subsequent executions'.

Bob Sherman, American actor and writer, from an interview with Michael Macomber in 1992, originally quoted in the 'Sandbaggers Information Service' newsletter on the internet. *The Sandbaggers* was a television series written in the 1970s about a small MI6 unit. Although it was designed to dramatic, in terms of atmosphere it is probably one of the most accurate portrayals of service life to have appeared on film. Its writer, Ian Mackintosh, had served in naval intelligence, not MI6, but he was either very lucky or very well connected in the intelligence world. He disappeared in mysterious circumstances (probably an unfortunate accident) in 1979.

'Most things turn out not to be as important as they seem. Even espionage. Sometimes especially espionage.'

Alan Judd, former "Foreign Service officer" in his spy novel *Legacy* (2001). For more about Judd see under "Agent Handling."

'Their only achievement in the biggest intelligence battle of the twentieth century, the Cold War, was to delay the West's victory and increase its human cost by infecting the West with the very disease that destroyed the Soviet Union – secrecy and paranoia. But just when it looked as if we had rumbled them, that we realized that they had perpetrated on us the greatest confidence trick of the century, they were saved by the new monster of terrorism. With fresh government support, new names, new acronyms, almost limitless funding, fresh faces and fresh targets, they once again became sources of great power in our society – frightening us, defining reality for us, directing our lives.'

Philip Knightley in *The Second Oldest Profession* (1987).

'My view always was – and experience has only tended to confirm it – that the results of a secret service are usually negligible.'

Brigadier General W.H.H. Waters, British military attaché of wide experience in intelligence matters, writing in *Secret and Confidential* (1926).

'The cost of the Secret Service has mounted even more astronomically than that of other government departments. It has the advantage of not having to account to Parliament for its expenditure, or to provide any public justification for its activities. Thus, there is no means, except by guesswork, of forming an opinion as to whether what is achieved is worth the money spent. I should myself doubt very much whether it was.'

Author and former MI6 officer Malcolm Muggeridge in his memoir *Tread Softly For You*

Tread On My Jokes (1968).

'Men whose business it is to detect hidden and secret things are very apt to detect things which have never been done. What excuse can a [spy] make even to himself for having detected nothing?'

Novelist Anthony Trollope in *He Knew He Was Right* (1869). Intelligence history abounds with examples of this. Sigismund Payne Best, an officer of military intelligence as well as MI6 was renowned for inventing agents. Occasionally he ran out of code names for them. One network had agents codenamed 'TABLE', 'DESK' and 'CHAIR'. They were well paid. One imagines that Best simply pocketed the money. He certainly had an extravagant lifestyle. For more about Payne Best see under "SIS."

Verification

'Although spies may not deliberately give false intelligence, they should each be questioned so that by the agreement or disagreement of their intelligence, you may judge whether they are speaking the truth and by this process of verification, you will know who betrays you and who renders you good service.'

George Monck (1608-1670), Oliver Cromwell's spy chief in Scotland from his book *Observations on Military and Political Affairs* (1670). See under "Agent Handling" for more about Monck.

'There have been determined hoaxers on nuclear missile technology who have got the physics right but the colours of buses on the nuclear base wrong'.

Alan Judd in *The Quest for C* (1999). Judd's point is that when a spy is checking a source's information, it is often the small details which really matter.

'... to the extraction of significant and accurate information from an agent leading questions are fatal. Agents respond like fortune-tellers to what they think their clients want.'

Compton Mackenzie, author and MI6 officer in *Greek Memories* (1939).

'Intelligence is not uniquely worthy of belief. Intelligence is uniquely worthy of scepticism'.

Lord Butler quoted in *The Economist* magazine 19 March 2005. Lord Butler conducted the inquiry into the intelligence which led to the UK's entry into the Iraq War. Intelligence which often turned out to be exaggerated or completely false.

'Renseignement unique, renseignement nul'.

"Unconfirmed intelligence is no intelligence". A maxim of the Deuxieme Bureau, the forerunner of the DGSE, the French Intelligence Service. Quoted in *Secrets of the Rue St Roch* by Janet Morgan (2004).

'In general, we find ourselves, when attempting to assess the value of secret reports, somewhat in the position of the Captain of the Forty Thieves when, having put a chalk mark on Ali Baba's door, he found that Morgiana had put similar marks on all the doors in the street and had no indication to show which mark was the true one.'

Laurence Collier, senior civil servant in 1939, lamenting the tendency of MI6 to report every single rumour it heard without assessing its validity. The remark was prompted in the intelligence crisis just after the signing of the Nazi-Soviet Non-aggression Pact in 1939 which led directly to the Second World War. MI6 later claimed to have known the date and the details of the Pact but to have thought that they were not worth passing on to the British Government. Quoted in *The Secret Servant* by Anthony Cave Brown (1988).

'The importance and accuracy of each piece of information collected by an army of agents can be more carefully analysed in terms of the other pieces of information which verify or contradict it.'

Wilhelm Stieber in his book *The Chancellor's Spy* (1979). Stieber was chief of the Prussian Central Intelligence Bureau, the very first German secret service. If you are wondering why a Prussian intelligence chief only published a book in 1979, it is because his book was not published in his lifetime and only "discovered" and translated much later.

Vigilance

'Our spies should be constantly on watch.'

Flavius Renatus. 4th Century AD. Yes, it sounds obvious but consider that the following events were not spotted by British spies despite plenty of signs: World War One, World War Two, the Falklands War, the end of the Soviet Union, etc. etc. Perhaps Renatus should have said: *"... on watch and not more stupid than a bag of ferrets."*

Walk-Ins

'Never turn away freeman or slave, by day or by night, though you may be sleeping or eating or bathing, if he says that he has news for you.'

Advice for officers of the Byzantine army, 10th Century AD. Walk-Ins means those agents who offer their services without being formally targeted and recruited first (which is the way that it is supposed to work.) The name comes from the idea that they might have just "walked in" to the embassy (and some have). In fact, almost all of the most successful spies in history, for all agencies, have been those who have made the first move. It even raises the question of whether the modern method of going out to recruit spies is worth all the time and expense of maintaining foreign espionage stations or whether we should return to the old days of simply waiting for disaffected members of the enemy to offer their services. A study of intelligence history presents an argument that we would not be much worse off.

Wallet Litter

'Even minutia should have a place in our [intelligence] collection, for things of a seemingly trifling nature when enjoined with others of a more serious cast may lead to valuable conclusions.'

George Washington writing about the Revolutionary War. This quote also appears under "Detail." It appears again here to illustrate a lesson of different kind. First, it is a shame that Washington did not heed his own advice. A packet of his letters was captured by the British during the War of Independence. Some of the letters contained valuable intelligence. At first, the intelligence seemed so good that the British thought that it was a trick. However, they then found a letter from Washington to his dentist. British officers reasoned that such a routine piece of mail would not be included with the packet unless the correspondence was genuine. They acted on the information and it proved to be right. However, certainly in terms of modern espionage, this was a dangerous conclusion to reach. "Wallet litter" is the general term applied to the little, seemingly inconsequential details that are provided to make an act of deception look genuine. The classic example is Operation Mincemeat from the Second World War in which the Allies allowed the Germans to find a corpse supposedly carrying valuable intelligence. In fact, it was a trick that was designed to mislead them about Allied landings in Africa. The Germans were convinced of its validity, at least in part, because of all the little bits of detail that were found on the corpse such as ticket stubs from a recent visit to London, letters to a girlfriend etc. So, in espionage, detail is important but it can also be dangerous. Like all intelligence, it needs to be evaluated with great care.

Wannabees

'It's a great game of chess that's being played – all over the world – if this is the world at all, you know. Oh what fun it is! How I wish that I was one of them! I wouldn't mind being a Pawn, if only I might join ...'

Through the Looking-Glass by Lewis Carroll (1871).

'There is something in the psychology of certain individuals that leads them to devote a great deal of time and ingenuity to seeking involvement with an intelligence service, as if their lives were thereby lent a greater and more vivid reality.'

Alan Judd in *The Quest for C* (1999).

'Something about a secret intelligence agency attracts an endless stream of letters, cards, telegrams, phone calls and personal visits from deranged, possibly dangerous, or merely daffy, citizens...'

David R. McLean in *"Cranks, Nuts and Screwballs"* in *Studies in Intelligence* No.9 (Summer 1965).

'Espionage as a subject has never been more popular than it is today, for reasons that I daresay Freudians would be all too ready to adduce. As John Le Carré has said, the spy's inevitable loneliness makes him an appealingly symbolic figure in the mid-twentieth century, when the individual, without faith or hope, or even a moral code to keep or break, feels himself to be helpless and alone in face of a menacing collectivity and the appalling means of destruction that have been devised in its name. The very fantasy of a spy's life, the loss of his own identity, his pursuit of pseudo-information through pseudo-relationships, makes him a sort of hero of our time.'

Author and former MI6 officer Malcolm Muggeridge from the Introduction to *British Agent* by John Whitwell (pseudonym of the MI6 officer Leslie Nicholson) (1966).

Warnings

'It often seems that the government, police and the intelligence services issue warnings merely to guard their own backs in case the worst happens.'

Historian Max Hastings quoted in *The Guardian* newspaper, 17 October 2005.

'It is pardonable to be defeated but never to be surprised.'

Attributed to Frederick the Great.

Wives of Spies

'I'm not sure I could bear another three years as an embassy wife. All those coffee mornings, those interminable bridge evenings, those dreadful dinners for people you'd never dream of talking to, just because they might be useful or because you owe them. I suppose it's the same with any job that's at all political. And having to be nice to the head of chancery's awful wife who's forever trying to queen it over you. And the school fees. We might be better off in a beach hut in West Wittering.'

Alan Judd, former "Foreign Service officer" in his spy thriller *Legacy* (2001).

WMD (Weapons of Mass Destruction)

'... if we do not want plutonium to bring about the end of civilisation, then we must look not to the spy but to the nuclear accountant as the guardian of our future.'

Science writer Tom Wilke quoted in *MI6* by Stephen Dorril (2000).

Women

'I'll back you up whatever other mistakes you make, but if you start employing women I'll not put out a hand to get you out of any mess you get yourself into.'

Author and MI6 officer Compton Mackenzie in *Water On The Brain* (1933). In this comic novel, Major Blenkinsopp, the hero, is getting his instructions from MI6 before heading abroad. Although fiction, Mackenzie wrote the book because he had been prosecuted for writing fact. So, he was forced to disguise fact thereafter but still wanted the truth about the profession to be known. Before the Second World War, women were almost never employed as intelligence officers and there was a terrible sense of misogyny when their employment was suggested. However, their work as agents was equal to that of any male spy and finally the lesson was learned.

'...a whore, a traitor, a liar, a killer and, most of all, an ingenious spy.'

Mathilde Carré, who betrayed the Interallié network in World War Two. Quoted in *Double Agent* by David Tremain (2018).

"The outstanding point about her is her complete lack of ordinary human understanding and sympathy, and her inability to judge any person or problem except in relation to herself ... She is fundamentally vicious, spiteful and amoral.'

MI5 character analysis of Mathilde Carré. (quoted above.)

'It is no disparagement of the sex to say that women do not make good spies ... just when they have won the intimacy of a man who can really tell them something important they cannot bring themselves to betray his confidence.'

Sir Basil Thomson, head of British Police CID and also the Home Office Intelligence Unit. Quoted in his book *Queer People* (1922). Thomson was an appalling judge of women and later was arrested when he was found in the company of a prostitute. He claimed he was conducting research.

'Never confide in women. Never give a photo to anyone, especially a woman.'

MI6 training manual from the First World War. Quoted in *SIX* by Michael Smith (2010). My problem is that women won't accept my photograph.

'Don't employ a bad character or a woman. Sooner or later they will fail you.'

Captain Ferdinand Tuohy, Intelligence Corps officer in World War One and author of *The Secret Corps* (1920).

'She is extraordinarily stubborn and must be treated gently ... Never mind, guys, I am some Bear when it comes to the ladies!'

Letter from German spy Georg Breekow to his controller Heinrich Flores in Rotterdam. He was writing about Lizzie Wertheim, a German agent living in Britain who was far more accomplished than he was. She wasn't about to be told how to do things by this amateur, hence the comment about her stubbornness. Although they were supposed to work together, she quickly got rid of him sending him to Westcliff to get naval intelligence which he proceeded to do by asking for a sea view and a telescope when he arrived at his hotel. Meanwhile she went to Scotland for a driving holiday with a friend, Mabel Knowles. Since Mabel was an American citizen, this was excellent cover. But sometimes spies are undone through no fault of their own – Mabel had forgotten her passport and because she needed this to register at hotels, she had to return to London. Lizzie continued alone and attracted attention because a police officer saw her and thought "she drove too well for a woman"! She was arrested on her return to London. Far from Breekow being "a Bear with women", it was he who fell under her spell. At the trial he did all he could to maintain the story that she was innocent. As a result, he was shot while she only got ten years despite being the brains of the partnership. He had to be dragged sobbing to the execution ground and asked to be blindfolded with one of her scented handkerchiefs. But the establishment was not about to let as dangerous a spy as Lizzie off so slightly. She was certified insane and sent to Broadmoor where the conditions were so bad that she died of tuberculosis in 1921.

On spotting suspicious letters:

'Women were found to be definitely better for the work. They have a more accurate memory for details of handwriting and are more methodical and painstaking.'

Spycatcher and Special Branch officer Herbert Fitch in his book *Traitors Within* (1933). But his view could vary:

'So much nonsense has been written recently about the sober business of espionage by emotional ladies who, having once extracted an unimportant secret from a soldier friend, now feel entitled to publish hysterical meanderings about their "adventures" ...'

Inspector Herbert Fitch again in *Traitors Within*.

'She must have been a woman of some ability from the many accounts received, for she inspired respect, and her identity was concealed for a considerable time, in spite of many attempts to discover it.'

Vernon Kell, Director General of MI5 writing about the "Frau Doktor" also known as "Tiger Eyes" or "the Lady with the Cigarette". This was supposed to be some German superagent who controlled German spying activities in Belgium in the First World War. Kell had never met her but he was speculating about what sort of woman she had been. In fact, the "Frau Doktor" had more to do with spy fantasies than reality and for many years it was thought that she had been a myth. For years the tales grew until she became a chain-smoking, whip-wielding, leather fetishist. Only recently have historians discovered several German female agents, one of whom may actually have been the basis for these (wildly exaggerated) stories. The best candidate is probably Dr Elsbeth Shragmuller, a talented spy but a million miles from the garish character presented in fiction. Quoted in *Female*

Intelligence by Tammy Proctor (2003).

'Fear all women! Eve is efficient as a spy. But as a spy-catcher, she is deadly.'

J. Bernard Hutton quoted in *Female Intelligence* by Tammy Proctor (2003).

'There will be female spies as long as men remain vulnerable to the wiles of attractive, wilful women.'

A.A. Hoehling *Women Who Spied* (1993).

'In effect, women fail in both the head and the heart, and also in character composition for the business on hand. Women are fundamentally inaccurate. They experience a constant "urge" to be working in the limelight, jibbing at the patient compilation of dull details which forms the basic job in spying.'

Captain Ferdinand Tuohy, Intelligence Corps officer in World War One and author of *The Secret Corps* (1920).

'He was terribly in love and on that I based my plan. It was perfectly clear that he would tell me everything if I questioned him cleverly enough. In order to gain his confidence I told him a most moving story.'

First World War German spy Genia Josifovna. Quoted in *Fifty Amazing Secret Service Dramas* (1937).

'By and large those women who make careers of intelligence work are not the best or the brightest.'

Anonymous female CIA officer. Quoted in *Women in Espionage* by M.H. Mahoney (1993).

'Added to which,' he gave me an appreciative look, 'you are so unlike one, who on earth would take you for a spy? No one in their right mind would ever suspect you to be more than a pretty young popsy.'

A senior MI5 officer to Charlotte Bingham who was at the time working as an MI5 secretary. Quoted in her memoir *MI5 and Me* (2018).

'Some women are born to be secret intelligence agents. The "baby-faced" Breton chit was one of them.'

The intelligence historian Margaret Richings writing about the French courtesan and spy Louise de Kéroualle. There is considerable debate about just how good a spy she was – or even if that was her principal role. It used to be thought that she had been deliberately sent by King Louis XIV of France to monitor the new King Charles II of England, but a lack of documentary evidence for this has led to doubts. She obtained a position of lady-in-waiting to the Queen and Charles fathered a son by her (Charles, Duke of Richmond). Whatever the case, she was a supreme example of female power in action: she was rewarded by both kings: she received jewellery and vast sums of money (equivalent to £50 million in modern terms in just one year alone.) Charles made her Duchess of Portsmouth, Louis made her Duchesse d'Aubigny. It seems that her power as an influencer and a gatherer of intelligence was based on "closeting", the concept of having private social meetings with select and influential people. (Interestingly, this is a practice that is continued in British politics today and Russian agents are particularly keen to penetrate these networks using money as a way in). Even if she was not an intelligence agent she was an excellent example of an "agent of influence", a source who secretly tries to move events in one country in the interests of another. She lived a full life and long enough to be present at the coronation of George I. Quoted in *Espionage* by Margaret Richings (1934).

'My father always maintained that very pretty women didn't become spies. He said they weren't attracted to it. For his plants at communist headquarters and so on, he always used what he called the Miss Smiths of this world – plain women with excellent shorthand and typing.'

Charlotte Bingham, author and daughter of John Bingham, former senior officer in MI5. Quoted in *The Sunday Times* newspaper in 2018.

'The employment of women as spies or as secret agents is not favoured in Britain.'

Sir George Ashton in *Secret Service* (1930).

'I was a Secret Service agent, not a ridiculous young girl.'

Marthe McKenna, British agent of the First World War in her memoir *I Was a Spy* (1932).

'Women ... can seldom disguise their cleverness....'

Lord Baden-Powell in *Aids to Scouting for NCOs and Men* (1914). It's probably best not say too much about Baden-Powell's knowledge of women.

'When women are employed as secret service agents, the probability of success and the difficulty of administration are alike increased. Women are frequently very skilful in eliciting information; they require no disguise; if attractive they are likely to be welcome everywhere, and may be able to seduce from their loyalty those whose assistance or indiscretion may be of some use. On the other hand, they are variable, easily offended, seldom sufficiently reticent, and apt to be reckless. Their treatment requires the most watchful discretion. Usually they will work more consistently for a person than for a principle, and a lover in the Intelligence Corps makes a useful intermediary.'

Colonel David Henderson in *'Field Intelligence: Its Principles and Practice'* (1904) considered by some to be "the bible of modern military intelligence".

'Secretarial assistance was provided by upper-class girls who alleviated the ardours of war for all who were fortunate enough to come into contact with them. The security of their persons was by no means inviolate. But where their work was concerned they were impregnable.'

Author and former MI6 officer Malcolm Muggeridge in his memoir *Tread Softly for You Tread On My Jokes* (1968).

'A woman's chief weapon in obtaining information is sex; having once secured an agent or informer by this means, she may easily over-reach herself and fall in love.'

The former MI6 officer Leslie Nicholson writing as John Whitwell in *British Agent* (1997).

'English women as a rule have little knowledge or experience of foreigners and are less capable of handling them than, say, a Frenchwoman.'

Leslie Nicholson in *British Agent* again (see above).

'The use of women in procuring intelligence for Germany is very considerable, and extends from ladies down to the professional "horizontales."'

Lt. Col. James Edmonds, a senior figure in early British intelligence. Quoted in *Female Intelligence* by Tammy Proctor (2003). The French secret service of the time also used to speak of *"la patriotisme horizontale"*.

'Women, it is interesting to learn from high authorities on the arts of espionage, are rarely effective or satisfactory agents in secret service.'

Hamil Grant from his influential 1915 history of espionage *Spies and Secret Service* (1915).

'In a female agent, charm and tact, beauty and manners, a la grande dame, and knowledge of the world and men are essential.'

Dr Karl Graves, *Secret of the German Secret Service* (1915). For more about Graves, see under "Agent Selection."

'A tyranny entails a secret police like the female spies employed at Syracuse.'

Aristotle, *Politics,* Book 5, Chapter 11, Line 12.

'They tend to become even less capable physically and less responsible mentally for several days out of every month. I'm talking about European women of course. American women may be quite different for all I know.'

Anonymous European intelligence officer quoted in *"A Dim View of Women"* in Studies in Intelligence 6 (Spring 1962). Proof, if ever it were needed, that some men involved in espionage are incredibly thick.

'The man is nothing, the woman is all.'

Leopold Blancjean, agent of MI6's Belgian *La Dame Blanche* train spotting network in the First World War talking about the recruitment of couples as spies – it didn't matter what the man thought, the trick was to convince the woman.

'The beautiful vamp who removes secret treaties from the pockets of Ambassadors after a couple of cocktails has, I fear, no counterpart in real life.'

Vernon Kell, first Director General of MI5. Someone should have introduced him to MI6 agent Amy Elizabeth Thorpe who once stole vital documents from the safe of a naval attaché while wearing nothing but a string of pearls.

'Women do not make good agents.'

Vernon Kell, first Director General of MI5. Quoted in *Female Intelligence* by Tammy Proctor (2003). If you are beginning to think that Kell was a crusty old twit, you would be right.

'There is one thing worse than male machismo and that is female machismo.'

General Vernon Walters of the CIA to General Galtieri leader of Argentina who had just invaded the Falkland Islands. Galtieri didn't believe that Margaret Thatcher would dare to send military forces halfway around the world to retake the Islands. Walters begged to disagree – and was right. Quoted in *A Spy Called Cynthia* by Anonymous (2022).

'It would have been a much easier task if we had known we were looking for a woman.'

Comment by Pete Lapp who was part of the FBI team trying to find Ana Montes, a DIA analyst (US military intelligence) who was working for the Cubans. It had been known for some time that there must be a spy somewhere in US intelligence working on Cuba but matters were confused because they thought they were looking for a man. This was because American agents who managed to get access in Havana found that Cuban records suggested this – possibly it was a deliberate ruse by Cuban intelligence to throw investigators off the scent. If so, it worked. Montes spied for Cuba for seventeen years and was quite possibly their greatest spy ever. She was finally caught in 2001 and sentenced to twenty-five years in prison for espionage. She was released in January 2023, aged 66, having served over twenty years of her sentence. She was unrepentant. Quoted on BBC News website 25 April 2013.

'For brilliant and effective espionage, and for courage that is truly awe-inspiring.'

CIA citation for Jeannie Rousseau. During the Second World War, she provided vital intelligence on Hitler's V-weapons and then survived incarceration and torture in three different concentration camps. That citation says all you need to know about female spies.

World Trade Centre attack ("9-11")

'The intelligence community struggled throughout the 1990s and up to 9-11 to collect intelligence on and to analyse the phenomenon of transitional terrorism. Many dedicated officers worked day and night for years to piece together the growing body of evidence on al-Qaeda and to understand the threats. Yet, while there were many reports on Bin Laden and his organisation, there was no comprehensive review of what the intelligence community knew and what that meant.'

The 9/11 Commission Report reporting on the inability of US intelligence agencies to prevent the 9/11 attacks. It isn't collecting intelligence that is the most important thing – it is what a country does with that intelligence once it has it. This is the most important rule of espionage.

<u>X</u>

Xenophobia

'Refuse to be served by a German waiter! If he says he is Swiss, demand to see his passport!'

The UK's *Daily Mail* newspaper circa 1908. Part of the nationwide spy scare that led to the establishment of the British intelligence services MI5 and MI6 in 1909.

'The assumed stupidity of the British was the most valuable asset and it was not until the war was over that the Germans became aware how completely their confidential channels of communication had been compromised.'

Professor Sir Alfred Ewing speaking at a lecture in Edinburgh 1927. In 1914, Ewing established "Room 40", the very first Admiralty decoding centre that was a model for all decoding centres that came after and which very probably won the war for Britain. To a modern reader, he seems a little like "Doctor Who" - he was described as *"a meticulous dresser with a penchant for striped waistcoats and bow ties..."* and he had even devised his own cipher machine which he had submitted for consideration to the Navy. But while a brilliant academic, he was not a natural leader and he was dismissed amid great bitterness in 1916. Quoted in *Spymaster* by David Ramsay (2008).

Continentals... *'do not associate arse with paper.'*

Sir Mansfield Cumming, first chief of MI6, explaining why agents could conceal messages in their rectums on the grounds that Germans were unlikely to search for it there. Quoted in *Armour Against Fate* by Michael Occleshaw (1989). There's an image you won't forget easily.

Y

Yuppies

'I was saddled with an overabundance of yuppie spies who cared more about their retirement plan and health insurance benefits than about protecting democracy. For them, the CIA was just a job.'

Former senior CIA officer Duane Clarridge in his book *A Spy For All Seasons* (1997). And yet there were plenty of earlier spies who did the job for the glory and paycheck. Old spies are like old people everywhere – tending to remember a golden past that never actually existed.

Z

Zero Dark Thirty

'*It makes sense to get behind the winning horse.*'

CIA memo discussing whether or not to co-operate with the makers of the movie *"Zero Dark Thirty"* and the advantages of doing so. The CIA thought that if they offered co-operation then they could make themselves look good after what had been, in fact, a very dark chapter in the Agency's history. Some believe that the finished movie perpetuates two myths: 1) that the CIA torture programme worked and 2) that intelligence obtained led the CIA to the hiding place of Osama Bin Laden. The Senate Intelligence Committee investigated these claims for five years and concluded that both claims were manifestly false. But this quote illustrates how modern intelligence services, far from remaining secret, are considering how to manipulate modern media to their own ends.

Zimmerman Telegram

'*Sir, do you want to bring America into the war?*'

Nigel De Grey, one of Britain's chief code breakers in the First World War, having burst into the office of the Director of the Naval Intelligence Division, Admiral Reginald "Blinker" Hall. This was at 1030am on 17 January 1917 at a period when Britain was at its lowest ebb. U-boat attacks had almost strangled the country's supply lines. Publication of the telegram, which urged Mexico to declare war on the United States, brought America into the war and ultimately secured victory for the Allies. Such was Hall's skill that the Germans never found out where the British had obtained the telegram nor that the British were reading their codes. Quoted in *Spymaster* by David Ramsay (2008).

Zinoviev Letter

[In 1924 the first ever Labour Government was facing a General Election. It lost largely because the *Daily Mail* published a letter which appeared to show that the Soviet Union was using sympathisers in the Labour Party to take power in Britain. In fact, the letter was a forgery. It had been leaked to the *Daily Mail* by members of the intelligence services in order to bring the Labour government down.]

'*The important aspect of the Zinoviev Affair is that it may indicate a tendency on the part of the secret services to slide from being the secret servants of the state into something very different: a "secret state" in its own right.*'

Quoted in *Plots and Paranoia* by Professor Bernard Porter (1988).

And that seems like a good note (and letter) on which to stop.

About the Author

Harry Ferguson was recruited into the Secret Intelligence Service (MI6) after graduating from Oxford University in the early 1980s. Following the fall of the Soviet Union, he was re-deployed to the National Investigation Service (NIS). There he worked undercover against international drugs and arms smuggling syndicates. The NIS was essentially the old Investigation Division of UK Customs and Excise, but in the 1990s, because its powers of search and operational flexibility were much greater than those of the police, it began recruiting former spies, special forces operators and other specialist technical personnel. It became the country's leading crime fighting force. At the end of the 1990s, the NIS was amalgamated with certain specialist police units into the National Crime Agency (NCA). This is often referred to as "the UK's FBI." Harry wrote two books about some of his work in the NIS: "Kilo 17" and "Lima 3."

In 2003, Harry was selected to be the MI6 representative in the BBC TV series "Spy". This was a reality television series in which ordinary members of the public were put through real spy training by Harry and Mike Baker of the CIA. With the end of the Cold War, recruitment for the intelligence services had changed from the classic "tap on the shoulder" days when Harry was recruited. It was hoped that a popular television series would attract a new and more diverse kind of recruit. Harry wrote the book of the series entitled "Spy". Sadly, the show was axed after just one series in the wake of the war in Iraq. However, the BBC exported "Spy" to more than one hundred countries overseas and Harry became one of the best known former intelligence officers in the world.

Since his MI6 and NIS service, Harry has worked in the world of media and private intelligence. He helped to design the "Science of Spying" exhibition at the Science Museum in London and then took the exhibition to America. He researched and wrote "Operation Kronstadt", the story of the greatest MI6 operation of the twentieth century. He appears regularly on television and radio news programmes as an expert in intelligence matters. He has appeared on other television shows all over the world, including on children's television programmes. He has demonstrated how to kill someone with a ballpoint pen on Japanese television and helped a Belgian TV crew to break into an art museum in an incident that became so notorious questions were asked in the Belgian Parliament. He also took part in a hunger strike to highlight the plight of Shaker Aamer, one of many innocent prisoners held in Guantanamo Bay.

Today, Harry is "mostly retired" although he does still lecture on the history and practice of espionage. At the time of writing, he has a TikTok channel: @theenglishspy

Printed in Great Britain
by Amazon

41896662R00110